Protestant History and Identity in Sixteenth-Century Europe

Volume 2

St Andrews Studies in Reformation History

Editorial Board:

Andrew Pettegree, Bruce Gordon and John Guy

Titles in this series include:

*The Shaping of a Community: The Rise and Reformation
of the English Parish c. 1400–1560*
Beat Kümin

*Seminary or University? The Genevan Academy and
Reformed Higher Education, 1560–1620*
Karin Maag

Marian Protestantism: Six Studies
Andrew Pettegree

*Antifraternalism and Anticlericalism in the German
Reformation: Johann Eberlin von Günzburg
and the Campaign against the Friars*
Geoffrey Dipple

Forthcoming:

*Reformations Old and New: Essays on the
Socio-Economic Impact of Religious Change c. 1470–1630*
edited by Beat Kümin

Protestant History and Identity in Sixteenth-Century Europe

Volume 2
The Later Reformation

Edited by
BRUCE GORDON

Ashgate

Aldershot • Brookfield USA • Singapore • Sydney

Published by
Ashgate Publishing Limited
Gower House
Croft road
Aldershot
Hants GU11 3HR
England

Ashgate Publishing Company
Old Post Road
Brookfield
Vermont 05036–9704
USA

Reprinted 1998

British Library Cataloguing in Publication Data

Protestant History and Identity in Sixteenth-Century
  Europe.
  (St Andrews Studies in Reformation History)
  1. Reformation—Europe. 2. Protestantism—History. 3. Europe—
  History—1517–1648.
  I. Series   II. Gordon, Bruce
  940.2´3

  ISBN   1–85928–294–4
         1–85928–175–3 (Two volume set)

Library of Congress Cataloging-in-Publication Data

Protestant history and identity in sixteenth-century Europe/edited
  by Bruce Gordon
        p.   cm.   (St Andrews studies in Reformation history)
    Includes bibliographical references and index.
    Contents: v. 1. The medieval inheritance—v. 2. The later
  Reformation.
    ISBN 1–85928–175–3 (set). ISBN 1–85928–294–6 (v. 1: cloth).
  ISBN 1–85928–295–4 (v. 2: cloth)
    1. Reformation—Europe. 2. Protestant churches—Europe—
  Doctrines—History—16th century. 3. Reformation—Historiography.
  4. Identification (Religion) I. Gordon, Bruce, 1962–
  II. Series.
  BR307.P76   1996
  274´.06—dc20   96–4270
                                                               CIP

Typeset in Sabon by Raven Typesetters, Chester and
Printed in Great Britain by Antony Rowe Ltd, Chippenham, Wiltshire

Contents

Notes on Contributors

Pamela Biel is a historian and translator living in Frankfurt, Germany. Among her publications is *Doorkeepers at the House of Righteousness. Heinrich Bullinger and the Zurich Clergy* (1991).

Christopher Bradshaw is a research student in the St Andrews Reformation Studies Institute. He is the author of the section on the English Protestant Reformers in the revised *Cambridge Bibliography of English Literature*.

Bruce Gordon is Lecturer in Modern History at St Andrews University. He has written *Clerical Discipline and the Rural Reformation* (1992) and is currently working on a history of the Swiss Reformation and a biography of Theodor Bibliander.

Howard Hotson is Lecturer in Early Modern European History at the University of Aberdeen, and his monograph on Johann Heinrich Alsted will be published by Oxford University Press.

Ute Lotz-Heumann is an academic assistant and research student at the Humbolt University, Berlin.

William G. Naphy is Lecturer in History at the University of Aberdeen and the author of *Calvin and the Consolidation of the Genevan Reformation* (1994). He is currently working on Calvin as lawgiver, and on plague spreaders in Early Modern Europe.

Bodo Nischan is Professor of History at East Carolina University, Greenville, North Carolina. He has written *People, Prince and Confession* (1994).

Andrew Pettegree is Director of the St Andrews Reformation Studies Institute and Reader in Modern History at the University of St Andrews. His books include *Emden and the Dutch Revolt* (1992) and *The Early Reformation in Europe* (1992).

Paul Regan is attached to the Department of History at Southampton University. He has written 'Cartography, Chorography and Patriotic

Sentiment in the Sixteenth-Century Low Countries' in *Studies in Medieval and Renaissance History* (1995).

David Watson is a research student in the St Andrews Reformation Studies Institute. He holds the Research Bursary of the Ecclesiastical History Society, and has contributed a paper to the Cambridge colloquium sponsored by the British Academy John Foxe Project.

Preface

This project emerged from one of the regular meetings of the European Reformation Research Group, an informal group of mostly young scholars whose research interests are concentrated on diverse aspects of the religious thought and practice of the Reformation era. At our meeting at Stonyhurst College in the summer of 1993 it became clear that many participants were presenting papers on a related theme: how sixteenth-century Protestants used their sources to craft a historical perspective which could justify the break with the medieval church. It seemed to us then that the group should take up the challenge of exploring this theme in greater detail; and it was decided to meet a year later in St Andrews and present papers on how we saw this phenomenon emerging in our own areas of research. During three days in early August of 1994 we heard papers which discussed a wide range of literary, theological and political texts, along with studies of marital, liturgical and social practices – all vital and interrelated components of the Protestant endeavour to articulate its historical place and identity. It was clear that our discussions benefited greatly from the diversity of methodological and intellectual approaches to such a broad theme. The range of perspectives offered was then broadened by the introduction into the group of a number of scholars from outside the Anglo-Saxon historical tradition – scholars who spoke on how these issues are being debated on the Continent.

Most of the essays in these volumes were read at that St Andrews meeting, whilst others were contributed by those who were not able to attend. The number of contributions required that the work appear in two volumes, divided along a rough chronological line. Although the division was of editorial rather than thematic necessity, the essays in the first volume explore the relationship between the Reformation and the medieval religious and intellectual culture; those in the second cover the period when Protestantism had become an established faith. While we have sought to cast our net as widely as possible, it is clear that even with 20 essays this subject is far from exhausted, and important areas of Europe have not been treated. Much work still remains to be done. Nevertheless, these books bear witness to the seriousness with which a group of young historians has taken up the challenge of exploring the fundamental suppositions of the Protestant Reformation.

I wish to thank the contributors for their efficiency in preparing their texts for publication. My colleague Andrew Pettegree supported this project from the beginning, and for his encouragement and advice I am extremely grateful. Professor Aldo Corcella of the University of Basilicata (Potenza), my research student Mark Taplin and my wife Rona Gordon Johnston rendered a considerable service in their assistance in the translation of several essays. As ever, James Cameron read my work and offered sage criticism. Julian Crowe of the St Andrews Computing Laboratory solved technical problems large and small, and for that I wish to express my gratitude. Professor Natalie Zeman Davis visited the St Andrews Reformation Studies Institute in April of 1995 and participated in a seminar discussion of the themes treated in these books. Her comments and suggestions were most helpful in the editing of this project. Above all, I wish to thank my wife Rona for her unflagging support and encouragement which made possible the editing of this book during a first year of teaching and marriage.

Bruce Gordon
St Andrews

Abbreviations

ARG	Archiv für Reformationsgeschichte
BHR	Bibliothèque d'Humanisme et Renaissance
BSHPF	Bulletin de la Société de l'Histoire du Protestantism Français
CH	Church History
CHR	Catholic Historical Review
CR	Corpus Reformatorum
DNB	Dictionary of National Biography
DTh	Deutsche Theologie
EHR	English Historical Review
EvTH	Evangelische Theologie
FKDG	Forschungen zur Kirchen- und Dogmengeschichte
GWU	Geschichte in Wissenschaft und Unterricht
HJ	Historical Journal
JEH	Journal of Ecclesiastical History
KuD	Kerygma und Dogma
LP	Letters and Papers, Foreign and Domestic, of the Reign of Henry VIII, eds J.S. Brewer, J. Gairdner et al. (21 vols, London, 1862–1932)
LuJ	Luther Jahrbuch
MQR	Mennonite Quarterly Review
NDB	Neue Deutsche Biographie
P&P	Past and Present
SCH	Studies in Church History
SCJ	Sixteenth Century Journal
STC	Short Title Catalogue of Books Printed in England ... 1475–1640
SVRG	Schriften des Vereins für Reformationsgeschichte
TRE	Theologische Realenzyklopädie
THR	Theologische Rundschau
TRHS	Transactions of the Royal Historical Society
WA	Luther, Werke (Weimar Ausgabe)
WATR	Luther, Tischreden
WABR	Luther, Briefwechsel
ZKG	Zeitschrift für Kirchengeschichte
ZThK	Zeitschrift für Theologie und Kirche

CHAPTER ONE

The Changing Face of Protestant History and Identity in the Sixteenth Century

Bruce Gordon

At the root of each attempt by Protestant writers of the sixteenth century to place their movement within the expanse of Christian history was the desperate need to answer the accusation flourished with such devastating effect by their detractors: where had their church been for a thousand years?[1] Opponents of the Reformation never tired of drawing attention to the apparent reality that whilst the church of Rome might have needed correction, it nevertheless formed a continuous, visible, and historical link with the ancient church.[2] The institutional church was much beleaguered in the fifteenth century: at the highest levels it was lamed by the prolonged struggle between papal supporters and conciliarists over ultimate authority, debates held against a backdrop of war and schism.[3] In urban and rural parishes reform-minded movements quickly took root, and some, such as Lollardy and the Hussites, though branded heresies, were in fact movements which reflected increased lay participation and interest in the work of the church.[4] Despite the confusion, however, at the close of the Middle Ages there were few who would question the truth that the church, even in its fractured state, was the body of Christ in the world.

The essence of the hierarchical church lay in its commission to administer all that the Son of God had given to the apostles, the power to save

---

[1] On Catholic polemical literature, see Beat Hodler, in Volume 1, Chapter 2; David Bagchi, *Luther's Earliest Opponents* (Minneapolis, 1991); R.A. Crofts, 'Printing, Reform, and the Catholic Reformation in Germany', *SCJ*, 16 (1985), 369–81; Bernd Moeller, 'Die frühe Reformation als Kommunikationsprozess' in H. Boockmann (ed.), *Kirche und Gesellschaft im Heiligen Römischen Reich des 15. und 16. Jahrhunderts* (Göttingen, 1994), pp. 148–64; and Remigius Bäumer's introduction to Wilbirgis Klaiber (ed.), *Katholische Kontroverstheologen und Reformer des 16. Jahrhunderts* (Münster, 1978), pp. vii–xxiii.

[2] R.N. Swanson, *Religion and Devotion in Europe, c. 1215–c.1515* (Cambridge, 1995), esp. chap. 3, 'Access to the Faith', pp. 42–91.

[3] Antony Black, *Council and Commune. The Conciliar Movement and the Council of Basle*, (London, 1979), pp. 9–26.

[4] Malcolm Lambert, *Medieval Heresy. Popular Movements from the Gregorian Reform to the Reformation* (reprint. Oxford, 1992), pp. 243–300.

and the power to damn. To the medieval mind, what distinguished the church from all other institutions was its role as sole guardian of God's revelation to humanity; a unique position which had at all times to be jealously defended against the incursions of secular rulers.[5] The extent to which the life and teachings of the church had permeated and informed all communal, cultural and economic relations of European society had become evident in the high Middle Ages with the emergence of the concept of Christendom – the belief that what united the peoples of the Latin West above all else was their adherence to the one holy, catholic and apostolic church. The bond between church and society was the final arbiter of human actions; it named and formulated the accepted religious life, it defined the crucial social distinctions of 'clerical' and 'lay', 'religious' and 'regular', and it set the boundaries of human belief and action by proscribing heresy and superstition and condemning immoral forms of commerce such as usury.

The Reformation turned this understanding of church and society on its head. Luther posited the question of how God and humanity are essentially related, and his conclusion, that this relationship exists through the unmerited gift of grace from God, radically transformed the manner in which Christian communities conceived of their history and identity.[6] The foundations of medieval church authority, with their emphasis upon consensus, authority and antiquity, were shaken, but certainly not destroyed. Luther's message soon revealed itself to be a chimera, a hybrid being whose relationship to human history was not uncomplicated. History in the sense of chronology was discredited as a means of measuring the verity of the church, but, as Luther understood full well, the nascent reform movement could not turn its face against God's historical plan; there remained for the evangelical cause the imperative of locating and explaining its historical place. It was inconceivable to the medieval/early modern mind that a new church, reform movement or theology could spring suddenly from the ground. Innovation was evil, the work of Satan, and reform movements had no alternative but to couch their intentions in terms of a return to first principles: the restoration of the 'pure church'.

---

[5] See the excellent book by Uta-Renate Blumenthal, *The Investiture Controversy: Church and Monarchy from the Ninth to Eleventh Century* (Philadelphia, 1988).

[6] The literature on this subject is enormous. H. Bornkamm, 'Luthers Bericht über seine Entdeckung der Iustitia Dei', *ARG*, 39 (1940), 117–28; Scott Hendrix, *Ecclesia in via: Ecclesiastical Developments in the Medieval Psalms Exegesis and Dictata super Psalterium (1513–1515) of Martin Luther* (Leiden, 1974); Martin Brecht, 'Iustitia Christi. Die Entdeckung Martin Luthers', in Bernhard Lohse (ed.), *Der Durchbruch der Reformatorischen Erkenntnis bei Luther. Neuere Untersuchungen* (Stuttgart, 1988), pp. 167–225; Alister E. McGrath, *Luther's Theology of the Cross* (Oxford, 1985), pp. 141–7.

All issues of reform, whether medieval or early modern, hinged on a historical argument whose logic held that through the course of human history the church had repeatedly fallen away from the intentions of its founder and was in need of correction. For the majority of reform-minded churchmen, the restoration of the church was to be accomplished through a vigorous reaffirmation of existing laws and institutions.[7] What distinguished the Reformation from the myriad of medieval reform movements was the manner in which it initially discarded this argument. As John Headley has argued, 'taking seriously the corrupted nature of God's creation, Luther insists that since the devil works so splendidly in the world, one must show another basis of authority than long time and majority opinion'.[8] This abandoning of a crucial tenet of the medieval church, which held to the intrinsic virtue of established church order, forced upon the evangelical reformers an agenda which they could hardly meet. How were they, on the one hand, to dismiss as spurious the unity of the Western church, whilst, on the other, claiming an authority for their local reformations which depended heavily on established forms of religion? The attack on the authority of the medieval church carried with it the responsibility to reclaim history and to establish another means of discerning the undoubted continuity of the church. For Protestants, the uncovering of history was a constituent part of establishing the Word of God as authoritative in the world: the true church, so the evangelical reformers argued, would find its history and identity in the study of the scriptures.

The essays in this volume bring into relief the variety of ways in which Protestants undertook the challenge to express their sense of identity and culture through a shared recollection of the past. In examining the uses of the past in the sixteenth century from the early years of the Reformation through to the age of orthodoxy and confessionalisation, we cannot but be impressed by the fluid nature of Protestant historical thought. This was necessarily the case, for the principal teachings around which the evangelical movements took shape, namely *sola scriptura*, justification by faith alone and the providence of God, had by nature an ambiguous relationship to institutions and communal structures. Protestants boldly declared the Word of God to be the sole legitimate basis of authority, but this claim did not enable them to obviate the dilemma that scripture is

---

[7] Harmut Boockmann, 'Das 15. Jahrhundert und die Reformation', in his *Kirche und Gesellschaft*, pp. 9–25; Josef Leinweber, 'Provinzial Synode und Kirchenreform in Spätmittelalter' in R. Bäumer (ed.), *Reformatio Ecclesiae. Beiträge zu kirchlichen Reformbemühungen von der Alten Kirche bis zur Neuzeit* (Paderborn/Munich/Vienna/Zurich, 1980), pp. 113–128.

[8] J.M. Headley, 'The Reformation as Crisis in the Understanding of Tradition', *ARG*, 78 (1987), 11–12.

frustratingly silent on questions of church polity and the organisation of the 'godly society'. The medieval church had overcome this stumbling block with its concept of the presence of the Holy Spirit in the church, guiding its institutions and sanctioning its decisions. Luther rejected this position. The whole creation of a Protestant history and identity had its provenance in the early recognition of the reformers that the Word of God had to be interpreted. At that point the reformers understood that despite their railing against human reason and traditions there would have to be an accommodation of the divine and human. The argument that the Word of God alone was authoritative was not new to the medieval theologians; what transformed the early modern world was the application of this principle to European society.

The Bible was the central cultural text of the Reformation. The truth of this statement is to be seen on several levels, as the essays in this volume explore. For the theologians the question of legitimacy rested upon finding a means to interpret scripture in a consistent manner.[9] The Bible was not merely a theological textbook but a mirror in which the evangelicals saw themselves and their enemies reflected; their religious leaders were the prophets, those suffering persecution were the Israelites in Egypt, their godly rulers were Josiah and Hezekiah, and their enemies were Pharaoh's servants. The Bible provided the language and imagery required to create a Protestant culture, but its force as an agent of change was predicated upon the existential bond which early modern people felt with the characters of biblical narratives.

In order to create a religious culture in which the popular understanding of scripture was consonant with the theological principles of the Reformation leaders, Protestant writers were forced into a tendentious presentation of both the Bible and the writings of long-dead luminaries of the church.[10] In martyrologies, chronicles, sermons and pamphlets the biblical stories were moulded to express the reality of the Protestant experience, whether of persecution, exile, triumph or of household order. The names of men such as Augustine, Bernard of Clairveaux, Hus and Savonarola were regularly invoked and emended versions of their writings cited to support the truth of the Protestant cause. This might appear to modern eyes as a gross act of mendacity, but the evangelical writers of the sixteenth century believed that God had chosen their time to reveal the truth of the Christian religion and they were his appointed agents. This gave them licence to administer a form of Ockham's razor to Christian history, finding the truth in earlier writers, no matter how greatly obscured, and excising the errors. The questions of authority,

---

[9] See Marshall in Volume 1, Chapter 5 and Ryrie in Volume 1, Chapter 6.

[10] On Crespin's shaping of material, see Watson, Chapter 3, this volume.

hermeneutics, theology and literary form which this radical approach to the past entailed stands at the centre of these essays.[11]

It should not surprise us that as soon as the Reformation began to take shape in the 1520s both Luther and Zwingli turned their minds to how the Bible was to be applied to society, in other words, to determine how divine and human righteousness are related.[12] Their shared conclusion was that human righteousness, which judges only the external actions of people, was a shadow of the righteousness of God upon which it is based. In practical terms for the Reformation this meant that the original sense of *sola scriptura*, which held that all that was not sanctioned by the Bible should be abandoned, was dropped. As has often been noticed, when the evangelical movements gained power there was a radical shift in how they interpreted and presented their fundamental position on the role of scripture in reformation.[13] In the face of practical difficulties attendant upon the implementation of reform, and the stinging criticisms of those groups who felt betrayed by the alliances made by the reformers with established political authorities, mainstream evangelical thought moved towards the position that all that was not proscribed by scripture was to be retained. For men such as Bernardino Ochino, it was the principle of *sola scriptura* which had inspired them to abandon positions of power and become refugees for their beliefs. What they discovered, however, when they moved into Protestant territories, was that the institutionalisation of the Reformation led to the same problems of coercion in matters of faith from which they were fleeing.[14] Thus in its early years a crucial distinction appeared in the Reformation which was borne out in subsequent decades: Protestants in power had a different perception of the past from those suffering for their faith.[15]

The European Reformation was essentially local in nature.[16] Whether in Zurich, Venice or Saxony it was through the media of preaching, printing and the 'acts' of reformation, such as iconoclasm, that the evangelical parties constructed a religious language suited to the particular

---

[11] For the variety of sources, see Parish in Volume 1, Chapter 10 and Lock in Volume 1, Chapter 11.

[12] Paul Althaus, *The Theology of Martin Luther*, trans. Robert C. Schultz (reprint. Philadelphia, 1988), pp. 251–73; W.P. Stephens, *The Theology of Huldrych Zwingli* (Oxford, 1986), pp. 295–309.

[13] See Headley's extremely useful discussion of how Luther changed the position he had held in his *Contra Henricum*, 'Reformation as Crisis', p. 16.

[14] See Campi in Volume 1, Chapter 8.

[15] On this point, see Regan, Chapter 6, this volume.

[16] See Thomas A. Brady Jr, *Protestant Politics: Jacob Sturm (1489–1553) and the German Reformation* (Atlantic Highlands, 1994), esp. chap. 1, 'The German Reformation as Political Event', pp. 2–12.

needs of their communities.[17] The broader principles of the Reformation (justification by faith etc.) fell on fertile soil when they were localised, or, in other words, when they were presented to the people in worship or preaching in terms with which they could identify. What we see emerging from the essays in this volume is a sense that Protestant history-making was situational, that it varied greatly depending upon the particular circumstances in which it was being nurtured. Whether in positions of power or exile, the Protestant understanding of scripture and history provided individuals and communities with a set of models which served as raw materials for the creation of identities.

The formation of a historical memory, and through this remembrance an identity, took place where evangelical teaching encountered local cultures. The greatest challenge faced by Protestant reformers and rulers was not simply to inculcate in the people a new faith, though that in itself was a Herculean task. The major undertaking was to penetrate local societies and disentangle established (though to the Protestants abhorrent) religious experiences and practices from the daily exchange and activities of the people. Religion and belief, in all their countless manifestations, whether within or outwith the church, were the primary categories of individual and collective identities in the early modern world. The establishment of a Protestant culture with a history and identity turned on the success of reformers in making the religion of the Word the basis of communal relations. Certainly local circumstances and attitudes such as anticlericalism and iconoclasm facilitated this process, but acts of violence and protest, though rich in symbolic and theological meaning, were not in the end an adequate foundation for the new religious culture. The writing of Protestant history served many purposes. It was in the first instance a polemical defence against charges of schism. But, as the Reformation began to settle, it was turned to the service of providing identities for individuals, groups and even nations in particular circumstances.[18] It was a struggle not only to establish the primacy of the Word, but to control words: to formulate a language which could be used to legitimate the Protestant cause and bring people into the new communities through the use of propaganda.[19] In this evolution it became mani-

---

[17] For a study in the formation and use of religious language in which the laity are shown to have had more than a passive role, see Lee Palmer Wandel, *Voracious Idols and Violent Hands: Iconoclasm in Reformation Zurich, Strasbourg and Basel* (New York, 1995).

[18] On the problems of building a national identity from a minority position, see Ute Lotz-Heumannin , Chapter 7, this volume, on Ireland.

[19] The best treatment of the subject remains R.W. Scribner, *For the Sake of Simple Folk. Popular Propaganda for the German Reformation* (reprint. Oxford, 1994). Scribner argues that propaganda was used both to revile papal belief and to present the Reformation 'through the familiar and traditional'. See his essay, 'Teaching the Gospel: Propaganda as Instruction', pp. 190–228.

festly evident that there was no one Protestant view of history, but several, and each acquired its voice and character from the local circumstances out of which it arose.

Very little in the Reformation was stable. Not only did the formulation of religious ideas take place amidst wars, persecution and plague, but the very language which the evangelical groups conscripted to their cause formed a brilliant prism, whose diverse colours transformed as it was manipulated. Terms such as church, authority, nation and even reformation itself were variously and often in contradictory ways used in the sixteenth century. Among Protestant groups there were competing notions of church and authority, and these rival positions were expressed through a wide range of historical, theological and literary materials. There were, without doubt, unifying themes and shared sources, above all scripture, the fathers of the church, medieval historians, legends and the liturgical traditions of the church, but these sources were moulded by writers to speak to particular circumstances. Patrick Geary, writing of the eleventh century, refers to Pocock's argument 'that when traditional relationships between present and past break down, those most affected by this rupture respond by reshaping an understanding of that which unites past and present in terms of some new continuity in order to defend themselves from the effects of this rupture'.[20] This was the experience of sixteenth-century European Protestantism. The question which these essays explore is how various groups shaped their histories by remembering and forgetting, by editing and deleting, by compiling and destroying.

The Reformation, with its attack on established norms of authority, its emphasis on vernacular and national cultures, and its enhanced role for the individual in religious life, ruptured European society. The extent of this rent must not tempt us to forget the enormous debt which Protestant historical thought owed to the medieval world from which it emerged.[21] Historical writing in the Middle Ages in general was notable for its lack of interest in both the individual and chronology. Essentially, as Gabrielle Spiegel has argued, medieval historical thinking was topological.[22] Figures and events were used by medieval chroniclers to

---

[20] P.J. Geary, *Phantoms of Remembrance. Memory and Oblivion at the End of the First Millennium* (Princeton, 1994), p. 8.

[21] Franz-Josef Schmale, *Funktion und Formen mittelalterlicher Geschichtsschreibung. Eine Einführung* (Darmstadt, 1985); Joachim Knape, *'Historie' in Mittelalter und früher Neuzeit. Begriffs- und Gattungsgeschichtliche Untersuchungen im interdiziplinären Kontext* (Baden-Baden, 1984).

[22] G.M. Spiegel, 'Political Utility in Medieval Historiography: A Sketch', *History and Theory*, 14 (1975), 323.

explain and legitimate contemporary religious and political life. Through the use of types, medieval writers attempted, in Spiegel's words, 'to establish genuine historical relationships between temporally distinct phenomena'.[23] Chronology was of little importance because to date an event was to condemn it to the past and lose its importance for the present, whereas the thrust of medieval historical thought was to 'break down barriers between past and present, to draw events out of the past and make them live in the present experience'.[24] Within this general understanding of historical writing in the medieval world we must be aware of variety, for whilst chroniclers did endeavour to make use of known facts and eyewitness accounts, more prophetic historians such as Joachim de Fiore saw earthly events as nothing more than signs of spiritual realities to be interpreted.[25]

This concern to bring the past into the present was also a major component of the other intellectual trend which shaped historical thought in the sixteenth century – humanism.[26] As has often been acknowledged, Renaissance humanist historiography emerged out of the political and social crises of the fourteenth and fifteenth centuries. In Italy, the study of history was the offspring of a new perspective on the past. Humanist scholars posed the question, how had Italy become disinherited from the greatness of the culture which was Rome?[27] To answer this question the humanists developed what John Stephens has called a 'novel consciousness of historical development'.[28] This took shape through the introduction of periodisation into history through the positing of a 'middle age' between antiquity and the present time. Renaissance historians sought to understand the political and social developments of their own age (i.e. the rise of powerful civic oligarchies and the collapse of imperial power) by drawing upon the ancient historians, especially Tacitus. This, however, was not simply a pious act of antiquarianism, for the historical endeavour of the Renaissance did not seek to revive lost societies, but

---

[23] Ibid., p. 322.

[24] Ibid., p. 323.

[25] Marjorie Reeves, *The Influence of Prophecy in the Later Middle Ages: A Study of Joachimism* (reprint. Notre Dame, 1993).

[26] The literature on Renaissance historical writing is enormous. To name a few useful works: Nancy S. Struever, *The Language of History in the Renaissance* (Princeton, 1970); G. Huppert, *The Idea of Perfect History. Historical erudition and historical philosophy in Renaissance France* (Chicago, 1970); Donald R. Kelley, *Foundations of Modern Historical Scholarship* (New York/London, 1970); Peter Burke, *The Renaissance Sense of the Past* (London, 1969); Eric Cochrane, *Historians and Historiography in the Italian Renaissance* (Chicago/London, 1981).

[27] Stephens, *Italian Renaissance. The Origins of Intellectual and Artistic Change Before the Reformation* (London/New York, 1990), p. 185.

[28] Stephens, *Italian Renaissance*, p. 186.

rather to study their rise and fall as recorded by their historians, and draw from these accounts historical principles applicable to the world of fifteenth-century Italy. In the revival of classical learning Renaissance humanists found the bond which joined them to Italy's glorious past, and they revelled in the wisdom of its authors, but, as Stephens argues, their need to explain their own situation created a historical perspective unknown to the ancients:

> Classical histories were informed by the feeling of a gulf between 'barbarism' and civilisation, with the culture of Greece and Rome near the light and the inferior peoples outside the Pale. The Romans had an idea of decadence, of a golden age in the past from which they had declined. The idea, however, was lacking to them of ancient and modern history, as well as the problem it pushed to the fore of explaining how modern times had come to pass.[29]

Humanism north of the Alps, whilst greatly indebted to the work of Italian humanists, their textual methodology, their unearthing of ancient texts, and their use of classical historians, looked to their past from another perspective. They did not share the historical problem which drove the Italian humanists to find the connection between Roman civilisation and contemporary Italian culture. The northern Europeans belonged to the class of 'barbarians', and their historical conundrum was to establish how the wisdom of the ancient world spoke to them. The key to this, as has been noted by scholars, was the writings of Tacitus. Here again, classical sources were enlisted for the service of contemporary problems. German, French and English humanists looked to the Middle Ages to validate their 'barbarian' past and Tacitus provided the material for an examination of the national customs and institutions which lay at the heart of these emerging nation states.[30] Northern writers sought to prove that access to the ancient world was not solely through Italian culture, and they made use of the new historical craft unleashed by the Renaissance to write national and cultural histories of their own peoples. The northern humanists took up the work of the fourteenth-century chroniclers who had begun to separate the sacred and profane. In the late Middle Ages the writing of history was removed from the hands of clerics and began to serve the interests of the emerging burgher classes. Civic chronicles extolled the virtues of the state and unified the social, political and historical interests of its peoples.[31] These chronicles, with their patriotic orientation, were eagerly read by humanists and reformers,

---

[29] Ibid., p. 191.

[30] Ibid., pp. 196–7.

[31] Richard Feller and Edgar Bonjour, *Geschichtsschreibung der Schweiz vom Spätmittelalter zur Neuzeit* (2 vols, Basle/Stuttgart, 1962), I. 20.

and they provided essential material for historians in the sixteenth century.[32]

Humanism provided the Reformation with the tools and methods necessary to create a wide-ranging intellectual culture. As Donald Kelley has argued, humanism gave history coherence and continuity through 'imputation of causal relationships, through literary devices such as orations and dialogues, and through extracting moral and political lessons from this reconstructed past'.[33] With the revolution brought about by the advent of printing there were significant scholarly developments which transformed the writing of history: classical, patristic and medieval texts were discovered, corrected and published; philology became an essential tool for historical research; a new archival spirit led scholars to scour the libraries of Europe in search of manuscript sources.

Although the debt of Protestant historical thought to both the medieval and humanist traditions was great, the nature of the reformation revolt against authority required that certain elements of these traditions were appropriated, and others rejected. The dispute between Erasmus and Luther was fundamentally about anthropology, the nature of humanity, and this brought into sharp relief underlying tensions between the Renaissance and Reformation.[34] The basic evangelical teaching on the sinfulness of humanity meant that only certain aspects of humanism could be employed in the service of articulating the true faith. Certainly the academic tools and perspectives which it provided to the scholarly world of sixteenth-century Protestantism were gladly accepted, but as the lives and work of such men as Castellio, Bibliander, Curione and Ochino demonstrated, Protestant theology and ecclesiology could never really come to terms with basic humanist principles.

The most important humanist legacy for the Reformation was the creation of a Protestant textual community, a Europe-wide circle of learned men who shared a common language and whose intellectual and religious exchanges took place through common modes of inquiry.[35] Calvin, Melanchthon, Bucer, and their Catholic opponents moved in the rarefied atmosphere of debate where the controversies of the ancient

---

[32] On the use of chronicles, see Bächtold in Volume 1, Chapter 4, and Naphy, Chapter 2, this volume.

[33] D.R. Kelley, 'Humanism and History', in A. Rabil (ed.), *Renaissance Humanism. Foundations, Forms and Legacy* (3 vols, Philadelphia, 1988), III. 249.

[34] Geoffrey Elton, 'Auseinandersetzung und Zusammenarbeit zwischen Renaissance und Reformation in England', in August Buck (ed.), *Renaissance–Reformation. Gegensätze und Gemeinsamkeiten* (Wiesbaden, 1984), p. 220.

[35] On this subject, see the stimulating work, Debora Kuller Shuger, *The Renaissance Bible. Scholarship, Sacrifice, and Subjectivity* (Berkeley, 1994).

church, with all their participants and decrees, were relived in the polemical exchanges of the sixteenth century. For example, François Baudouin, in response to the Colloquy of Poissy, published in 1566 a history of the Council of Carthage (411) with notes comparing Beza to the leader of the Donatist party.[36] The attack on the Calvinists and their views on the church was undertaken in terms of the condemnation of the Donatists. Calvin's reply was made in kind. The whole academic debate between Protestant and Catholic humanists moved on a level where the language and history of both scripture and the early church were appropriated and used as though there were no temporal distance.

In this textual community, as Shuger argues, the past is 'type and (rhetorical) figure of the present'.[37] The temporal differences between past and present are minimalised, for scripture is the mirror of the past. Shuger quotes T.H.L. Parker's assessment of Calvin's New Testament commentaries:

> We almost forget which century we are in; we hardly know whether the participants are they or we. We are talking about Judaizers in Galatia – no, we are not, they are Romanists in France and Switzerland – indeed, we are not talking about the Judaizers at all, we are joining in the controversy, we are taking sides . . . [38]

The beginning point for the Protestant vision of the past was with those men who served as leaders of the movement. For all their differences, what united this disparate cast of men was a shared belief that they had been called as one of God's prophets.[39] This self-identity, which drew its inspiration from the prophetic figures of the Old Testament, entailed an intimate connection between their inner spiritual conversion and the outer religious and cultural realities around them. For each of these men, the essential message of the Word of God was present as a spiritual reality to their self-understanding. Each of the principal reformers, whether Luther, Zwingli, Müntzer or Calvin responded to the charges of sectarianism by affirming that they were instruments of God, chosen by him to fulfil his will.[40]

---

[36] I am grateful to Dr J.A. Alexander of St Mary's College, University of St Andrews for this information.

[37] Shuger, Renaissance Bible, p. 22.

[38] Ibid., p. 23.

[39] Klaus Peter Voss, Der Gedanke des allgemeinen Priester- und Prophetentums. Seine gemeindetheologische Aktualisierung in der Reformationszeit (Wuppertal/Zurich, 1990).

[40] On Luther's understanding of office, see B.A. Gerrish, 'Doctor Martin Luther. Subjectivity and Doctrine in the Lutheran Reformation', in Peter Newman Brooks (ed.), Seven-Headed Luther. Essays in Commemoration of a Quincentenary 1483–1983 (Oxford, 1983), pp. 2–24.

The role of prophet was variously interpreted. Luther, in the early years of the Reformation, denied Catholic accusations that he claimed for himself a special office and authority. But, as Mark Edwards has argued, in response to those whom he saw as 'fanatics', Luther moved ever closer towards identifying himself with St Paul, seeing himself in the role occupied by the biblical prophets.[41] Luther set down the terms of being a true prophet and used these to vilify his opponents. As with Zwingli and Calvin, Luther held that the role of the prophet was intimately connected with the preaching of the Word of God.[42] All these reformers held that Reformation and history were in the end divine, not human works. The beginning and end, together with the substance of Reformation, was Jesus Christ, the Word of God. It was the timeless relationship between Christ and his church which, for the reformers, provided the historical continuity which they had rejected in the institutional church.

For Luther, the historical continuity of the church was based upon the profession of faith, and was, therefore, wholly dependent upon the will of God.[43] This, however, was not to turn the church into some ethereal body, for, as Oberman writes:

> The Church is visible, but as a suffering communion of Christians. It is endowed with great riches, which are accessible only through faith. It is unique and unified, but scattered all over the world. Bishops and doctors are its servants, allowing the Gospel to be preached in sermon, sacrament, absolution of sins, praise of God – and martyrdom: as in the days of the early church so will it be until Judgement Day. Persecution and pressure will increase, and yet the adversary will not be able to vanquish the Church.[44]

Luther held that the true church in the world stood in contrast to the ostentatious pomp and glory of the institutional church. The Reformation would necessarily cause disruption and strife, for the Devil, in the form of the institutional church, was at war with the preaching of the Gospel. He would seek to destroy those few who belonged to the true

---

[41] M.U. Edwards, *Luther and the False Brethren* (Stanford, 1975), p. 200.

[42] Bernd Moeller, 'Was wurde in der Frühzeit der Reformation in den deutschen Städten gepredigt?', *ARG*, 75 (1984), 176–93; Hans-Jürgen Goertz, *Pfaffenhass und gross Geschrei* (Munich, 1987), pp. 134–47; R. Scribner, 'Preachers and People in the German Towns', in his *Popular Culture and Popular Movements in Reformation Germany* (London, 1987), pp. 123–43; Bruce Gordon, 'Preaching and the reform of the clergy in the Swiss Reformation', in Andrew Pettegree (ed.), *The Reformation of the Parishes. The Ministry and the Reformation in town and country* (Manchester, 1993), pp. 63–84; T.H.L. Parker, *Calvin's Preaching* (Edinburgh, 1992).

[43] Wriedt in Volume 1, Chapter 3.

[44] H.A. Oberman, *Luther. Man between God and the Devil* (New Haven/London, 1989), p. 270.

church on account of their faith. What would characterise the true church was that it would be persecuted and might even fall into apostasy. At every moment what provides the church with continuity is not the historic witness of its members, no matter how few, but the presence of the Word of God.

It is for this reason that although Luther enjoyed speaking of men and women in the past who had witnessed to the truth in times of darkness, he rejected the notion that they constituted a continuous succession of the true church.[45] Martyrs such as Hus and Savonarola served as examples to Christians, providing them with encouragement that they were not alone in their struggle, but no more. For theological reasons, Luther rejected this human chain as a basis for the church, but as the Reformation began to take shape, this position was modified.

For both Luther and Melanchthon history sprang from the pages of scripture, and the history of the church was to be understood in terms of its faithfulness to the Word. To understand history it was crucial to read the works of pagan antiquity and chronicles of the medieval world; they provided the methods and the details for the comprehension of human history. But, in the end, human history was part of a great divine plan, the *Heilsgeschichte* (history of salvation) which revealed God's true purpose for creation.[46] Luther saw his prophetic role as part of God's plan to bring about the end of the world through the preaching of his Word.[47] Melanchthon, who was more committed to the academic study of history, which he regarded as a key to understanding theology, developed this position in ways which made history-writing an important polemical tool of the Reformation.[48] Melanchthon concentrated on demonstrating how the whole history of Germany was to be understood in terms of the conflict between the papacy and empire.[49] The model of martyrdom which the Lutherans came to employ so successfully as a means of encouraging the faithful was transposed to the whole German nation: Germany had borne witness to the faith and had suffered at the hands of tyrannical Rome. This became the dominant theme of German Protestant historians during the sixteenth century, reaching its zenith in

---

[45] J.M. Headley, *Luther's View of Church History* (New Haven/London, 1963), p. 102.

[46] Wriedt in Volume 1, Chapter 3.

[47] R. Kolb, *For All the Saints. Changing Perceptions of Martyrdom and Sainthood in the Lutheran Reformation* (Macon, GA, 1987), p. 25.

[48] On Melanchthon, see S. Wiedenhofer, *Formalstrukturen humanistischer und reformatorischer Theologie bei Philipp Melanchthon* (2 vols, Berne, 1976); Heinz Scheible, 'Melanchthon Zwischen Luther und Erasmus', in Buck, *Renaissance–Reformation*, pp. 155–80.

[49] Kolb, *For All the Saints*, p. 25.

the *Magdeburg Centuries*.[50] Matthias Flacius, its chief historian, structured the material so as to demonstrate Germany's divine mission.[51]

Lutheran historical writing developed some key concepts which remained constant through the sixteenth century: the connection between Word and history, the development of church history within a national context, and the emphasis upon the chain of witnesses.[52] The apocalyptic atmosphere in which Luther formulated his Reformation message slowly diminished as the reformer began in his later years to look more favourably upon the medieval world, and freely admitted that those essential signs of the church which he outlined in his work *On the Councils and the Church* (1539) were discernible in the medieval church. Luther appeared to move towards seeing more continuity in institutions. As Gordon Rupp has commented: 'Luther never unchurched the whole Roman Church, though he thought that those only were saved who relied wholly on Christ's merits for salvation: "Some children and some old people (but very few) who at the end of their lives turned to God." '[53]

As Robert Kolb has argued, what distinguished Lutheran writers from other Protestants was the centrality of doctrine to their portrayal of history.[54] Their work was not concerned with providing the faithful with emotional, dramatic accounts of the stirring deeds of earlier generations. The principal martyrology of Germany pales in comparison to those produced in areas where persecution was a lived experience, as in the work of Crespin, Haemstaede and Foxe;[55] Rabus's work is dull and poorly constructed. A more accurate reflection of the nature of Lutheran history writing is found in the *Magdeburg Centuries*, which equates the history of Christianity with the history of doctrine.[56] The work was not intended

---

[50] On the relationship between Melanchthon and the Magdeburg Centuriators, see Robert Kolb, 'Philipp's Foes, but Followers Nonetheless. Late Humanism among the Gnesio-Lutherans', in Manfred P. Fleisher (ed.), *The Harvest of Humanism in Central Europe. Essays in Honour of Lewis W. Spitz* (St Louis, 1992), pp. 163–5.

[51] Gerald Strauss, 'The Course of German History: The Lutheran Interpretation', in Gerald Strauss (ed.), *Enacting the Reformation in Germany. Essays on Institution and Reception* (Aldershot, 1993), pp. 684–5. On Flacius as church historian, see Thomas Haye, 'Der Catalogus testium veritatis des Matthias Flacius Illyricus – eine Einführung in die Literatur des Mittelalters?', *ARG*, 83 (1992), 31–48.

[52] Martin Brecht, 'Luther und die Probleme seiner Zeit', in Volker Press and Dieter Stievermann (eds), *Martin Luther. Probleme seiner Zeit* (Stuttgart, 1986), pp. 58–74.

[53] Gordon Rupp, *The Righteousness of God. Luther Studies* (reprint. London, 1968), p. 325.

[54] Kolb, *For all the Saints*, p. 97.

[55] See the contributions by Watson (Chapter 3) and Pettegree (Chapter 4), this volume.

[56] Kolb, *For All the Saints*, p. 97.

for the laity, but for ministers who could read Latin. It drew upon traditional themes of individual witnesses of faith, persecution and martyrdom, but its primary purpose was didactic: ' . . . for the pastor who wanted to use martyr stories or to trace some history of the confession of the church, the Centuriators provided not only a systematic organisation and analysis of the relevant material but also a wide overview of the history of the church'.[57]

In Germany the Lutherans constructed a historical discourse based on the history of right faith and teaching. This enabled Protestant writers to reclaim those parts of ancient and medieval church history which they found acceptable. Thus Hus and Savonarola could be cleansed and presented as godly witnesses to the truth in times of darkness.[58] In addition, the Lutheran focus upon the papacy and Rome as the source of all corruption made possible a more positive view of the other offices and structures of the church, particularly diocesan and parochial, which were retained and employed by the Protestants. Luther had claimed that he had been forced out of his father's house by the papacy, now he could return and claim his legacy. In many ways, the history of the Lutheran Reformation in the sixteenth century was more about coming to terms with the middle ages than making a break with them.

For most German Protestants the experiences of martyrdom and persecution were remote. Although the situation in the empire was precarious as long as Charles V opposed the Reformation, from 1530 onwards the Protestants began to construct a religious culture which enjoyed the protection of powerful territorial princes. A distinctly Lutheran identity could be shaped through education, marriage laws and worship, all of which stressed the natural ordinances of family, work and station.[59] The Lutheran Reformation emphasised vocation and the fulfilment of one's Christian duty in the diligent performance of one's calling. This had profound implications for all levels of society, and Susan Karant Nunn has shown how this process of identity formulation was applied to women. In examining the sermons of Johannes Mathesius, she had concluded:

> A salient difference between men and women is that among men, a variety of vocations are in evidence, whereas for womankind there is a single, unified calling, that of Christian housewife and mother. On this point Mathesius was, as he believed himself always to be, in complete agreement with Luther, his hero and his model. No matter what women's actual livelihoods and vicissitudes might be, their

---

[57] Ibid., p. 101.

[58] On the editing of medieval writers to make them appeal to Protestant audiences, see Ryrie in Volume 1, Chapter 6.

[59] On the implications of the reformation for the structuring of familial relationships, see Biel, Chapter 8, this volume.

identity and their satisfaction were to be derived from their ties to husband, children and home.[60]

The establishment of a Lutheran sense of history and identity necessarily meant the conquest of other views and perceptions. Theologically, Zwinglianism and radical thought, deprived of meaningful political support, were vilified and increasingly marginalised.[61] As Heinz Schilling has demonstrated for northwestern Germany, the more the Lutheran Reformation produced 'a new consensus on belief and ritual in the towns and, in addition, established a legally and institutionally independent town church', the easier it was for dissenting voices to be identified and eradicated.[62] Schilling's arguments are persuasive. The European civic mentality was dominated by concepts of 'peace' and 'unity' which cut across social, political and economic lines. Despite innumerable internal conflicts, it was clear that no one group wanted to undermine the basic communal structures which held together urban and civic life in Germany.[63] In the early Reformation, nervous magistrates in southern Germany accepted the evangelical religion only when popular support threatened to sweep them away.[64] The seeds of triumph of a Lutheran identity were sown when the Reformation moved to accommodate itself to existing political structures, mollifying anxious magistrates and territorial princes with assurances that preaching the Word of God was a means, and not an impediment, to increased political centralisation and social stability. This crucial turn in the early Reformation shaped the manner in which Protestant history and identity were to be expressed in Germany. As T. Brady has recently written, the Peasants' War of 1525 'created a memory shared by the Reformation's chief actors, which acted as a powerful mortgage on decisive action for change and encouraged prudence and political sobriety on all sides'.[65]

---

[60] S.C. Karant-Nunn, 'Kinder, Küche, Kirche: Social Ideology in the Sermons of Johannes Mathesius', in Andrew C. Fix and Susan C. Karant-Nunn (eds), *Germania Illustrata. Essays on Early Modern Germany Presented to Gerald Strauss* (Kirksville, 1992), p. 312. On the relationship between domestic and public piety, see Patrice Veit, 'Private Frömmigkeit, Lektüre und Gesang im protestantischen Deutschland der frühen Neuzeit: Das Modell der Leichen Predigten', in R. Veirhaus (ed.), *Frühe Neuzeit – Frühe Moderne? Forschungen zur Vielschichtigkeit von Übergangsprozessen* (Göttingen, 1992), pp. 271–95.

[61] Heinrich R. Schmidt, 'Die Häretisierung des Zwinglianismus im Reich seit 1525', in Peter Blickle (ed.), *Zugänge zur bäuerlichen Reformation* (Zurich, 1987), pp. 219–36.

[62] Heinz Schilling, 'Alternatives to the Lutheran Reformation and the Rise of Lutheran Identity', in Fix and Karant-Nunn, *Germania Illustrata*, p. 111.

[63] Ibid., p. 113.

[64] Heinrich Richard Schmidt, *Reichstädte, Reich und Reformation* (Stuttgart, 1986), pp. 313–14.

[65] Thomas A. Brady, Jr, *Protestant Politics*, p. 9.

The construction of a Protestant history was a victory for the elites. It is clear that the Lutheran Reformation eventually managed to leave its stamp on local communities, thus effecting the creation of a Protestant identity.[66] This was achieved to the point, as we shall see in Brandenburg, where Lutheran parishioners were able to discern the Calvinist rituals which were being imposed upon them and voice their objections.[67] This victory came, as Strauss has said, 'owing to the hard work done by ruling elites in state, church, academy, and publishing house whose concrete interests these discourses defined in intellectual terms'.[68]

The Lutheran form in Germany, however, must not be regarded as normative for the evolution of Protestant identities and history. Within Germany alternative voices, such as the Hutterites, with their curiously diffident attitude towards church history, survived and indeed laid down roots.[69] Such voices were driven to the periphery of German society, largely to the rural areas, leaving the cities and towns to the Lutheran, and later Calvinist, parties. In other parts of Europe, however, contrasting patterns of reform and identity emerged.

In the Swiss Confederation the reformed tradition had its roots in the preaching of Huldrych Zwingli, who, like Luther, interpreted the Reformation and his role in it as the work of God. Much of the vast literature dedicated to the subject has failed to grasp the extent of the differences between the theologies of Luther and Zwingli. Their superficial agreements masked what surely was the greatest and most poignant manifestation of the central dilemma of the early Reformation – the inability of two legitimately ordained authorities to agree on a fundamental question of scriptural interpretation, the Last Supper. Whereas Luther looked for the hand of God in the final struggle with the Devil, which revealed the last times, Zwingli saw the God who is pure and holy and demands that his people be likewise. This God is active in history,

---

[66] Veit, 'Private Frömmigkeit'; C. Scott Dixon, 'Rural Resistance, the Lutheran pastor, and the Territorial church in Brandenburg Ansbach-Kulmbach, 1528–1603', in Pettegree, *Reformation of the Parishes*, pp. 85–112. Dixon speaks about the resistance which was unleashed by the imposition of the Lutheran reformation on the people.

[67] See Nischan, Chapter 9, this volume.

[68] Gerald Strauss, 'Comment on "Jewish Magic" and "The Devil and the German People"' in Steven Ozment (ed.), *Religion and Culture in the Renaissance and Reformation* (Kirksville, 1989), p. 130.

[69] Klaus Deppermann, 'Die Argumente der deutschen Täufer und Spiritualisten gegen ihre Verfolgung', in Silvana Seidel Menchi (ed.), *Ketzerverfolgung im 16. und frühen 17. Jahrhundert* (Wiesbaden, 1992), pp. 231–48. See also Dipple, in Volume 1, Chapter 9.

striking down the godless and protecting his chosen peoples. Zwingli's vision was of an outward reforming of society, the creation of an all-embracing visible church which took its inspiration from both the historical books of the Old Testament and the church of Constantine.

At the core of Zwingli's evangelical reform was a memorial. The central rite of the church was its remembrance of the Last Supper.[70] This memory was made authentic through the presence of the Holy Spirit, who lifted local communities out of their parochial setting and grafted them on to the body of the universal church.[71] For Zwinglians, the unifying link between past, present and eternity was the reality of the Word of God. The accounts of the Bible are not for the faithful merely pious stories, but events of their own history. They find their identity in the people who populate the pages of scripture.[72] Thus Swiss reformers and humanists appropriated the deliverance language of the Old Testament as a means of portraying Swiss history. The whole thrust of Zwingli's thought was backwards. In contrast to Luther, Zwingli's faith was 'fixed to the Christ of the past and not directed toward the Christ who is coming'.[73]

The Zwinglian Reformation offered an alternative form of Protestant history, but one which was no less exclusive. From the beginning, with its assumption of the unity of the civic society and the church, it was directed toward the urban, burgher classes.[74] As would become so disastrously clear, it had little to offer to the numerically dominant rural population. It constructed a view of the Swiss past which may have made sense to anti-Habsburg sentiments, but the Zwinglian historical identity failed as a polemical tool to make the Reformation acceptable to most of the Swiss Confederate states.[75] It was a tendentious creation too clearly aligned with the hegemonic interests of Zurich.

The speed with which Zwingli had to formulate his theology and ecclesiology was remarkable, and much of his thinking was shaped by

---

[70] The most profound explication of Zwingli's eucharistic position remains J. Courvoisier, *Zwingli. A Reformed Theologian* (London, 1964).

[71] Fritz Büsser, 'Zwingli und die Kirche. Überlegungen zur Aktualität von Zwinglis Ekklesiologie', in his *Die Prophezei. Humanismus und Reformation in Zürich* (Berne, 1994), pp. 77–94.

[72] Fritz Büsser, 'Zwingli, der Exeget', in *Die Prophezei*, pp. 26–55.

[73] S. Strehle, 'Fides ut Foedus: Wittenberg and Zurich in Conflict over the Gospel', *SCJ*, 23 (1992), 10.

[74] Hans Christoph Rublack, 'Zwingli und Zürich', *Zwingliana*, 16 (1985), 393–426.

[75] On the debate within the evangelical party over how to deal with the Catholic Orte, see my forthcoming article 'Toleration in the Early Swiss Reformation: the Art and Politics of Niklaus Manuel of Berne', in Robert Scribner and Ole Grell (eds), *Tolerance and Intolerance in the European Reformation* (Cambridge, 1996).

the attacks made by his critics, above all the Anabaptists.[76] The rejection of infant baptism as non-scriptural was the most serious challenge to mainstream evangelical thought in the 1520s.[77] It forced Zwingli to rethink the relationship between the Old and New Testaments, and it was his attempt to counter the devastating logic of the Anabaptists which led him to the notion of the covenant, the central tenet of the Reformed teaching on church and history.[78] The idea of the Christian church as a continuation of God's covenant with the Israelites appealed on many grounds, not the least of which was the way in which it strengthened Zwingli's use of scripture as the mirror of society. Although the language of the Swiss, or later the Dutch, as the 'elect people' was abandoned, the concept of a 'relationship of mutual responsibility, contingent not only on the faithfulness of God but also upon that of man' provided the Reformation with a most useful means of articulating its history and identity.[79]

The Zwinglian model of the 'godly society', which placed all authority over the church in the hands of pious rulers who were to exercise power in accordance with the Word of God, drew its inspiration from a topological reading of the Old Testament.[80] The rulers of Zurich, Berne and Basle took upon themselves the roles of Israelite kings, and the reformers cast themselves as Nathan and Samuel, the prophets of Israel.[81] This historical creation proved highly exportable and an attractive advertisement for the Swiss model of reform, especially in England under Edward VI.[82] In the concern of English writers to employ myths and historical memories to construct a literary vision of national identity, the Old Testament model of the godly society proved highly adaptable.[83]

This accommodation of civic unity with evangelical thought proved, however, a fleeting moment in the course of the Reformation. Ultimately,

[76] Werner Packull, 'The Origins of Swiss Anabaptism in the Context of the Reformation of the Common Man', *Journal of Mennonite Studies*, 3 (1985), 35–59; James Stayer, 'Die Anfänge des schweizerischen Täufertums in reformierten Kongregationalismus', in Hans-Jürgen Goertz (ed.), *Umstrittenes Täufertum, 1525–1975* (Göttingen, 1977), pp. 19–49.

[77] Adolf Fugel, *Tauflehre und Taufliturgie bei Huldrych Zwingli* (Berne, 1989), pp. 177–212.

[78] J. Wayne Baker, *Heinrich Bullinger and the Covenant. The Other Reformed Tradition* (Athens, Ohio, 1980).

[79] See Regan, Chapter 6, this volume.

[80] Bruce Gordon, 'Zurich and the Scottish Reformation: Rudolf Gwalther's Homilies on Galatians of 1576', in James Kirk (ed.), *Humanism and Reform: The Church in Europe, England and Scotland, 1400–1643*, SCH, Subsidia 8 (Oxford, 1991), pp. 207–20.

[81] Baker, *Heinrich Bullinger*, esp. pp. 55–80.

[82] See Bradshaw, Chapter 5, this volume.

[83] On England, see Andrew Hatfield, *Literature, Politics and National Identity* (Oxford, 1994).

as Bullinger and others would learn, the interests of the two were quite incompatible.[84] Through the imposition of moral legislation and social control, the urban reformers sought to build God's church on earth, but the results were anything but satisfactory.[85] As the Reformation began to see the advent of religious wars and the migration and exile of refugees it had to look for another way of explaining its history and identity. This, above all, was provided by John Calvin.

Calvin was perhaps the most dextrous of the sixteenth-century reformers because he spoke to people on so many levels. His humanist credentials were impeccable: his views of textual criticism, scriptural exegesis, philosophy and history were all moulded by the humanist education he received in France. Calvin's understanding of history revealed his humanist roots. History for Calvin, whether pagan or sacred, was worthy of study because it reveals both the good and evil of human nature and the providence of God. In his sermons on Job, Calvin wrote:

> It is not enough to have our eyes open and to note well and mark what God does during our lives, but we must profit from ancient histories. In fact this is why our Lord has wanted us to have some notable judgements left in writing, so that the memory of them would remain for ever. And we should not only profit from what is contained in Holy Scripture, but when we hear what is spoken by the histories written by the pagans, we should also have the prudence to apply to ourselves what God has done.[86]

Calvin saw history as charting the moral degradation of human societies. The pagan world of antiquity was to be admired for its remarkable achievements, but not without reservation. Calvin loathed the ancient Romans, whom he saw as decadent, cruel and tyrannical; they were cynical manipulators of religion and thereby worthy forefathers of his own enemies in Rome.[87]

Calvin was greatly influenced by Renaissance humanism and its moral interpretation of history. The key, however, to human history was the providence of God, which Calvin argued was to be discerned by human minds. Calvin was not interested in a hidden God, for it is the revealed works of God which give meaning to human existence and induce piety. It is the certainty which the faithful can have about God's providence which brings relief from the overwhelming anxiety of human existence:

---

[84] Hans Ulrich Bächtold, *Bullinger vor dem Rat. Zur Gestaltung und Verwaltung des Zürcher Staatswesens in den Jahren 1531 bis 1575* (Berne, 1982).

[85] Bruce Gordon, *Clerical Discipline and the Rural Reformation. The Synod in Zurich, 1532–1580* (Berne, 1992).

[86] Quoted in W.J. Bouwsma, *John Calvin. A Sixteenth Century Portrait* (1988), p. 169.

[87] Ibid., p. 146.

Yet, when the light of divine providence has shone upon a godly man, he is then relieved and set free not only from the extreme anxiety and fear that were pressing him before, but from every care. For as he justly dreads fortune, so he fearlessly dares commit himself to God. His solace, I say, is to know that his Heavenly Father so holds all things in his power, so rules by his authority and will, so governs by his wisdom, that nothing can befall except he determine it.[88]

Calvin shared with Luther the belief that faith distinguishes the true church from the false, and it is the faith of the church which provides its historical continuity. Unlike Zwingli and Bullinger, however, Calvin was not prepared to associate the church with human political structures. The elect would always remain a gathered church of the few, and although they live in civil society and take on its offices, the goals of the church must not be confused with those of civic unity.[89] Calvin was more concerned to speak of the God who is immanent in the world, comforting those suffering persecution and exile. These people could find the assurance of their salvation in the pages of scripture, for, as Zwingli had shown, biblical history was also their history. This message was at the core of Calvinist writings as they spread across Europe. Crespin and Haemstaede, in their martyrologies, provided afflicted Calvinists with examples from history which would educate the faithful into Christian living during persecution. Pithou's history was intended 'to demonstrate the importance of witnessing to the inner truth of conscience and its energising effects on others'.[90]

The various Protestant movements of the sixteenth century understood that historical writing is a powerful vehicle for the expression of ideology. All history has the feature of shaping: in the Reformation there existed whole networks of people gathering material which could be moulded to create memories of the religious past of both individuals and communities. In the first instance, the reformers turned to history because they were forced to in order to defend themselves against charges of schism, but during the course of the Reformation historical writing acquired other roles. The Protestant Reformation was concerned with the creation of new communities, both local and national, which conformed to their understanding of God's designs for humanity. Communities, to the early modern mind, required a collective memory of

---

[88] John Calvin, *Institutes of the Christian Religion,* ed. John T. McNeil (2 vols, Philadelphia, 1960), I. 17.1, 224.

[89] On this point, see Heiko Oberman, 'Europa afflicta: The Reformation of the Refugees', *ARG,* 83 (1992), 104–5.

[90] Mark Greengrass, 'Nicolas Pithou: experience, conscience and history in the French civil wars', in A. Fletcher and P. Roberts (eds), *Religion, Culture and Society in early modern Britain: Essays in honour of Patrick Collinson* (Cambridge, 1994), p.16.

the past which defined their identity and gave meaning to their institutions and rites. The basic tool of the reformers in the creation of communities was scripture, which not only revealed God's will, but provided the people with stories and characters with which they could identify. The Protestant writers employed images and metaphors in their writings which were taken from scripture and intended to shape the minds of men and women, and to influence their perceptions and ways of acting. There was no one means of achieving this, and indeed the Bible provides diverse and seemingly contradictory images and examples. This proved a strength of the Protestant endeavour, for its creation of communities took place within a variety of social and political networks and its fundamental messages were shaped to meet the needs of those situations. The experiences of the Zurich magistrates were not those of the Calvinist refugees during the French Wars of Religion. The challenge for historians is to read the texts which these various groups have left us, attentive to the conditions which produced them. As Gabrielle Spiegel, writing of an earlier period, reminds us, 'inextricably associated with these histories is a wide range of social and discursive practices, of material and linguistic realities that are interwoven into the fabric of the text, whose analysis as a determinate historical artefact in turn grants us access to the past'.[91]

---

[91] G. Spiegel, *Romancing the Past: The Rise of Vernacular Prose Historiography in Thirteenth-Century France* (Berkeley, 1993), p. 9.

CHAPTER TWO

'No history can satisfy everyone':[1] Geneva's Chroniclers and Emerging Religious Identities

William G. Naphy

In 1532 Antoine Froment delivered the first public Protestant sermon in Geneva. He declared that the people of Geneva, and their ancestors, had slowly fallen under the sway of Antichrist whose power had spread as a contagion for a thousand years. Antichrist was aided by false prophets whom Froment explicitly identified as the priests and monks of the Catholic church. In addition, he delivered a concise rendition of the clerical attack against him and his supporters:

> You have sprung up preaching a new Law, casting down our ancient Law, tested by time and approved by good men everywhere, by Councils, by Universities, by the great teachers who have gone before. Your law is but a seven day wonder and a novelty troubling everyone everywhere. Ours is the faith of the ancients.[2]

Thus, Froment accurately identified the historical problem facing his co-religionists as they assaulted the bastions of late medieval Catholicism. How could the Catholic faith whose origins lay obscured in the mists of time be replaced by a new religion? Change and novelty were the curses hurled against Froment. He realised that to shape the present and determine the future of Christendom, it was essential to capture the past. The heroes and heroines of biblical history, the saints and teachers of the ages and the wisdom of the classical world were objects to be fought over. Out of this struggle would come not only innovative views on history but also, crucially, new ways of understanding oneself and one's opponents.

In examining and assessing the manner in which Genevans resolved this issue we are assisted by a host of eyewitness accounts of the events, for the city is extremely rich in journals and memoirs for the first half of the sixteenth century.[3] Before plunging into a detailed analysis of the use

---

[1] A. Froment, *Les Actes et Gestes merveilleux de la Cité de Genève* (Geneva, 1854), p. xxvii.

[2] Froment, *Actes*, pp. 23–33, passim.

[3] Geneva has many chronicles. The earliest extant is E. Mallet (ed.), 'La plus ancienne chronique de Genève, 1303–35. Fasciculus temporis', in *Mémoires et documents de la Société de l'histoire et d'archéologie de Genève* (hereafter MDG), 9 (1855), 291–320.

of history and the emergence of religious identities we might profit from a discussion of the sources and authors themselves.[4]

Geneva is surprisingly rich in Catholic accounts. The best known is the chronicle of Jeanne de Jussie, secretary of the Poor Claires of Geneva.[5] Jeanne recorded the events of the period 1526–35 (the Poor Claires left Geneva in 1535).[6] It appears that her work was substantially finished by 1546 although it remained unpublished until 1611.[7] This late date explains the anachronistic, and incorrect, title, 'The Leaven of Calvinism', which replaced Jeanne's own title, 'The Commencement of Heresy in Geneva'. Her account is supplemented by two other Catholic sources. Jean Balard, an ironmonger, long-serving Genevan councillor (1515–55) and Syndic (1525, 1530) left a journal of the events of 1525–31.[8] This lengthy and detailed record is an almost daily account of the events and is similar to the other major Catholic source, *The Memoirs of Pierrefleur*.[9] These memoirs provide a journal of the events in the wider francophone area of the Swiss Confederation for the years 1530–61. Guillaume Pierrefleur, the author, was a local dignitary in the Savoyard village of Orbe, conquered by Protestant Berne in 1535.[10] Although faithful to the old faith, Pierrefleur was able to serve as the village's governor four times under Bernese rule (the last in 1577). His work is of a more general nature than those of De Jussie or Balard but provides details on a grander chronological and geographical scale. Most interestingly for an understanding of the developing identities of the Catholic and Protestant factions forming in the midst of dramatic change,

---

[4] The authors were closely interconnected. Balard, Farel, and Claude Roset (Michel's father) were all involved in the Rive dispute which led to the adoption of the Reform. Froment and Dentière were well-known for their work in Geneva. Dentière tried to entice the Poor Claire nuns out of their convent. Bonivard was a prominent Genevan cleric. Finally, Pierrefleur, the Orbe magistrate, had a close relative (perhaps his sister) in the Poor Claires' convent.

[5] J. de Jussie, *Le Levain du Calvinisme, ou commencement de l'heresie de Genève* (Geneva, 1865).

[6] On the Poor Claires: T. Dufour, 'Notice sur le couvent de Saint-Claire à Genève', in *MDG*, 20 (1879–88), 119–33.

[7] On De Jussie: M. Bossard and L. Junod (eds), *Chroniqueurs du XVIe siècle* (Lausanne, 1974), pp. 153–7; A. Rilliet, 'Notice sur Jeanne de Jussie', in De Jussie, *Levain*, separately numbered after p. 293; M. Godet et al., *Dictionnaire historique & biographique de la Suisse* (8 vols, Neuchâtel, 1921), IV. 311; and H. Feld, ' "Es gat ein Christenman über fäld": Die Begegnung von humanistisch geprägter Theologie und mittelalterlicher Volksfrömmigkeit in der Zwinglischen Reformation', in W. van't Spijker (ed.), *Calvin. Erbe und Auftrag* (Kampen, 1991), pp. 181–202 esp. pp. 193–202.

[8] J. Balard, *Journal du Syndic Jean Balard* (Geneva, 1854). See Godet, *Dictionnaire*, I. 518.

[9] G. Pierrefleur, *Mémoires de Pierrefleur* (Lausanne, 1856).

[10] See Godet, *Dictionnaire*, V. 292 and Bossard, *Chroniqueurs*, pp. 85–7.

Pierrefleur and Balard remained in governments officially devoted to the reform. Clearly, their ultimate loyalty and personal identity was to the local community, their friends, families and lands.[11]

Unsurprisingly, there is a greater wealth of sources for the Protestant point of view. The earliest published works are by Marie Dentière, a former abbess from Tournai, and Froment's wife.[12] Her first work, published in 1536, was *The war and deliverance of the city of Geneva*.[13] She followed this, in 1539, with a historically detailed epistle addressed to the Queen of Navarre.[14] This latter work, attacking the treatment of Calvin and Farel by Geneva's pro-Bernese magistrates, was suppressed by the state and ushered in magisterial censorship in Geneva.[15] Dentière's letter highlights the fact that, only a few years after the adoption of the reform, history was being used against other Protestants.[16] Personal identity and self-awareness amongst the adherents of the new faith progressed rapidly to the point at which individuals felt compelled to differentiate themselves even within the narrow, nascent confines of Genevan Protestantism.

In addition, Geneva also produced three other chronicles of events in the city. The first was written by the early preacher of the reform, Antoine Froment, Dentière's husband. His work, on the *Marvellous*

---

[11] Cf. another minor Catholic work: Jean Gacy, Father-Confessor to the Poor Claires, composed and published (1536) *La deploration de la Cité de Genève sur le faict des Heretiques qui l'ont tiranniquement opprimée* (scc A. Montaiglon [ed.], *Recueil de poesies françoises des XVe et XVIe siècle* [Paris, 1856], 4, 94–102). It presents a short but vitriolic attack on Geneva's religious changes (and includes the earliest surviving printed use of Eidgenot, p. 95: 'Les Anguenotz m'ont fait sedicieuse').

[12] There is an extensive literature on Dentière: Godet, *Dictionnaire*, II. 657; I. Backus, 'Marie Dentière: un cas de féminisme théologique à l'époque de la Réforme', in *Bulletin de la Société de l'histoire du Protestantisme français*, 137 (1991), 177–95, and her 'Le guide des Femmes disparues', in A. M. Käppeli (ed.), *Graffiti Propose* (Geneva, 1993), pp. 20–39; also J. D. Douglas, 'Marie Dentière's use of Scripture in her Theology of History', in M. S. Burrows and P. Rorem (eds), *Biblical Hermeneutics in Historical Perspective* (Grand Rapids, 1991), pp. 227–44, and her 'A Report on Anticlericalism in Three French Women Writers 1404–1549', in P.A. Dykema and H.A. Oberman (eds), *Anticlericalism in Late Medieval and Early Modern Europe* (Leiden, 1993), pp. 243–56.

[13] M. Dentière, 'La Guerre et Deslivrance de la Ville de Genève', in *MDG*, 20 (1879–88), 337–76.

[14] Dentière, *L'Epistre tres utile faicte et composee par une femme Chrestienne de Tournay* (Geneva: Girard, 1539 falsely labelled Anvers: Martin, 1539). Cf. A.L. Herminjard, *Correspondance des Réformateurs* (Geneva, 1874), 5 (1539–40), 295–304.

[15] See my *Calvin and the Consolidation of the Genevan Reformation* (Manchester, 1994), pp. 27–43 and esp. 124.

[16] Cf. Anonymous, 'Poême sur les événements Genevois de 1538 à 1540'. The two surviving copies are in the Musée d'histoire de la Réformation, Institut d'histoire de la Réformation, Bibliothèque publique et universitaire de Genève, Qca5 and Archives d'Etat de Genève, Histoire de Genève opuscules, G235/11.

events and deeds of the city of Geneva, discusses the period 1532–33 and
was completed by 1554.[17] Michel Roset wrote the second major chronicle.[18] His father, Claude, was Geneva's secretary (1535–55) and Michel
succeeded to the post (1555–59). A devout Calvinist and patriotic
Genevan, he served as Syndic 14 times between 1560 and1612. Upon his
death the city recognised his devotion to Geneva by conferring upon him
the title 'père de la patrie'.[19] His *Chronicles* cover Genevan history up to
1562. The greatest difficulty with this chronicle is that it is a second-gen-
eration retrospective on the emergence of Genevan Protestantism. Roset,
born in 1535, more than any other chronicler, Catholic or Protestant,
was writing as a second-hand witness to the events. The usefulness of his
work is that it represents the culmination of the process whereby history
is used to shape and buttress a confessional identity.

Without minimising the works of the above authors it is true to say
that the greatest, most prolific chronicler of Geneva was François
Bonivard. Bonivard, former prior of St-Victor, Geneva's Cluniac
monastery, was the author of several historical, philosophical and linguistic works.[20] Educated at Pignerol, Turin and Freiburg (Breisgau)
Bonivard possessed the best local mind before and after the Reformation.
He was a devoted though not uncritical supporter of Calvin's reforming
work in Geneva. The majority of his historical works date from the
period 1550–66. None were published in his lifetime (nor were those of
Froment or Roset); the state refused to grant them a licence because of
their frank criticism of Geneva's magistrates and its military protector,
Berne, during 1530–55.[21]

Together these sources cover the sweep of opinion available for an

---

[17] Froment, *Actes*. For details on Froment's life see Godet, *Dictionnaire*, III. 279 and
Bossard, *Chroniqueurs*, pp. 217–9. The transcript of the 1534 heresy trial of Baudichon de
la Maisonneuve (a leading Genevan Protestant) in Lyons presents the views of numerous
individuals from both parties. cf. *Procès de Baudichon de la Maison Neuve accusé d'hérésie
à Lyon 1534*, ed. J.G. Baum (Geneva, 1873). On De la Maisonneuve, see Godet,
Dictionnaire, IV. 640.

[18] M. Roset, *Les Chroniques de Genève* (Geneva, 1894).

[19] See Godet, *Dictionnaire*, V. 557f.

[20] These are: F. Bonivard, *Advis et devis de la source de l'idolatrie* (Geneva, 1856); *Advis
et devis des lengues* (Geneva, 1865); *Advis et devis de l'ancienne et nouvelle police de
Genève* (Geneva, 1865); *Chroniques de Genève* (2 vols, Geneva, 1867). An alternative version of the *Chroniques* exists only in a Turin manuscript. Micheline Tripet (Geneva's city
archivist), at the time of writing editing this manuscript, kindly allowed me full access to
her transcription of this fascinating document.

[21] Bonivard has been the object of a number of studies: Godet, *Dictionnaire*, II. 235;
Bossard, *Chroniques*, pp. 13–17; H. Bressler, *François Bonivard* (Geneva, 1944); J.J.
Chaponière, 'Notice sur François Bonivard, Prieur de Saint-Victor, et sur ses écrits', *MDG*,
4 (1845), 137–304; J.E. Berghoff, *François Bonivard. Sein Leben und seine Schriften*
(Heidelberg, 1923).

assessment of Geneva's Reformation. The voices of merchant magistrates are heard along with those of humanist clerics. Devout religious adherents compete with fervent patriots. Women and men, rich and poor, in prose and poetry, strive to understand the events swirling about them, to place the present in an historical context, to decide who they are and what they stand for and against. All this was complicated in Geneva by the crucial need for the city and its residents to justify and legitimise their revolt against Savoy as well as their Reformation.

As one might expect, the Protestant authors turn most frequently and naturally to the Bible for historical precedents and examples to explain contemporary events. As a historical and theological book it presented events within the context of divine, prophetic interpretation. The Bible remained the best source of historical models; its stories of good and evil, truth versus deceit were familiar. The average person may not have understood biblical teaching on the eucharist or election but it hardly took a Renaissance education to understand idolatry and apostasy or the danger of divine wrath. These dangerous sins and their consequences were a common idiom, familiar to all.

For Protestants, though, the control of scripture in interpreting contemporary events was crucial. As Froment said above, they were accused of fulfilling the prophecies about the false teachers of the latter days. Dentière met the need both to control biblical stories and rebut the charge of novelty with true ingenuity. She compared the tardy arrival of evangelical truth with the appearance of children to Abraham and Sarah, and Zachariah and Elizabeth.[22] The latter allusion was especially valuable as it recalled John the Baptist, the harbinger of Christ, the 'voice of one crying in the wilderness' who assailed Israel's apostasy which had brought Roman tyranny.[23] This image was very useful as Dentière wished to overthrow papal idolatry and exalt in the simultaneous deliverance of Geneva from Savoyard tyranny. Quite naturally she then identified the Duke of Savoy as Pharaoh, whose power over Israel was destroyed after a long period of bondage.[24]

Froment makes frequent use of this latter historical model. Geneva is Israel in exile. However, the city is also Jerusalem, unheeding of Jeremiah's words, bound in its apostasy and idolatry, its stubbornness inviting divine retribution.[25] It is not the Protestant preacher (the new Jeremiah or Elijah) who troubled Geneva (the new, tormented Jerusalem)

---

[22] Dentière, *Guerre*, pp. 340f; Herminjard, *Correspondance*, p. 300. Cf. Gen. 21:5f. and Luke 1:13–24.

[23] John 1:23.

[24] Dentière, *Guerre*, p. 348 and Exod. 1:13f.

[25] Froment, *Actes*, pp. xiv–xix (passim), 167, 179. Cf. Jer. 6:6f.

but the city's ruler (the Ahab-like bishop): 'It is you, O King, who troubles Israel, not I'.[26] The holy host of righteous kings and prophets were paraded forth as examples to be followed in overthrowing idolatry while those who led Israel to destruction were reborn under the contemporary guise of clerics, monks and nuns: Elijah and Hezekiah versus Ahab and Jezebel.[27]

However, one is somewhat surprised by the lack of biblical allusions in Roset and Bonivard. Their greatest concern, justifying the secular revolution, finds scant use for such models. In one area, though, they all make use of the Bible. This is the clear, consistent identification of the pope with the Antichrist of Christian eschatology. For Dentière the pope is a supporter of idols, abomination, blasphemy, the Antichrist.[28] Froment is no less certain that God's poor people are enslaved by the 'great tyranny of the Antichrist'.[29] Bonivard speaks of the Guises, the great persecutors of French Protestants as having renounced 'Christ to adore the image in Rome and to persecute the faithful of Christ with fire and sword'.[30] Most horrible of all to Bonivard is the pope's Beast-like claim to divine omnipotence.[31] Roset sees the triumph of the reform as the culmination of biblical eschatology, 'the ruin and final destruction of the Antichrist and his followers', a verbatim account of the assertion on the post-Reformation commemorative plaque placed above the portal of the Maison de Ville.[32]

How does scripture fare in the hands of the Catholics? Old Testament assaults on idolatry are too dangerous while allusions to Antichrist seem to be equally self-defeating. Already their opponents have captured great swathes of the Bible; idols are associated with saint's cults and Antichrist and Babylon with the pope and Rome. Balard even uses the phrase 'the Pope Antichrist', though he makes no other use of biblical images.[33] Pierrefleur, likewise, has no recourse to the scriptures, though he mentions that Farel is called a devil, among other things. His one obvious allusion to the Bible is to mock a Protestant image. He discusses a book, *The testament and death of Pierre Viret's wife*, which the Genevan

---

[26] Froment, *Actes*, p. 6. Cf., 1 Kgs 18:18.

[27] Froment, *Actes*, pp. 131f (Hezekiah, 2 Kgs 18:3f; Asa, 1 Kings 15:11f.), 134 (Jezebel, 1 Kgs 18:13), 193f. (Gideon, Judg. 7:5f. The Bernese captain only diminished his army by dismissing the fainthearted).

[28] Dentière, *Guerre*, pp. 364, 375; Epistre, sig. b6ʳ.

[29] Froment, *Actes*, p. 23.

[30] Bonivard, *Police*, p. 311. Cf. Rev. 13:15.

[31] Bonivard, *L'Idolatrie*, p. 13. He finds repugnant the pope's assertion that he will not use his power to free souls from purgatory.

[32] Roset, *Chroniques*, pp. 8, 226f. Cf. Rev. 18.

[33] Balard, *Journal*, p. 268.

authorities confiscated and suppressed in 1551. Pierrefleur says that the Catholics had laughed at the notion that on her deathbed Elizabeth Turtaz had said that she beheld the heavens opened and chairs prepared for Viret and Farel.[34]

De Jussie, however, is happy to use biblical models. The Bernese soldiers, who sacked churches as they passed through Vaud and Gex, are likened to the servants of Caiaphas beating Jesus and Pilate's soldiers scourging Christ. She identifies Luther with the Antichrist by calling him 'the Prince and Great Heresiarch' who has 'renewed all heresies' but has been thwarted by God who will not 'abandon His bride, the Church'.[35] She speaks of the persecution of the church and the infection of the people by 'this abominable and detestable sin' which invites 'the wrath of God . . . divine judgement'.[36] She also reports with enthusiasm the denunciation of Farel by Amadée de Gingin, Abbot of Bonmont. The good abbot lambasted Farel for failing to show any sign of divine vocation or approbation such as Moses was able to show Pharaoh.[37] Thereafter, she explicitly refers to 'these doomed preachers of the Antichrist'.[38]

The most frequent use of scripture by a Catholic is in a poem by Gacy, the father-confessor at De Jussie's convent. He recalls the laments of Rachel, of Anna, and of Naomi at their sorrowful situations.[39] He then bewails the decline of 'grieving Geneva' seduced by the 'Anguenotz' who are 'blind men' whose 'eyes are shut by scales'.[40] The supporters of reform are 'beasts', a 'detestable sect'.[41] Farel is a 'demoniac' associated with Belial.[42] Viret was driven from his native Orbe like a leper.[43] Geneva, unlike faithful France, had become 'a bottomless pit', a 'Gehenna' surging with 'infernal flames'.[44] For all of Gacy's fervid and evocative use of scriptural allusion, the Catholics have less recourse to

---

[34] Pierrefleur, *Mémoires*, pp. 21f., 185. All copies of the book, B. Textor, *Le testament et mort de la femme de Pierre Viret* (Geneva: Jean Girard, 1551) were destroyed but manuscripts circulated in Orbe. See 'Fiches alphabétiques d'Herminjard', *MHR, IHR*. Cf. Stephen's vision, Acts 7:56 and Rev. 4:4.

[35] De Jussie, *Levain*, p. 33.

[36] De Jussie, *Levain*, p. 35. Cf. Eph. 5:23–7.

[37] Taking the role of Pharoah whose heart was hardened by the Mosaic 'signs' was probably counterproductive. Cf. Exod. 7:9–13, De Jussie, *Levain*, p. 49. Also Pierrefleur, *Mémoires*, p. 25: 'ceux qui annoncent la nouvelle Loy ne font aucun miracle'.

[38] De Jussie, *Levain*, p. 51.

[39] Gacy, 'Deploration', p. 94. Cf. Matt. 2:18 (Rachel); Ruth 1:3–18 (Naomi); 1 Sam. 1:9–11 (Anna, Samuel's mother).

[40] Gacy, 'Deploration', p. 95. Cf. Matt. 15:14; Acts 9:18.

[41] Gacy, 'Deploration', p. 97.

[42] Gacy, 'Deploration', p. 97. Cf., 2 Cor. 6:15.

[43] Gacy, 'Deploration', p. 98. Cf. Num. 12.

[44] Gacy, 'Deploration', p. 101. Cf. Ezek. 20:47f.

the Bible for historical imagery and models to interpret contemporary events. The Protestants, for their part, seem most comfortable with the Old Testament denunciations of Israel's apostasy and idolatry or New Testament eschatological warnings of the impending decline of the new Israel into similar sins.

However, in one area associated with scripture both Catholics and Protestants are agreed. Both are rabid in their identification of their enemies with the Jews and, to a lesser extent, the Turk.[45] Rather than indulge in a lengthy enumeration of this phenomenon one can discuss the broader categories used in this particular method of attack. Some epithets in this area are meant to recall biblical passages. Catholics and Protestants are fond of recalling Caiaphas who led the Jews in delivering Jesus to Pilate.[46] Froment associates Catholic practices with the synagogue.[47] He was joined by Dentière in alluding to scribes and Pharisees.[48] General use of the term 'Jew' as abuse is found in Bonivard, De Jussie and others.[49] Almost as frequently, the opposition is labelled 'Turk' recalling the very present threat to the Christian West posed by the then still expanding Ottoman Empire.[50] Finally, it is worth noting that these terms can be used by Protestants against their co-religionists; for example, the anonymous author of The events of 1538–40 mentions Caiaphas when attacking Calvin's magisterial opponents.[51] The frequency and virulence of these epithets strengthens the sense of visceral hatred developing. Both sides are identifying one another not only with past or future adversaries of God's Word but also with the perceived contemporary enemies of Christ within and without Christendom, the Jews and Turks.

The references to Jews have the advantage of linking present realities to biblical events. However, this is not the only use made of non-biblical personages or contemporary history. Perhaps not surprisingly, as Bonivard is the sole chronicler with a thorough training in the classics, he is the only author to make regular use of ancient history.[52] Most importantly he uses classical and church history to demonstrate that the decline

---

[45] Cf. Matt. 27:25, the traditional proof-text for 'Christ-killers'.

[46] Dentière, Guerre, p. 350; Roset, Chroniques, p. 165; De Jussie, Levain, p. 9.

[47] Froment, Actes, p. 68.

[48] Froment, Actes, pp. 26–9, 36f., 39; Dentière, Epistre, sig. b8r.

[49] Bonivard, L'Idolatrie, p. 148; De Jussie, Levain, pp. 23, 55, 64; Froment, Actes, pp. 70f.; Dentière, Guerre, p. 362.

[50] Bonivard, L'Idolatrie, pp. 144f.; De Jussie, Levain, pp. 23, 54; Froment, Actes, pp. 70f., 134; Dentière, Epistre, sig. a2r.

[51] Anon., 'Evenements', p. 9.

[52] See, Des lengues, pp. 157f. (Luther and Epicurus), p. 189 (on More's Utopia); Police, p. 44 (on Geneva's chief military post, Capitaine Général and the Arthurian Siege Perilous),

of Christianity dates from the reign of Constantine the Great.[53] Bonivard is also the author who makes the greatest effort to link the reformers of his day with their 'predecessors' Wyclife, Hus and the Waldensians.[54] However, this connection has a negative application as well. Catholics use it to show that the new ideas form yet another link in the great chain of heresy.[55] In general, though, the use of contemporary events, recent history or classical allusions is avoided. Name-calling seems the easiest and most natural form of abuse.[56] One is obviously a Christian if opposed by Antichrist, Caiaphas, Pharisees, Pharaoh, Jezebel, Jews and Turks – simplistic yet effective.

One area of contemporary events is noted by Catholics. Signs and wonders are frequently mentioned, especially by De Jussie. Before examining her rather problematic use of miraculous events one should consider the approach of the other authors. For the most part, signs, especially comets and strange heavenly lights, are mentioned with regularity by the pro-Catholic magistrates Pierrefleur and Balard.[57] However, they rarely make any attempt to interpret their relevance to earthly events.[58] The few Protestant references to wondrous events are equally lacking in interpretative significance to the chroniclers.[59]

---

p. 103 (on the lewd paintings of Roz Monet and the Emperor Heliogabulus). His witty wordplay of Pope Paul IV engaging in papelardise not paillardise (L'Idolatrie, p. 118). Cf. Dentière, Guerre, p. 353. She says that transubstantiation makes claims even an alchemist would avoid. Her husband, Froment (Actes, p. xxvi) refers to Cicero, Horace; also Socrates (pp. 166f.). Cf. Bonivard, Police, pp. 149–51; L'Idolatrie, p. 4 (on worshiping Greco-Roman gods and the cult of saints, e.g. Mars as St George) and Froment, Actes, p. xxiii. Also Bonivard, Police, p. 93 (comparing Catiline to Perrin).

[53] Bonivard, L'Idolatrie, pp. x–xi, 6f., 11f. (on damage to church by Constantine and Charlemagne).

[54] Bonivard, L'Idolatrie, pp. 8, 81–3, 134.

[55] Dentière, Epistre, sig. c2r–v, c3r; Froment, Actes, p. 4; Pierrefleur, Mémoires, p. 389.

[56] Cf. De Jussie, Levain, p. 61 on outlawing name-calling.

[57] Pierrefleur, Mémoires, pp. 65 (Sep. 1531, comet), 68 (spirit of priest dying at Orbe seen in the neighbouring village of Nozeroy), 91 (Sep.–Dec. 1532, comet), 220f. (25 Feb. 1543, three suns appear in the sky), 368 (12 Jun. 1560, a great fire seen over Lake Geneva. The local fisherman believed the end of the world was nigh); Balard, Journal, pp. 91 (7 Feb. 1527, earthquake), 153 (5 Apr. 1528, comet), 304 (7 Nov. 1530, comet).

[58] Cf. Mémoires, p. 381: an earthquake and men fighting in the sky prophesies war amongst the Swiss.

[59] Froment, Actes, p. 195 (flash of light and thunder heard in Geneva at the same time as a nearby battle). Roset, Chroniques, pp. 152 (Nov. 1530, comet), 157 (12 Aug. 1530, comet), 165 (29 Sep.–14 Oct. 1532, comet), 234 (16 May 1536, strange lightning), 264 (May 1539, comet). All before his birth in 1535. He does, however, relate one event (Chroniques, pp. 386f.) he must have witnessed. In August 1556 the cross which had been left on the steeple of Geneva's main (cathedral) church was blasted away by a bolt of lightning amid universal acclaim.

With De Jussie, though, one sees miracles coming into their own as proof of God's favour towards Catholics and celestial condemnation of Protestants. However, her examples are so incredible that one is hard pressed to accept that even she believed them. One particularly outrageous example will suffice. The eternal nature of the struggle between the forces of good and evil is apparent in her reference to the execution of a Protestant who died without absolution. His corpse was exposed on the gibbet next to that of an executed (absolved) Catholic woman. After a year on the gibbet, this good woman rose to the defence of the faith by turning to bite the newly exposed Protestant corpse. Geneva's Protestants, horrified by this obvious condemnation of their faith, vainly separated the two corpses with pikes; the lady bit the Protestant again. De Jussie claims that this was witnessed by thousands.[60] Surely this is a cautionary tale, a parable elevated to the level of history. It is a fantastical account meant to awe the faithful and warn them of the manifest evil of this new heresy.[61] The overwhelming majority of her examples fall into this category: many involve (Catholic) corpses refusing to rot and white doves descending from on high to light upon the heads of these ruddy-faced, sweet-scented witnesses.[62]

Two broad areas remain to be considered. First, the extent to which these authors were aware of the issues and groups involved in the emerging Protestant movement and the necessity, if any, of communicating this awareness to their readers. Finally, some comment must be made on the broader historical issues: the greatest charge levelled at the Protestants, the one which occasioned the most difficulty for them, was that of novelty. Laying aside historical examples, curses, signs and wonders, the fact remained that these preachers were proposing a break with the ancient customs and practices of the church and their ancestors.

The terms used to describe the emerging Protestant and Catholic adversaries are fairly consistent. Both groups are aware that the usual Catholic label for Protestants is 'Lutheran' while Protestants call themselves 'evangelicals'.[63] Occasionally, Catholics refer to themselves as

---

[60] De Jussie, *Levain*, pp. 89f.

[61] Including her assertion that the first Protestant eucharist was celebrated with bread and cheese. De Jussie, *Levain*, p. 64.

[62] Cf. De Jussie, *Levain*, pp. 24 (desecrated Host spirited away), p. 26 (two days' supply of bread lasted 12), p. 28 (1530 plague outbreak as divine punishment for heresy), p. 28f. ('trois fort beaux & excellens chevallier' protected the convent from the plague-spreaders), p. 32 (Aug. 1532, a comet marking the death of Loyse of Savoy, Queen of France. However, see p. 48 where the same comet is unexplained); as well as references (pp. 68, 87, 102f.) to undecayed Catholic corpses.

[63] For example, Froment, *Actes*, p. 47 ('contre eulx qu'on appelloit Lutheriens, ou Evangelistes'); Balard, *Journal*, p. 268 ('la loy de levangile quilz appellent Lutherienne'); and Pierrefleur, *Mémoires*, p. 1 ('secte Lutheriane, que à présent veulent estre appellée Evangile').

'good Christians' though Protestants, too, are inclined to appropriate this epithet.[64] Usually the Catholics refer to their party as 'Catholic' though conscious of the Protestant preference for the term 'papist'.[65] There is also a non-sectarian use of the phrases 'the party of the mass' and 'the party of the sermon/preachers'.[66]

The use of 'Lutheran' by Catholics implies no ignorance of the differences amongst the Protestants. On the contrary, Pierrefleur seems well appraised of the issues separating Protestants; thus, he uses the term 'Lutheran' as a generic designation bereft of theological or sectarian nuances.[67] For the most part the Protestant authors follow the same pattern.[68] They are aware of the disputes between Zwingli and Luther but appear to be untroubled by the designation.[69] Dentière is the sole author who repudiates the term outright; she lumps Lutherans in with Papists, Jews, Turks, and Anabaptists.[70] Froment makes an attempt to separate the term from the person and party of Luther by giving a detailed explanation of the reformer's name. He says, imitating a Lutheran play on words, that the name comes from the German word 'lauter', i.e. the French 'clair', ('brilliant' or 'clear'). Hence, he argues that the Catholics are actually accusing them of preaching 'clear' doctrines.[71] The explana-

---

[64] Cf. De Jussie, *Levain*, p. 24 ('un bon Chrestien') and Dentière, *Epistre*, sig. a2ʳ (in the title, 'une femme Chrestienne'). Cf. Dentière's pleading with the Genevan sisters and De Jussie's scandalised response (*Levain*, p. 173).

[65] Cf. Pierrefleur, *Mémoires*, pp. 16 ('bons catholiques'), 48f. ('la Religion chrestienne qu'ils nommoyent papistique'). Baum, *Baudichon*, p. 25 ('Crestiens tenans le party contraire ausdicts Lutheriens').

[66] Pierrefleur, *Mémoires*, pp. 81 ('les uns veulent le presche, les autres la messe'), p. 272 ('le party de la messe . . . party du presche'); Froment, *Actes*, pp. 159 ('au lieu de la doctrine des Prebstres, de leurs messe et ceremonyes, one receu une Reformation Evangelique'), p. 192 ('pour fayre prescher et deffendre l'Evangile'), p. 218 ('la loy du Pape et la Messe').

[67] Pierrefleur, *Mémoires*, pp. 185f. (Antinomianism noted), pp. 238f. (eucharistic debates mentioned), pp. 265f. (Osiandrian disputes in Prussia). Cf. Balard, *Journal*, p. 328 for the 'Lutheran' defeat at Kappel.

[68] Balard, *Journal*, p, 268; Pierrefleur, *Mémoires*, p. 1; Baum, *Baudichon*, p. 18. Cf. a Protestant use in Roset, *Chroniques*, p. 148 ('de l'Evangile, qu'on appelloit Luthériens').

[69] Bonivard, *L'Idolatrie*, pp. 147, 158. Bonivard is harsh on the leading Lutheran princes. Bonivard also comments on Farel's unwillingness to accept any 'innovations' from Basle or Zurich; cf. *Chroniques* (Turin manuscript), fo. 196ᵛ. Roset, *Chroniques*, p. 241 on the eucharist.

[70] Dentière, *Epistre*, sig. a2ʳ, b3ʳ. Her title says, 'Faulx chrestiens, Anabaptistes & Lutheriens' and she claims transubstantiation is consubstantiation.

[71] Froment, *Actes*, pp. 70f. Cf. his 'ont heu la lumiere evangelique par laquelle voyr clerement de present' (p. 168). See also J. Grimm and W. Grimm, *Deutsches Wörterbuch* (Leipzig, 1885), VI. col. 380 ('der ist der lauter schwan, darvon Husz zuvor 100 jaren geweizaget', in J. Mathesius, *Sarepta* [Nürnberg, 1587], 93a) and col. 381 ('lauther' for 'lauter', clear, in F.L. von Soltau, *Einhundert deutsche historische Volkslieder* [Leipzig, 1836], no. 278 from the sixteenth century). New High German and Middle High German both have 'luther' for 'lauter'.

tion is awkward though ingenious.[72]

There is also extensive agreement between the two groups on the issues which separate them. Maisonneuve's prosecution at Lyons for heresy in 1534 is especially useful. He and the witnesses against him manage to mention almost every point of contention.[73] Dentière, in 1539, discusses the similarity, as she sees it, of transubstantiation and consubstantiation. The refusal to swear is seen to be Anabaptist.[74] Psalm-singing and catechisms are noted by Pierrefleur.[75] Even the Protestant debates on predestination are known at Orbe.[76] There is also unanimous agreement that schism in the church arose, in part, from clerical immorality and abuse.[77]

Both groups use contemporary events as they happen to identify themselves. In effect, they create a history of the Reformation as it happens. In Geneva and the francophone Swiss lands we discover a self-analysis by Protestants and Catholics which is somewhat surprising, especially to historians of the French Religious Wars. In Geneva the Protestants win, while in the Pays de Vaud and Gex the Bernese work tirelessly after 1535 to root out Catholicism. A majority finally vote for the new faith in Orbe in 1555; only then can the mass be abolished.[78] As a result, in these chronicles one sees the Catholics portraying themselves as victims. They are the persecuted. Their churches and books are destroyed. They are the martyrs of the faith, the 'poor Christians'.[79] These phrases are noticeably

---

[72] See the agreement on Anabaptists. For example, Dentière, *Epistre*, sig. c2ᵛ; Roset, *Chroniques*, p. 240; Pierrefleur, *Mémoires*, pp. 96–8, 138–40; and Bonivard, *L'Idolatrie*, p. 147. However, cf. Bonivard, *Des lengues*, p. 166 on Anabaptist charity.

[73] Baum, *Baudichon*, p. 36 (transubstantiation), pp. 44f. (eating meat during Lent), pp. 54ff. (purgatory, veneration of the Virgin), p. 58 (vernacular Bibles), p. 61 (church laws not binding), pp. 67–9 (relics), p. 76f. (cult of the saints), pp. 79–81 (mass), p. 101 (pope), p. 102 (priesthood of believers).

[74] Cf., however, Baum, *Baudichon*, p. 49: 'lequel [Baudichon] a reffusé prester de serement, disant qu'il est deffendu en l'evangille de iurer & soufftit dire ouy ouy, non non'. Cf., Roset, *Chroniques*, p. 240. Roset says that those refusing the Confession of 1537–38 were, therefore, Anabaptists. Hence that old chestnut that Calvin's opposition was Anabaptist. Cf. W. J. Bouwsma, *John Calvin. A Sixteenth-Century Portrait* (Oxford, 1988), pp. 19–21.

[75] Pierrefleur, *Mémoires*, pp. 93, 199.

[76] Pierrefleur, *Mémoires*, pp. 37f.

[77] Cf. De Jussie, *Levain*, p. 35. Also Balard, *Journal*, pp. 268f. Pierrefleur, *Mémoires*, p. 256 mentions the scandal of a pregnant nun.

[78] Pierrefleur, *Mémoires*, pp. 299f. De Jussie, *Levain*, p. 37 praised the constancy of Orbe's Catholics.

[79] Pierrefleur, *Mémoires*, pp. 186–8 (gravestones and churches demolished to repair castles) and De Jussie, *Levain*, pp. 9–16 (on the progress of the Bernese army through the Pays de Vaud). Froment, *Actes*, p. 59 says the people of Fribourg considered the monk, Verly, killed at Geneva to be a martyr just like St Thomas of Canterbury. Cf. De Jussie, who is the most explicit in referring to martyrdom: 'à ce benoit martyr' and 'le beau-frere du martyr' (Verly, p. 67f.); the execution of Cartellier (p. 3); the murder Lord Ponvoire (pp. 4f.); and of an unnamed merchant (p. 59).

absent from the pages of the Protestant chronicles. Indeed, even the Protestants show a certain humility before the example of the Poor Claires leaving Geneva.[80]

The best that the Protestants can do is to detail the deceit and immorality of the old ecclesiastical structure. They gleefully relate the combination of bellows and stones used by Genevan monks to make dead unbaptised infants appear to revive long enough to receive the sacrament.[81] The Protestants enumerate the fake relics discovered when the churches are cleansed as well as the various devices for producing their miraculous movements and noises.[82] However, as victors the Protestants can only exult over the ruined churches and convents of their foes. It is the Catholics who parade forth the slain monks and preachers, the defiled images, the burned churches and, most pathetically, the Poor Claires in their cloaks and sandals walking alone to refuge through driving rain and clinging mud.[83] Terror, pillage, murder, fire and sword are charges hurled against the Protestants by the bewildered, defenceless adherents of the faith of their fathers.[84]

This rather naturally leads to the final historical issue. How can a 'new' faith ever replace the ancient customs and teachings of the Catholic church? This is the constant question directed at the Protestants by the Catholics. Pierrefleur stares with open-mouthed wonder at the Protestant enthusiasm for innovation; 'they must change everything'.[85] Apart from Froment's mention of the thousand years of deceit which had afflicted the church only Bonivard makes any attempt to rebut this charge. He presents a reasoned defence of the assertion that Catholics, from Constantine the Great, have been innovators while the Protestants wish to restore the ancient, pure faith of Christ and the apostles.[86] However, most Protestants seem content to respond to the abusive term 'innovators' by simply shouting back 'deceivers, idolaters, Papists'.[87]

---

[80] On their departure, see the historical comments at the end of De Jussie's text (Levain, p. 286, an armed escort was provided by the syndics, and pp. 291f., small donations were sent to the new convent at Annecy by the government until at least 1728).

[81] Froment, Actes, pp. 151ff.; Roset, Chroniques, p. 197.

[82] Froment, Actes, p. 146 (e.g. St Antony's arm was actually the 'pible du cerf'); Roset, Chroniques, p. 214, where it is 'le membre génératif d'un cerf, tout sec'.

[83] Froment, Actes, pp. 163f. decries the stubbornness of the Poor Claires. Cf. their reaction to the sacrilegious abuse of the Host, Levain, pp. 28f.

[84] See De Jussie, Levain, esp. pp. 9–16.

[85] Pierrefleur, Mémoires, p. 72: 'Nos lutheriens, ne cessans tous les jours à faire quelque innovation'.

[86] Bonivard, L'Idolatrie, pp. 11–19 dates the 'sad' history of the church and canon law from Constantine's day.

[87] Herminjard, Correspondance, p. 299 gives a wonderful outburst from Dentière: 'Mais en abjurant et retournant baiser la pantouffle de ce grand serrurier, adversaire de Jésus, sont vénéficiéz, prébendéz, rentéz, corronez et mittréz' – the letter was condemning Calvin's Protestant opponents of 1538!

The danger of facing the charge of innovation directly was apparent to Bonivard. He is fully aware of the host of reasons for accepting the Reformation which had no regard for a restored pristine Christianity. In his treatise *On the Deformed Reformers* he reveals why Protestants prefer biblical models to contemporary ones: 'Why have the great lords, these powerful principalities embraced the Reform?' he asks.[88] Henry VIII wants a new wife and the wealth of the church.[89] The Teutonic knights want lands and dynastic security.[90] Magistrates want power and covet ecclesiastical wealth.[91] What Bonivard fails to find is any real enthusiasm for an ethical understanding of the Gospel or reform.[92] He even draws the conclusion that the new clerical elite does not differ drastically from the old. The new morality is as immoral as the old; society has not been reformed.[93]

Who are these Protestants, then? How do they see themselves fitting into the great sweep of history, the working out of God's plan in time? First and foremost, in francophone Swiss lands during 1530–55 they are the victors. They cannot link themselves to the ancient martyrs of church history. To the extent that they use history it is to identify their age with two biblical periods. They are the new Israel enslaved in idolatry, led out of captivity and exile by new prophets. Moses, the law-giver, Hezekiah, the good king and Elijah, Jeremiah and Isaiah, the prophets of old are brought to life in the persons of the preachers and magistrates of their day. The Protestants are also the remnant saved from the clutches of Antichrist and Babylon by God's intervening power. They are God's servants and champions cleansing Israel of idols, marching victoriously over the wreckage of the Beast's Babylon.

The Catholics see these conquerors as heretical monsters. They are stunned and bewildered by the wanton destructiveness of the Protestants.[94] They evidence no desire to call upon history to defend themselves. They need only catalogue the atrocities of their opponents to validate their perception that they are victims, martyrs. Historically, they have no identity problem. The Catholics are secure in the knowledge that they are faithful to the ancient customs, faith and law of 'Holy Mother Church'.[95] All history is implicitly called to their defence when they affirm their determination despite persecution 'to live and die in the

---

[88] The treatise is in Bonivard, *L'Idolatrie*, pp. 133–63 (see, p. 141).

[89] Bonivard, *L'Idolatrie*, p. 139.

[90] Ibid., p. 158.

[91] Ibid., p. 160.

[92] Ibid., p. 159

[93] Ibid., p. 162.

[94] De Jussie, *Levain*, pp. 9–16.

[95] Cf. Baum, *Baudichon*, p. 59; Pierrefleur, *Mémoires*, p. 69.

ancient customs and faith of our fathers and ancestors'.[96]

History, its use and control, is a problem which the Protestants must resolve. The lack of Catholic concern seems to be predicated upon an assumption that 'possession is nine-tenths of the law'. It is incumbent upon the Protestants to capture history from the Catholics, to mould it to their use, to prove that they are not innovators, but restorers. In such a struggle modern figures such as Henry VIII or even the great, loyal churchmen of the past are simply not useful models. As the victors the Protestants must locate historical models to justify these sweeping changes, to prove themselves to be men and women cleansing, not sacking, the churches; revealing not rewriting the law. In this struggle the full panoply of medieval homiletical abuse was divided up as booty. In the end, Genevan Catholics were left with images of the persecuted church while Protestants were able to claim the Old Testament admonitions against idolatry and New Testament eschatology.

For the Catholics of Geneva there is only confusion and defeat. They were horrified by the violence they saw about them. Nuns were driven out, churches levelled, innovations swirl around them like autumnal leaves. Reading their histories we realise that they were so stunned that they could do no more than bear witness to the horrifying procession of events. Their acceptance of the need for reform but resistance to innovation complicated their interpretation of events and hindered development of a clear self-identity. As late as 1555 Pierrefleur still hoped for reconciliation and an end to innovation.[97] Having lost the battle to retain the old faith at Orbe he wrote, 'seeing and hearing these desolations I then wept and lifted up mine eyes to heaven praying to God that He would end these disputes within His Church'.[98] While the Protestants begin to emerge from this period of conflict with a clearer sense of self, most Catholics would echo the words of Froment, 'one side says one thing,

---

[96] See, Balard, *Journal*, p. 147 (Swiss Catholics: 'voulans vivre comme leurs predecesseurs'); De Jussie, *Levain*, p. 14 (Jeanne's Abbess: 'mais sommes deliberees vivre & mourir en nostre saincte vocation icy en nostre Convent'); Pierrefleur, *Mémoires*, p. 310 (Orbe Catholics: 'ils estoyent tous unis, voulans vivre et mourir en la Loy de nostre Mere Saincte-Eglise et selon les ordonnances d'icelle'). Cf. De la Maisonneuve in Baum, *Baudichon*, p. 9 ('il croit en la foy & comme ses predecesseurs ont creu, & croit le sacrement de l'aultier, de confession & autres').

[97] See Pierrefleur's generous comments: on Calvin, 'un grand & scavant docteur' (*Mémoires*, p. 37); Corauld, Calvin's co-worker in 1538, 'homme scavant selon sa pratique' (p. 184); and even André Zebedée (whom Pierrefleur disliked), 'homme rouz et cholere, bien superbe' (p. 201). In 1559, Pierrefleur reports enjoying a Protestant play ('histoire/farce'): '[La histoire] fust jouée magnifiquement, avec grand assemblée de peuple. La ditte histoire tendant la pluspart en derision des Prestres et de toutes gens ecclesiastiques' (p. 348).

[98] Pierrefleur, *Mémoires*, p. 317.

the other the opposite and the poor people don't know which way to turn'.[99]

For their part, because they dominated the political situation and were themselves persecutors, the Protestants could not call upon the biblical and historical images of martyrs. They saw the fate of their co-religionists in France and elsewhere but they were wary, in their dominant position, of using these historical models which are so often associated with other Protestant groups. Their aversion to 'martyrdom' is equivalent to the Catholic silence on 'idolatry'. The Genevan Protestants identify the latter as the biblical and historical Achilles' heel of the Catholics and emphasise the cleansing, restoring work of Old Testament prophets and kings. In Geneva, the Protestants saw themselves as Hezekiah grinding the idolatrous altars to dust and overthrowing the pagan high places; they are Elijah calling down celestial fire to scatter the followers of Baal. That is history, an identity, a justification they can use. It is vibrant, alive, destructive and victorious.[100]

---

[99] Froment, *Actes*, p. 33.

[100] Cf. the change to the city's motto which was 'post tenebras spero lucem' and became 'post tenebras lux'. Cf. Roset, *Chroniques*, p. 211 and Froment, *Actes*, pp. 166f.

CHAPTER THREE

Jean Crespin and the Writing of History in the French Reformation

David Watson

> Those who apply their spirits to compiling histories must aim at this principal goal, to propose as in a mirror, the strength, wisdom, justice and admirable kindness of God living and eternal.[1]

Jean Crespin's *Livre des Martyrs* was one of the core texts of the French Reformation. In successive editions between the first of 1554, and 1619, when the book achieved its final definitive shape, the book grew from a small collection to a vast compendium of martyr stories. Its successive editions elaborated an enormously influential vision of French Protestantism, sketching a history of evangelical commitment and suffering going back to the first decade of the evangelical movement. French Protestants could find encouragement in the witness of their suffering brethren, and the book achieved almost canonical status, on occasions apparently being read aloud as part of divine service.[2]

The man responsible for this publishing phenomenon was Jean Crespin, one of the most influential of the first generation of Frenchmen who joined Calvin in Geneva.[3] Crespin, a native of Arras, fled France in 1545 and arrived in Geneva in 1548, and soon built up one of Geneva's largest publishing houses. His martyrology became one of the business's most important, and presumably lucrative, projects.[4] But it was impor-

---

[1] Preface to Jean de Hainault, *L'estat de L'Eglise* (Crespin, Geneva, 1564), sig. aa 2ʳ. The following abbreviations are used as standard throughout this chapter: J. Crespin, *Recueil de plusieurs personnes qui ont constamment enduré la mort pour le nom de nostre Seigneur Jesus Christ* (Geneva, 1554) (Crespin 1554); J. Crespin, *Recueil de plusieurs personnes qui ont constamment enduré la mort pour le nom du Seigneur* (Geneva, 1556) (Crespin 1556); J. Crespin, *Histoire des vrays tesmoins de la verité de l'Evangile* (Geneva, 1570) (Crespin 1570); J. Crespin, *Histoire des martyrs persecutez et mis à mort pour la verité de l'évangile, depuis le temps des apostres jusques à présent*, ed. D. Benoît (3 vols, Toulouse, 1885–89) (Crespin 1619).

[2] As for instance in the Norman church of Le Mans in 1561. See Glenn Sunshine, 'From French Protestantism to the French Reformed Churches: The development of Huguenot Ecclesiastical Institutions, 1559–1598' (University of Wisconsin–Madison PhD thesis, 1992), p. 164.

[3] On Crespin, see J.-F. Gilmont's excellent biography, *Jean Crespin. Un éditeur réformé du XVIe siècle* (Geneva, 1981). Hereafter Gilmont, *Crespin. Un éditeur réformé*.

[4] For the publishing of Crespin's house see the exhaustive bibliography of Gilmont, *Bibliographie des Editions de Jean Crespin 1550–1572* (2 vols, Verviers, 1981).

tant too in another sense, since the *Livre des Martyrs* gave Crespin the opportunity to articulate a Protestant view of the function and purpose of history-writing. It is worth briefly pondering Crespin's statements on this matter before turning to a broader examination of the function and purpose of Crespin's martyrology within the general canon of Protestant history-writing.

The martyrology was one of a number of historical projects published by Crespin's house in this period. One of his most important projects was the publication in French, for the first time, of Johannes Sleidan's *Commentaries on Religion and the State in the reign of Emperor Charles V* (first published in Latin in 1555; in French in 1556) and his further work, *Of the Four Greatest Empires* (published in Latin in 1556 and in French in 1557).[5] Covering the events from the origins of the Reformation in 1517 to February 1555 in 25 books, Sleidan's *Commentaries* were at the forefront of sixteenth-century Protestant history-writing, and have been called ' . . . the fullest, broadest and most famous contemporary narrative of the Protestant Reformation'.[6] In the preface to Sleidan's *Oeuvres*, Crespin writes admiringly of Sleidan's ability and objectivity in his writing of history: 'Several have attempted to write about what has happened during our times, but there have been very few who have illustrated the councils and enterprises of Princes in such integrity and truth, as Jean Sleidan has done . . . '.[7]

Crespin draws a flattering comparison between Sleidan, who was not satisfied with hearsay but sought out the truth from public acts and town registers, and Thucydides who, in writing his history of the Peloponnesian War, even paid his enemies for information in order to secure the truth.[8] This would appear to be the model of historical methodology which Crespin wishes to emulate.

A less celebrated exponent of the historian's craft was Jean de Hainault, whose work Crespin also published for the first time in 1556. Although Hainault's *L'estat de l'Eglise* is now far less well-known than Sleidan's *Commentaries*, at the time it proved extremely popular, and Crespin published four editions of Hainault's work between 1556 and

---

[5] For work on Sleidan and Reformation history in English, see A.G. Dickens, 'Johannes Sleidan and Reformation History' in R. Buick Knox (ed.), *Reformation Conformity and Dissent. Essays in honour of Geoffrey Nuttall* (London, 1977); A.G. Dickens and J.M. Tonkin, *The Reformation in Historical Thought* (Oxford, 1985). Also D.R. Kelley, 'Johann Sleidan and the Origins of History as a Profession', *Journal of Modern History*, 52 (1980), 577–98.

[6] A.G. Dickens, 'Johannes Sleidan and Reformation History', in R. Buick Knox (ed.), *Reformation Conformity and Dissent*, p. 17.

[7] Jean Sleidan, *Oeuvres* (Geneva, 1566), sig. * ii.ʳ.

[8] Ibid., sig. * ii.ʳ.

1562. This work tells the story of 15 centuries of the history of the church, gathered together from histories of olden times and medieval chronicles. As with Sleidan's *Commentaries*, the preface to this work was written by Crespin and it does show, to some extent at least, what Crespin saw as the purpose of history-writing. For Crespin, divine action is all-powerful, and the reader should not be surprised if history tells how kingdoms, once decadent and wasted can be restored; for they should expect such things of God.[9] Crespin sees in the lessons of history some individual lessons of morality. The reader is reminded that no matter how wealthy, magnificent or long-established a monarchy is, it is in no position to resist the admirable judgement of God. The preface to *L'estat de L'Eglise* is built on the theme of those oppressed being exalted by Providence, and those of overbearing arrogance being justly punished. For example, Crespin argues that ' . . . there is a true painting which represents to life what wisdom God works in breaking the councils of the arrogant who abuse their power'.[10]

Furthermore, he sees no limit to the power of the Lord in punishing the arrogant:

> We see the crowns of Kings fall to the ground: the sceptres of Emperors break and smash: the glory of republics wither. And it is the ambition, proud ingratitude, and insatiable greed of those who are ordained to rule and do not recognise God, who are the cause of such reversals and such mutations.[11]

These are clearly covert assurances to the Reformed community in France that God will, in his own time, deal with the abuses of power by the monarchy, and deliver his chosen people. Before this will be done, however, those under persecution will have to endure hardships and danger: 'But the spiritual kingdom of the Son of God, which is his church, must not be judged by the dangers of the present life: for it is preserved in the middle of impetuous waves'.[12] Crespin then cites Isaiah 60:19–20 to assure the Reformed that their day will come: 'Thy sun shall no more go down; neither shall thy moon withdraw itself: for the Lord shall be thine everlasting light, and the days of thy mourning shall be ended'.

For Crespin, obviously, history must be written faithfully, with no other motives than to tell the truth and let the lessons of history educate and guide present happenings. These introductory pieces tell us something of Crespin's attitudes and perceptions of the historian's task. We

---

[9] Preface to Jean de Hainault, *L'estat de L'Eglise* (Crespin, Geneva, 1564), sig. aa 2^r.

[10] Ibid., sig. aa 2^r.

[11] Ibid., sig. aa 2^v.

[12] Ibid., sig. aa 2^v–aa 3^r.

are given a profounder insight into his view of history-writing in an extensive preface introducing the 1570 edition of his martyrology.

In this *Préface monstrant une conformité des persécutions et martyrs de ces derniers temps à ceux de la première église* . . . , Crespin expounds his sense of the continuity of history.[13] It is not an especially sophisticated theological or historical précis, although his aim is clear: to demonstrate that the martyrs of his time and of his faith bear comparison with those of the early church. This passage is important for elucidating Crespin's views, as it is an original piece of writing, rare among the many works produced by Crespin. A part of the preface is given over to the biblical martyr stories of Jesus, Stephen and John the Baptist, although in a very direct and simple fashion, very much as a short paraphrase of the biblical text. The reader is shown how John the Baptist, like the reformers, taught a new doctrine and in turn, chastises those in charge of the church for falsifying the doctrine of God, both actions that would bring home to even the most uneducated reader the conformity of times past and times present.[14]

Aspects of Christ's story are also held up for comparison with contemporary events by Crespin, aspects that bear direct relation to situations in which his readers would have found themselves. The reader is told how Christ also had enemies, who called him to dispute and who excommunicated him. According to Crespin, Christ was accused of, among other things, teaching without legitimate authority, disrupting the religion ordered by Moses according to the Word of God and seducing the people. The readers are assured by Crespin that their path is following that of Christ, who also condemned salvation by good works alone. Indeed, Crespin asks, what were the causes of Christ's persecution? The reply could suitably be a description of the failings of the authorities in more recent times, 'One of the principal [causes] was great blindness in this people, who glorified themselves in being the people of God: and besides this, the hypocrisy and malice of rulers, who are not at all able to suffer that their traditions, their abuses and their vices were removed from them once again'.[15]

Fittingly, Stephen, the first Christian martyr, is also included, as Crespin draws an analogy between the persecuted church of the apostle's times and his own. Not only was he the shining example for all Protestant martyrs, but it seems he also shared some of their fundamental beliefs. He believed, according to Crespin, that salvation would not be secured by good works, but only by faith.

---

[13] See Gilmont, *Crespin. Un éditeur réformé*, pp.183–9.
[14] Crespin 1570, Preface, sig. a4ʳ.
[15] Crespin 1570, Preface, sig. a5ʳ.

These accounts in the preface to the 1570 edition are striking for their brevity and simple message. Why Crespin sees fit to include this in his edition of 1570 rather than beforehand is uncertain. But it is possible to see this edition as the culmination of Crespin's attempts to create a new genre of book, which sets the persecution of his contemporaries into the wider context of the history of the church. In reformulating his martyrology in this way Crespin may have been influenced by an increased awareness of the work of Sleidan, Hainault and perhaps of the Dutch martyrologist, van Haemstede.[16]

Crespin's view of history is conventional and, within the context of the new Protestant history-writing, orthodox. He sees all the goodness of the primitive church being wiped out by the arrival of 'miserable idolatry' in the form of the papacy. He also shares a contemporary faith in the omnipotence and omnipresence of divine action. Crespin's view of history accommodates only divine action, seeing the goal of the historian to propose to readers, as if in a mirror, ' . . . the strength, the wisdom, the justice and the kindness of God'.[17]

Yet this is not to say that history does not provide a cautionary tale to those responsible for the persecution of the truth. Crespin warns not only the enemies of the Gospel, such as archbishops, cardinals, bishops and the entire Roman hierarchy, but also kings and queens, dukes and lords, chancellors and presidents, councillors, lieutenants, commissioners and governors of towns and provinces. Terrible judgements will befall great houses and others in charge of persecuting Christians.[18]

Crespin gives the reader several instances of retribution from the Bible. For example, from Exodus 14, he cites the story of the pursuit of Moses and the Israelites from Egypt by Pharaoh. The Israelites are allowed by the Lord to cross the divided sea, which crashes down upon the cream of Egypt's troops when they attempt to cross. He also, cites the story of Ahab in 1 Kings 16–22, whose house and wife were both brought to ruin by his greed and defiance of the Lord.[19] From Acts 12, Crespin relates the story of Herod Agrippa, the murderer of the apostle James, who met death eaten alive by worms, because he did not give praise to the Lord. The fate of all these characters as well as others from classical history,

---

[16] Adriaan van Haemstede, *De Gheschiedenisse ende den doodt der vromer Martelaren* (Emden, 1559). This process continues in the 1582 edition, after the death of Crespin, with Simon Goulart expanding this section into a whole new first book on the persecutions of the early church.

[17] Preface to Jean de Hainault, *L'estat de L'Eglise* (Geneva, 1564), sig. aa 2ʳ.

[18] And c.f. below, p. 56.

[19] Crespin 1570, Preface, sig. a7ᵛ. Cf. also C.H. Parker, 'French Calvinists as the Children of Israel: An Old Testament Self-Consciousness in Jean Crespin's *Histoire des Martyrs* before the Wars of Religion', *SCJ*, 24 (1993), 227–47.

such as Mark Anthony and Diocletian, are mentioned by Crespin as indications of the vengeance of God. These are all well-known stories and figures, whose fates, and the role of God's actions in them, would not be lost on Crespin's readership.

It is here, in these prefaces, that Crespin attempts to fit the suffering of his contemporaries into the wider picture of the persecution of the church and thus create a Protestant scheme of history that links the first Christian centuries with contemporary events. He also writes most directly on what he sees as the historian's task, and the purpose of history-writing. Whether Crespin always lived up to the lofty purposes expressed in these introductions is something that needs to be tested in an examination of the text itself, and more particularly of the working methods which Crespin employed in his own original work, the *Livre des Martyrs*. The martyrology was a work which evolved only gradually towards the monumental tome of the 1570 edition. Its successive redactions tell us a great deal of the difficulties Crespin faced in assembling his information, and of his practical approach to the business of history-writing.

Obviously in any modern critical assessment of the value of Crespin's book, an examination of his use of and approach to sources is crucial. Bearing in mind that Crespin's status as a refugee from France largely confined him to Geneva, he was entirely reliant on what sources of information he could secure within the city. Not surprisingly, in the circumstances Crespin made extensive use of other contemporary literature. Often, if anyone died a martyr, it was not long before his fate found a wide readership, through a *Flugschrift* or pamphlet. There is little doubt Crespin either had some of these to hand, or at least knew of them; numerous of Crespin's accounts of early evangelical martyrs are derived from German, Latin, or Dutch *Flugschriften* from 1523–30.[20]

One example where it is possible to locate the source of Crespin's account is in the history of Henry of Zutphen. This preacher was a student of Luther's and arrived in Meldorf in December 1524, where he began to preach.[21] But as a result of considerable agitation by the prior of the local Dominicans, and with the cooperation of other church leaders and civil authorities, certain peasants of the neighbourhood were per-

---

[20] See Bernd Moeller, 'Inquisition und Martyrium in Flugschriften der frühen Reformation in Deutschland', in Silvana Seidel Menchi (ed.), *Ketzerverfolgung im 16. und 17. Jahrhundert* (Wolfenbüttel, 1992), pp. 21–48.

[21] On Henry of Zutphen see *Bibliographie des Martyrologes Protestants Néerlandais* (2 vols, The Hague, 1890), I. 539–629.

suaded to kidnap Henry. After they had accomplished this, they drank themselves into a frenzy and lynched him on 10 December 1524. After his death, Luther wrote a small book about Henry's death, *The Burning of Brother Henry* in response to a request that he console the Christians in Bremen who grieved about the loss of their pastor.[22] He based the story on letters and oral reports and framed it in the style of a passion narrative. Luther's story is mirrored almost exactly by Crespin's account in his 1554 edition as he retells the story, copying much of what Luther wrote. This includes standard embellishments of a martyr story such as the inability of the wood in the pyre to be lit and Henry's refusal to die in spite of his many wounds, thus forcing the mob to resort to strangulation to kill him. It is clear that Crespin simply adopted Luther's account wholesale.

In this particular case, Crespin had an almost contemporary account of the background and story of Zutphen's martyrdom. This account of Luther's was clearly historically quite unreliable, and had been embellished with classic martyrs' tales. It is, however, at least a story of a martyrdom, a story that Crespin could use to inspire the faithful and act as an examplar, a mirror, of how the faithful should behave. Doubts over its objectivity, arising from its purpose and authorship, must be borne in mind.

Another example, and this time a story of particular interest to Crespin's anticipated French readership, is the story of Louis de Berquin, a Flemish nobleman of modest income.[23] Eventually executed in 1529, he was tried on three separate occasions by the Parlement and the Sorbonne, only to be released by the king's pardon. This was a well-known story, and on this occasion Crespin had available to him a valuable contemporary source: a letter from Erasmus to Charles d'Utenhove dated 1 July 1529.[24] This forms the backbone of Crespin's account.[25] From it Crespin draws considerable detail regarding the intricacies of Berquin's case, despite the fact that in the letter Erasmus admits to not having known Berquin personally. But Crespin is also selective. Omitted from Crespin's account is any mention of Berquin's recantation of 1526;

---

[22] *WA*, XVIII. 215–50. English translation in J. Pelikan and H.T. Lehmann, *Luther's Works* (55 vols, Philadelphia, 1958), XXXII. 265–86.

[23] On Berquin, R.J. Knecht, *Francis I* (Cambridge, 1982); P.G. Bietenholz and Thomas Deutscher, *Contemporaries of Erasmus. A Biographical Register of the Renaissance and Reformation* (3 vols, Toronto, 1985–87), I. 135–40. M. Mann Phillips, *Erasme et les débuts de la réforme française* (Paris, 1933).

[24] The original letter in *Opus epistolarum Desiderii Erasmi Roterdami*, ed. P.S. Allen (12 vols, Oxford, 1906–58), VIII. 209–16. Cf. E. and E. Haag, *La France Protestante*, (10 vols, reprint. Geneva, 1966) II. 215–22.

[25] Crespin 1570, pp. 70ᵛ–71ʳ.

something that would not have lain easily with Crespin's portrayal of Berquin as a paragon of constancy.[26]

Contemporary documents of this sort, although extremely valuable, are comparatively rare in the acknowledged sources for Crespin's collection. For the most part, and especially when dealing with the native French martyrs, Crespin had to construct his own narrative, and often one can only speculate as to the precise source of his information. Undoubtedly, on occasions, Crespin had access to some first-hand materials. Sometimes he quotes directly from letters of the martyrs to their parents and friends, as well as reproducing confessions of faith given as their testimony.[27] Such a compilation would have proved a formidable task. The preface to his first edition of 1554, however, gives us an insight into how he hoped to gather his material, and how this process could lead to a vast array of historical documentation of varying relevance and reliability. In it he requests of the faithful, in the name of Jesus Christ, 'the great leader and captain of martyrs', that they gather all the relevant information they can; to recall ' . . . all that they were able to hear, and that could be gathered of their constancy, their words and letters, their replies, the confessions of their faith, their words and last exhortations; in order to hold them all in the rememberance of the Church forever'.[28]

In his preface to the edition of 1570, he repeated his plea for help and collaboration. Exhorting the faithful to apply themselves rigorously to the task, he called upon them to follow the model of the primitive church, its zeal and activity and its painstaking care to put down in writing the acts of the martyrs and to conserve the registers as very precious treasures.[29]

It seems that his appeals were largely heard. Indeed, for the accounts of some martyrs, he is remarkably well-informed. For example, for the Spanish Protestant Juan Diaz, murdered by his brother in Neuburg in 1546, Crespin's account stretched to nearly 15 000 words.[30] Crespin was

---

[26] See N. Weiss, 'Louis de Berquin, son premier procès et sa rétractation d'après quelques documents inédits (1523)', *BSHPF, 67* (1918), 180–81.

[27] For example, confessions given by Claude Monier in 1551 (Crespin 1570, pp. 182^r–4^r). The letters and confessions of Godefroy de Hamelle, executed in 1552 (Crespin 1570, pp. 186^r–91^r) and Pierre Brully, executed in 1545 (Crespin 1570, pp. 134^v–40^r).

[28] The preface of the 1554 edition is reproduced in Crespin, *Histoire des martyrs persecutez et mis a mort pour la verité de l'evangile. depuis le temps des apostles iusques a Present*, ed. Daniel Benoit (3 vols, Toulouse, 1885), I. xxxv.

[29] Crespin 1570, sig. a5^{r-v}.

[30] Crespin 1570, pp. 151^v– 160^v. On Diaz see A.G. Kinder, 'Spain' in A. Pettegree (ed.), *The Early Reformation in Europe* (Cambridge, 1992), p. 231. Also note the account of Pierre Brully. Minister of the church at Strasbourg, he probably met Crespin for the first time in September–October 1544 while visiting Tournai, Lille, Valenciennes, Douai and Arras. Brully's execution in 1545 was the probable reason for Crespin's flight. The account of his death is approximately 9 300 words long. See G. Moreau, *Histoire du Protestantisme à Tournai jusqu'à la veille de la Révolution des Pays-Bas* (Paris, 1962).

personally acquainted with Diaz; the Spanish reformer was a member of the group of pupils of Guillaume Budé whom Crespin encountered on his first trip to Paris.[31] Thus those martyrs who were either known to Crespin personally, or who had maintained before their deaths a correspondence with the Reformed community in Geneva, were written about at great length by Crespin. For the accounts of the five students of Lausanne, executed in Lyons in 1553 after a prolonged period of imprisonment during which they corresponded regularly with their friends in Geneva, Crespin produces an exceptionally well-documented account of their suffering and martyrdom. Approximately one-quarter of the first edition's 690 pages is taken up with their epistles and confessions of faith.[32]

This contrasts strikingly with much shorter accounts of some other martyrs of the French Reformation. Some are so brief as to be almost wholly uninformative. The account of Jean L'Anglois from Burgundy, martyred at Sens in March 1547, for instance, amounts to a mere 60 words. All we are told is that he was an advocate, condemned by the Parlement of Paris for maintaining the truth of the Lord.[33] This is presumably all the information Crespin had to hand when compiling his first collection in 1554, and a large proportion of the accounts of native French martyrs are of this nature.[34] This suggests that for all his desire to create as complete a collection as possible, Crespin was simply not well-informed of the circumstances which led to many of the executions of evangelical believers in France up to the time of the first publication of his martyrology; and this despite the fact that by this point refugees from all parts of France were settled in some numbers in Geneva.[35] When Crespin had information to hand he certainly included it, even if it is nothing more than a stray letter or treatise of the imprisoned, which makes no mention of their present predicament, as it may well have been written several years previously.[36] This technique at times gives the book a somewhat random quality, as is evident from the last account in the edition of

---

[31] Gilmont, *Crespin. Un éditeur réformé*, p. 36. The source for Crespin's account of Diaz is an earlier publication: Claude Senarlens, *Historia vera de morte sancti uiri Ioannis Diazii Hispani* . . . (Basle, J. Oporinus, 1546).

[32] Crespin 1554, pp. 325–495.

[33] Crespin 1554, p. 639. On L'Anglois, see also Haag, *La France Protestante*, VI. 264.

[34] For example, in Crespin 1554, the accounts of Hubert Burré, Gillot Vivier, Macé Moreau, Maurice Secenat, René Poyet and François Bribard are all less than 50 words in length.

[35] William G. Naphy, *Calvin and the Consolidation of the Genevan Reformation* (Manchester, 1994).

[36] For example, Crespin's accounts of the first victims of the Marian persecution in England are a patchwork of details, letters and treatises.

1554, that of Richard Le Fevre.[37] The account of this martyr from Rouen is added in at the last minute, Le Fevre having only been martyred a month before Crespin's first edition appeared in August 1554. In this case the appearance of this last account may be taken to show the efficiency of Crespin's contacts in France by this stage, but the policy of including such recently arrived material certainly took little regard overall for the shape or form of his collection.

In some cases, therefore, Crespin obviously received sufficient information about the accused to ascertain the dates, places and circumstances of their arrest and execution. For other matters, such as the details of the proceedings and interrogations, it was more difficult for Crespin to secure information which the public would not be privy to, as the accused would be alone in front of the judges. This is especially the case if the authorities, as was apparently the case, sometimes burnt the trial documents along with the accused (perhaps they too having realised the propaganda value of the trial records). Crespin himself tells us how he attempted to overcome such problems. In the case of the martyr Pierre Denocheau, executed in Chartres in 1553, Crespin tells us that Denocheau

> . . . had a method of leaving, in writing, in the prison, his confession, based on the pure doctrine of the Gospel, which we have inserted here, as if we have plucked it from the middle of the fire. Few people ignore the difficulty which there is in recovering the judicial acts and confessions of those who were held prisoner for the true doctrine, all the more so because Satan knew to suggest this trickery to the brains of his henchmen, to burn entirely the cases with those executed.[38]

Access to the trial documents would be easier if the judges were sympathetic to the cause of the Reformed. Agrippa d'Aubigné, in his *Histoire Universelle*, tells us the Reformed religion was 'primarily taken up by men of letters, so there were few enough seats of justice in France where there was not some officer in favour of this doctrine. By this method, those who compiled the huge *Livre des Martyrs* authenticated their reports by acts and entire cases taken from clerks'.[39]

If we were able to confirm that documents of this sort were indeed made available to Crespin, it would greatly enhance a generally positive assessment of Crespin's accuracy and reliability. Unfortunately, such a

---

[37] Crespin 1554, p. 666–87.

[38] Crespin 1570, p. 274ᵛ.

[39] Agrippa d'Aubigné, *Histoire Universelle*, ed. A. de Ruble, (10 vols, Paris, 1886–1909).

conclusion is not generally suggested by the evidence. In the first place the early editions of Crespin contain only a few examples of direct quotations from official trial records.[40] Now, as we have seen, when Crespin had contemporary documentation he usually used it, regardless of its quality and direct relevance. The fact that Crespin does not quote readily from such documents suggests that they were not generally available to him.[41] A more likely source than official trial documents would in any case have been confessions and letters written by the prisoners themselves. Some martyrs found a way of writing up their interrogations from memory and confiding them to some courageous friends, who apparently would pass the material on to Crespin. One of these martyrs was Jean Sorret, a Walloon member of the Reformed church at Tournai, executed in 1569.[42] Writing to fellow members of his congregation, he requested: 'I beseech you not to show my interrogations to anyone, at least until after my death, for besides the fact that they have been written with great speed, if it is known that anyone gave me assistance to get these to you, they will be in great danger, because I know they fear God'.[43]

However, although Crespin makes great use of letters, or confessions written by the accused to their friends, sisters or brothers, it is difficult to know how or in what state he received them. And yet how Crespin treated these raw materials is crucial in establishing his editorial freedom, and his willingness to tamper with the testimonies. Often, with a great deal of time to pass, the prisoners would write letters of great length. We have little or no indication of the conditions in which these letters were written, but despite any hardships the letters as presented by Crespin were often crammed with a remarkable quantity of biblical and patristic citations. Even bearing in mind the much greater biblical literacy of the sixteenth century, their proficiency was suspiciously remarkable. One could understand this level of accomplishment in the case of students of theology, such as Pierre Navihères or Bernard Seguin, two of the five students of Lyons, yet the same fluency and quality of citation is also often

---

[40] For instance, the sentences handed down on the 14 martyrs of Meaux, executed in 1546, are to be found in Crespin 1570, pp. 161^v–3^r. Equally, the pronouncements of the Court against Jean Brugière, from Issoire, are reproduced in Crespin 1570, p. 171^v.

[41] A comparison of the trial documents of the heresy court of the Parlement of Paris, the so-called *Chambre Ardente*, for the years 1547–49 with Crespin's account of these same martyrs brings home the very different preoccupations of these two types of documentation. See N. Weiss, *La Chambre Ardente* (Paris, 1889); David Watson, 'French Protestantism in the time of trial. Jean Crespin and the Chambre Ardente' (unpublished paper, St Andrews Reformation Studies Institute, December 1994).

[42] On Sorret, see Moreau, *Histoire du Protestantisme à Tournai*, p. 242n.

[43] Crespin 1570, p. 707^r.

evident in letters written by more humble martyrs: merchants, book-sellers, tradesmen.[44]

An excellent example of this phenomenon is provided by the case of Jean Chambon, highwayman and thief, who was imprisoned for several months at the same time as the five students of Lyons. While in prison, he was visited by Pierre Berger, pastry-chef and future martyr. He was converted.[45] According to Bernard Seguin, one of his fellow prisoners, Chambon spent nearly his whole time clasped in irons, his feet in stocks and his hands bound by manacles.[46] Despite these manacles, he found a way of sending a letter to the five students asking for some book of consolation. This letter was published by Crespin and in it we learn of the difficult conditions in which it was written:

> If my letter is awkward to read, excuse me. For I only have bright-ness by a hole to pass my hand, and cannot cut my feather quill, which is therefore worthless. Moreover, I write in great pain, more than you could believe, yet I must write secretly, for it is forbidden for me, and they have taken away from me ink and paper. I have only obtained this with great difficulty, and there is only a servant who knows this.[47]

Obviously, conditions in the prison were not conducive to writing, yet Chambon the highwayman wrote like a theologian.[48] In the words of the *Histoire Ecclesiastique*, 'In an instant, by manner of speaking, he was transformed from a murderer to an excellent preacher of the truth'.[49] Chambon did indeed write skilfully. His account of his fellow prisoner, who was also converted, does seem the work of more than just a common thief:

> He who also entered blind into these prisons of Rouen, but, by the pain and example way of our brother Pierre Berger, he will leave, by

---

[44] The confessions of the five students include a wide variety of citations. For example, Seguin draws, to some extent, from nearly every book of the New Testament and many from the Old Testament. The other four students are equally proficient. In addition, the confessions of the above-mentioned Godefroy de Hamelle and Pierre Brully show similar biblical expertise. Examples of more humble martyrs being remarkably well-educated include the merchant Pierre Millet (Crespin 1570, pp. 524r–4v), Guillaume Cornu, an apprentice dressmaker (Crespin 1570, pp. 623r–4v), and Jean de Lannoy, a tapestry-maker (Crespin 1570, pp. 577v–8r). There are also the examples of the labourers Jean Cornon and Estienne Brun astonishing their more learned accusers with the depth of their biblical knowledge (Crespin 1570, p. 85r and Crespin 1570, pp. 94v–5r).

[45] Crespin 1570, p. 237v.

[46] Ibid., p. 215r–v.

[47] Ibid., p. 238v.

[48] A. Piaget and G. Berthoud, *Notes sur le livre des martyrs de Jean Crespin* (Neuchatel, 1930), p. 39.

[49] J. Baum and E. Cunitz, *Histoire ecclésiastique des églises reformées au royaume de France* (3 vols, Paris 1886–1909), I. 110.

the mercy of our good God, with the light of truth. I even reckon that he has acquired all the gold of this world. For if Jacques is killed, Pierre will stay in order to teach the blind.[50]

Chambon is desperately keen to die in the right manner. He asks the five students to teach him how to be led to death, where he wishes to say something for the honour and glory of God and for the salvation of his soul. According to Crespin, the letter is in Chambon's own language, and there are some vulgar references, more befitting a brigand. Chambon recalls of his two months of incarceration, that ' . . . I was not able to turn or move, so that often I had to piss under me'.[51] Aside from the occasional vulgar phrase, the rest of his letter is written well and with knowledge. Now it is possible that Chambon was a man of some education. But it seems equally likely that the refinement so obvious in his writing was added by Crespin in his compilation of the events and material.

Interestingly, this letter of Chambon's does not appear in the first edition of the martyrology of 1554, and its later appearance does raise questions as to the changing nature of the accounts in the collection, and to what extent they may have been refined by Crespin. For example, the changes undergone in the account of one of the proto-martyrs of French Protestantism, Jacques Pavanes, martyred in 1525, are important not only for the fact that they significantly increase the length of Crespin's account, but because they show a significant doctrinal development between successive editions. These are changes which must raise some doubts as to the reliability of what appears if these are to be treated as simple historical, narrative accounts. The considerable variations between the editions of 1554 and 1570 bring to light discrepancies in Crespin's developing account of this martyr which indicate a growing concern with doctrinal precision, even to the point of introducing new material which identifies these early evangelicals more clearly with Crespin's Calvinist readership. As an example, when discussing Pavanes' unflinching commitment to his beliefs when in front of the judges, ' . . . he maintains a pure confession of the Christian religion' in the edition of 1554 becomes ' . . . he maintains a pure confession of the Christian religion and above all the matter of the Holy Supper' in the 1556 edition, a manifestly more explicit reference to a doctrine of primary importance to Calvinists, indeed all orthodox Protestants.[52] In the same way, the account of Pavanes' death in the 1556 edition ends with the words, '. . . soon after (he) was burnt alive in Paris at the place de Greve, in the year 1525' whereas a comparison with the 1570 edition

---

[50] Crespin 1570, p. 238.
[51] Ibid., p. 238.
[52] Ibid., p. 263.

shows the addition of the following references to the Lord's Supper: ' . . . soon after (he) was burnt alive in Paris at the place de Greve, in the year 1525 to the great honour of the doctrine of the Gospel and edification of several of the faithful, who until then were unaware of the true usage and institution of the Holy Supper of the Lord Jesus Christ'.[53]

Sensitivity to which edition one is using, and the ways in which it varies from its predecessors, is crucial for one turning to Crespin for matters of historical fact. Undoubtedly some such changes would have resulted from Crespin's concern to provide the fullest and most accurate account of these martyr narratives and his wish to incorporate new material as it came to hand. But was this the likely reason for Crespin's elaboration of the account of the execution of Pavanes – events which had happened some 40 years previously – particularly when in this case the new materials smoothly accommodated Pavanes's views to those of Crespin's present readership?

This process of accommodation is perhaps most obvious in cases of this nature, concerning martyrs of the earliest years of the French Reformation, a time when doctrine was inevitably still fluid and unsettled. Tales from the early evangelical period were clearly embellished with successive editions, and in ways which brought them more into the Calvinist mainstream.

But what of those accounts where the doctrine of the martyr was not attested to, or only vaguely described? Crespin actually admits to tidying up or 're-dressing' some of the documentation received, if it was too long or poorly written. But it would be a more serious matter if this process extended to shifting the doctrinal emphasis to something more congenial to Crespin or his intended readership. Certainly if it could be demonstrated that Crespin was prone to such a process, it would call for more circumspection in the use of Crespin as a historical source than some recent historians of the French Reformation have shown.

As an example of this one may take the story of Alexander Canus. This passage contains a confession of faith, like many of the accounts of martyrs, and modern historians have built considerably on their analysis of Crespin's account. David Nicholls is not the first to put great store by Crespin's account of Canus' beliefs: 'But there is no doubt that the eucharist and other Catholic sacraments did come under attack at an early date. If Alexander Canus, burnt in 1534, made the "only explicit sacramentarian confession of faith", he was far from alone in attacking the mass.'[54]

Emile Leonard also put great emphasis on this confession as an indica-

---

[53] Ibid., p. 68[v].

[54] D. Nicholls, 'The Nature of Popular Heresy in France', *HJ*, 26 (1983), 271.

tion of how the beliefs of the early French evangelicals were increasingly being influenced by a Zwingli-oriented theology.[55] Yet our only indication of a source for Canus's beliefs comes from Crespin's account of the condemned preaching a sermon to bystanders and to the crowd at his execution, which Crespin claims some of them had written down. For an event which proves to be so critical for modern interpretations of the theological orientation of the French Reformation at this date, this cannot be adequate verification, particularly given what we now know of Crespin's apparent licence with these early martyr accounts.

For other narratives the source seems to be Crespin himself. When Crespin describes the election of Pierre Le Clerc as minister of the new church at Meaux in 1546, Crespin described his duties as, 'declaring the word of God and administering the Sacraments'.[56] This probably says more to us of Crespin's own bias and preoccupations than actual events, since this is simply a classic formulation of the Calvinist view of the marks of the true church.[57] One is led to wonder whether what one has here is the relating of a historical event, as occurred among the evangelicals at Meaux in 1546, or Crespin's own understanding of what should have occurred at the formation of a church. Yet Henry Heller, for one, accepts this quite uncritically, as an accurate recording of historical fact.[58] Crespin's writing here was more probably as a guideline and as a description of doctrinal policy for nascent Calvinist churches rather than the faithful recording of events.

By including statements of faith supposedly professed by the condemned, Crespin sought to provide some doctrinal guidance, unity and coherence to his readers at a time when many of them might have found themselves in similar situations; and at a time when the growth of the evangelical movement was so rapid that it threatened to overwhelm any controls sent out from Geneva and develop all sorts of diverse influences. One important aim of the *Livre des Martyrs* was an attempt to secure some degree of direction in the beliefs of its readers. This is more than a technical or historiographical point, since such embellishments of his text by Crespin, if that is what they are, have greatly affected our understand-

---

[55] E. Leonard, *A History of Protestantism* (2 vols, London, 1975), II. 233.

[56] Crespin 1554, p. 271.

[57] Compare the passage in J. Calvin, *Institutes of the Christian Religion*, ed. J.T. McNeill (2 vols, Library of Christian Classics, 1960), p. 1023: 'Wherever we see the Word of God purely preached and heard, and the sacraments administered to Christ's institution, there, it is not to be doubted, a church of God exists.'

[58] 'Meaux was the first French protestant community in which it could be said that the two essential markings of a Calvinist church, that is to say, preaching and the proper administration of the sacraments by a minister, were carried out.' H. Heller, *The Conquest of Poverty, The Calvinist Revolt in Sixteenth century France* (Leiden, 1986) p. 132.

ing of the French Reformation. For example, as a result of dependence upon Crespin's text, it has been generally accepted that a speech made by the martyr Constantin as he was being driven to the stake in Rouen in 1542 is the first indication of the spread of Calvin's *Institutes* within France. As Heller writes, 'Constantin was quoting the 1541 edition of the *Christian Institutes*'.[59] A cursory inspection of both passages suggests that this may indeed be a valid observation. This is Crespin's account of Constantin's words: 'Vrayement, nous sommes l'ordure et les balieures du monde, lesquelle puent maintenant aux hommes mais resiouissons-nous: car l'odeur de nostre mort sera plaisante et precieuse devant Dieu . . .'.[60] Compare Calvin's *Institutes*: '. . . c'est à scauoir, devant Dieu miserables pecheus, envers les hommes, contemnez et dejectez, et mesme si tu veux, l'ordure et ballieure du monde: ou si on peut encores nommer quelque chose plus vile'.[61]

Heller concludes, 'At Rouen the martyr Constantin had a passage from the Christian Institutes on his lips at the time of his death in 1542. From that time onward evangelicals in that city began to be referred to as Calvinists rather than Lutherans.'[62]

Yet two problems arise here. First, on the evidence presented thus far of Crespin's willingness to elaborate these early martyr tales, he was probably not beyond inserting such a quotation to embellish the story of someone who had been dead for 12 years. And even if Crespin could be relied on not to tamper with the testimony of Constantin, is it not more likely that he was quoting the Bible, 1 Corinthians 4:13, just as Calvin had done? 'Nous sommes blasmez, et nous prions: nous sommes faits comme baillieures de ce monde, et comme la raclure de tous iusques à maintenant.'[63]

Although Crespin does not reveal to us the nature of Constantin's profession or trade, or intellectual abilities, it seems by the nature of his title that he did not come from the higher levels of society, and therefore there was a fair chance that he did not read Latin. So, bearing in mind that the first French edition of the *Institutes* appeared in 1541, and Constantin was executed in 1542 (having possibly been arrested the year before), it is not intrinsically likely that Constantin could have absorbed the substance

---

[59] Ibid., p. 16n.

[60] Crespin 1554, p. 636.

[61] J. Calvin, *Institution de la religion chrestienne. Texte de la première édition française (1541) réimprimé sous la direction de Abel Lefranc par Henri Chatelan et Jacques Pannier* (Paris, 1911), dedicatory epistle, p. xi.

[62] Heller, *Conquest of Poverty*, p. 116.

[63] Jean Bonnefoy, *La Sainte Bible* (Geneva, 1566?). In addition, the second part of Constantin's remark is surely more likely to be a paraphrase of Ps. 116:15, 'La mort des bien-aimés de l'Eternal est précieuse à ses yeux'.

of Calvin's new book to the extent that these words were on his lips at the moment of his martyrdom. A balance of plausibility favours the contention that either Constantin was quoting from scripture, or that Crespin inserted the quotation himself. Certainly either conjecture is as plausible as the generally accepted view that Constantin's declaration is clear evidence of the early penetration of Calvin's *Institutes* into France.

Thus although Crespin in the preface to his original edition declared that he wanted to reproduce the accounts as faithfully as possible, without miracles or flights of fancy, it is clear that the pedagogic purposes of the book weighed as heavily with him as strict fidelity to a demanding standard of historical accuracy. Perhaps such a standard is in any case anachronistic in a culture which retained a highly developed sense of divine activity and providential intervention. While Protestants rejected bogus miracles and saint cults, they recognised that if theirs were the true religion it would certainly be visited by manifestations of divine favour. This might take several forms: either the horrific examples of judgements on their enemies which provided the cautionary aspects of these tales, or counter-examples of martyrs showing miraculous powers in the course of their execution.

Crespin includes several instances of persecutors of the faithful being visited with a swift retribution. The long account of the destruction of the Waldensians in 1545 contains one such example. In the story of the massacre at Cabrières and Merindol, Jean de Roma, a Jacobin monk, was so fierce in his persecution that

> he fell ill of a strange and horrible illness, which was so contagious that he was taken to the hospital, and more and more no-one dared approach him, for the smell and infection which emanated from his body and his flesh which was all ulcerated and lice-ridden: so much that he himself was not able to suffer his smell, in this way often crying, 'Who will deliver or kill me?'[64]

Furthermore, the edition of 1570 includes a whole section of judgements of God, presented in the shape of a letter to King Henry II. In this letter, Crespin sees divine retribution as the root of Henry's misfortune. In reference to the outbreak of war with Charles V in 1552, and the alliance between Henry II and Maurice of Saxony the previous year, Crespin writes: 'When you made the Edict of Chateaubriand, God sent you war: but when you deferred its execution and even made enemies of the Pope by entering Germany in defence of religious liberty, your affairs prospered beyond all riches'.[65]

Pierre du Chastel, Bishop of Orleans, also met an unfortunate end.

---

[64] Crespin 1570, p. 126ᵛ.
[65] Ibid., p. 473ʳ.

Having turned his back on the Reformed cause, he continued his persecution of Orleans. As a direct consequence of this, however, he was '... touched in the pulpit by God's finger, and struck by an illness unknown to doctors, which burned the greater part of his body, and left the rest as cold as ice, before he died, moaning and crying'.[66]

Antoine Duprat, Chancellor of France, also paid for his crimes against the evangelicals. Having given the first orders to kill the faithful, '... he died in the house of Nantouillet, cursing and despising God, and was found with his stomach pierced and worm-eaten'.[67] Equally unfortunate was Claude des Asses, councillor of the Parlement of Paris. After dinner on the day which he had given the order for the faithful to be burnt, in the process of a lewd act with a chambermaid, he had a fit of apoplexy and died.[68]

None of this should be surprising, reflecting as it does the very different sense of historical authenticity prevalent in the sixteenth century. But it should cast further doubt on the uncritical use of Crespin's work as a narrative source, particularly when it is used, as has so often been the case, to draw important conclusions regarding the nature of the beliefs of French evangelicals in this period.

Undeniably, for the purpose of educating and inspiring the faithful, Crespin's *Livre des Martyrs* was an outstanding collection. The bravery of the martyrs was consecrated in the words of Crespin. For the faithful, repressed and persecuted, the martyrs provided the example to follow. In order to secure '... the restoration of the ruins of the Church of the Lord', the inspiration given by these brave men and women was priceless to the Reformed cause.[69]

In the preface to his edition of 1570 Crespin spoke of his intentions and editorial licence, claiming all he sought was to write of the life, the doctrine and the fortunate end of those faithful.[70] He himself complained

---

[66] Ibid., p. 473[r].

[67] Ibid., p. 473[r].

[68] Ibid., p.473[r].

[69] Crespin 1619, p. xxxv.

[70] See Crespin 1570, preface, sig. a7[r]: 'Et au regard des escrits et confessions, je n'y ay rien mis sans avoir eu ou de l'escriture mesme de ceux qui sont morts, ou apprins de la bouche de ceux qui les ont solicitez, ou extrait des registres des greffes, ou bien receu de fidèles tesmoins. J'ay trouvé quelquefois des choses obscures, comme escrites en cachots ténébreux et souvent de sang que les povres martyrs s'estoyent fait sortir par faute d'encre; *les autres, en assez mauvais langage, selon qu'ils estoyent de diverses nations ou gens de mestier, que j'ay fait traduire et redresser le plus fidèlement que faire se pouvoit.* De leurs interrogatoires et responses qui ont esté quelquefois tirées des greffes, tout y est coustumièrement si confus et couché à l'appétit des greffiers, ou ignorans ou malins, que besoin a esté d'en donner extrait sommaire, en gardent une mesme substance des demandes et responses. Bref, en ce dernier point, tout mon but a esté d'escrire la vie, la doctrine and la fin heureuse de ceux qui ont suffisant tesmoignage d'avoir scellé par leur mort la vérité de l'Evangile.'

of the unreliability of human witnesses. And before one judges Crespin too harshly for his lack of historical sophistication and seeming haste in compiling his collections, it is well to remember that his martyrology was only one of many projects he was involved with. Unlike Foxe and Haemstede, he had the going concern of a printing workshop to maintain. Indeed, it was one of the busiest of any in the Reformed community, producing 267 editions of works in the 22 years he was in charge, not to mention his other duties as a leading member in the Reformed community in Geneva.[71]

Mention should also be made of how the situation of his readership in France affected the development of his collection. Before 1562, editions of the *Livre des Martyrs* were targeted at a clandestine readership. Under the terms of the Edict of Coucy (1535), reading of the book could lead to the death penalty for those found guilty. Consequently, the book remained a pocket-sized volume until the outbreak of civil war in France allowed its free circulation within Reformed communities. Beginning in 1564, the folio size of the volume indicates that this was now a book for open use, displayed in Protestant households next to the Bible.[72]

Crespin sees the fruits to be gained by the edifying merits of the accounts. These are teaching aids, drawing from the confessions of faith, doctrinal information and an encouragement to serve God through their shining example. In examining this, it must be separated from twentieth-century ideals of unbiased, objective and impartial histories and historians. For Crespin, the role of history was to teach, guide and act as examplar. He saw that history could, and should, be used as a mirror to advance the cause that he saw as the rightful church of Christ. As he wrote in the preface to the edition of 1570:

> I hope therefore that this history will serve not only the faithful of the Church, in order to put in front of them the works made so admirable by God, but also the poor, ignorant people in order to force them to remember the merits of the cause of those condemned and slaughtered for the truth of the Gospel, so that they can judge at their leisure whether if there had been reason to perpetrate so much cruelty.[73]

---

[71] See Gilmont, *Crespin. Un éditeur réformé*. Also, Gilmont, *Bibliographie des Editions de Jean Crespin 1550–1572*, I.

[72] It could be argued that in earlier editions, Crespin was possibly withholding information given the limited size of his book. However, in my opinion, the difference in lengths between accounts within the same volume shows that the amount of information included is dependent on how much he has available, and not on anything else. Indeed, it is revealing that he apologises in the introductions to his editions of the late 1550s for the poor chronological order of his work, claiming sections of information were included as he received them, rather than withholding information depending on other constraints.

[73] Crespin 1570, preface, sig. a7ʳ.

In this Crespin was fully consistent with the intentions of other
Protestant historians of the sixteenth century. To Crespin and his like the
past was a repository of edifying and instructional texts, guiding those
who followed in the path of true Christians in a very direct way. To
understand this pedagogic purpose is not to diminish the art and craft-
manship of Crespin's work; but certainly it makes one more aware of its
limitations as a historical source.

CHAPTER FOUR

Adriaan van Haemstede: the Heretic as Historian

Andrew Pettegree

Adriaan van Haemstede is, in many ways, the great exception among the sixteenth-century martyrologists. Haemstede's *Geschiedenisse der vromer Martelaren* (1559) is no less international a collection than the other great compilations of Foxe, Crespin and Rabus, but it is certainly the least well-known, and the least studied.[1] While John Foxe's *Acts and Monuments* remains an inexhaustible quarry and source of insight for historians of the English Reformation, Haemstede's work is hardly known outside the much smaller world of Dutch Reformation historians: his skills as a writer have barely been recognised.

Part of the reason for this is straightforward enough. Haemstede's martyrology, although a core text of the emerging Calvinist church in the Netherlands, was never published in any language other than Dutch, a fact sufficient in itself to guarantee it a certain honourable obscurity.[2] And there is also the matter of the author's strange and troubled personal history. The sixteenth-century martyrologists were persons of honour and reputation among their contemporaries, and their careers generally reflect this. By the time of his death in 1572 Jean Crespin was one of Geneva's leading citizens, the friend of Calvin and Beza, and the publisher of over 200 books.[3] John Foxe's work similarly brought him honour and the respect of many distinguished friends and patrons, while Ludwig Rabus was successively cathedral preacher at Strasbourg and

---

[1] The best work on Haemstede is a doctoral dissertation by Auke Jelsma and the articles by Gilmont cited in notes 15 and 16 below. A.J. Jelsma, *Adriaan van Haemstede en zijn martelaarsboek* (The Hague, 1970). This chapter owes a great deal to the intellectual insights of my doctoral research students David Watson and Christopher Bradshaw, and of my colleague Bruce Gordon, all of whose help I gratefully acknowledge.

[2] The translations of extracts cited below are my own. For a further flavour of Haemstede's style see the translated extracts reproduced in Alastair Duke, Gillian Lewis and Andrew Pettegree (eds), *Calvinism in Europe, 1540–1610* (Manchester, 1992), pp. 136–41.

[3] On Crespin see J.-F. Gilmont, *Jean Crespin, un éditeur réformé du XVIᵉ* (Travaux d'Humanisme et Renaissance, 186, 1981). For his publishing see J.-F. Gilmont, *Bibliographie des éditions de Jean Crespin* (2 vols, Verviers, 1981). See also the chapter by David Watson in this volume (Chapter 3).

superintendent of the Lutheran church at Ulm.[4] Haemstede's career was altogether more troubled and turbulent. Dismissed by one church and excommunicated by another, Haemstede ended his life a condemned heretic and in penniless obscurity, abandoned by the church to which he had given such distinguished if erratic service. So complete, indeed, was his fall from grace, that it is not entirely clear when and where Haemstede died: his end is recorded only by an eliptical reference in the list of ministers of the Dutch church in London. His indigent wife, meanwhile, was left to rely on the generosity of the exile church at Emden, Haemstede's last and most consistent supporter.[5]

This in itself is extraordinary enough, and I shall explore below how this troubled personal history may have influenced the reception of Haemstede's work. But Haemstede's book is also strikingly distinguished by the circumstances of its composition. Most of the martyrologists wrote their work in conditions of reasonable comfort and personal security, at one stage removed from the turbulent and harrowing events they were describing. Crespin naturally gathered his materials in Geneva, where he had resided for six years and built up a considerable business before he turned his attention to his *Livre des Martyrs*.[6] Foxe worked first in exile in Frankfurt and Basle, safe if not financially comfortable. The definitive edition of his work then emerged after his return to England, where Foxe enjoyed the hospitality of the Duke of Norfolk's London home in convenient proximity to the Aldersgate offices of his printer John Daye.[7] Haemstede, remarkably, composed most of his work during his years serving as minister to the secret Calvinist church of Antwerp, a position which necessarily implied both danger and considerable personal hardship. The hardship introduced strain into his relationship with the congregation; the danger left a searing impact on his writing.[8]

It is fair then to say that when writing of contemporary martyrs Haemstede experienced the dangers and costs of commitment to the faith

---

[4] On Foxe, J.F. Mozley, *John Foxe and his Book* (London, 1940); William Haller, *Foxe's Book of Martyrs and the Elect Nation* (London, 1963); *DNB*, VII, 581–90. On Rabus, F. Pijper, *Martelaarsboeken* (The Hague, 1924); Robert Kolb, *For All the Saints. Changing Perceptions of Martyrdom and Sainthood in the Lutheran Reformation* (Macon, GA, 1987).

[5] 'Adrianus Hamstedius . . . denatus in Frisia a. 1562'. Jelsma, *Haemstede*, p. 205. For the appearance of Haemstede's wife requesting alms from the Emden consistory see *Die Kircheratsprotokolle der reformierten Gemeinde Emden, 1557–1620*, ed. Heinz Schilling and Klaus-Dieter Schreiber (2 vols, Cologne/Vienna, 1989–92), I. 124.

[6] Gilmont, *Crespin*. For the published works of the years before 1554 see Gilmont, *Bibliographie des éditions de Jean Crespin*, I. 1–41.

[7] On Foxe and Daye, C.L. Oastler, *John Daye, The Elizabethan Printer* (Oxford Bibliographical Society, occasional publications 10, 1975), pp. 26–8.

[8] For the Antwerp years see Jelsma, *Haemstede*, pp. 18–81.

with an immediacy which the others could not match. As minister in Antwerp Haemstede would have shared in the trials and difficult decisions of life in communities 'under the cross'. As minister he would have comforted, and possibly have been confronted by grieving families; he almost certainly witnessed some of the executions which he describes so movingly. These were events which at one point threatened to destroy the Antwerp community, and led to angry recriminations between Haemstede and the congregation. For it was Haemstede's actions which in 1559 brought about the largely unnecessary confrontation with the city authorities which stimulated a new wave of persecution and necessitated the precipitate flight of most of the community's leading members. These included Haemstede himself, who made a hurried departure to Emden after the publication of a proclamation offering a reward of 300 gulden for his capture.[9] His martyrology was published in Emden with his own rapidly completed foreword less than eight weeks later.[10]

So it is not surprising that Haemstede's book is characterised by an exceptional closeness to its subject. This is the aspect which has thus far principally commended Haemstede's work to scholars of the Dutch Reformation: Haemstede as eyewitness and participant has been one of the best sources for the Dutch Reformation movement. Yet even with the rather different focus of this present study, devoted to Haemstede's qualities as a historian, it is clear that the circumstances of Haemstede's life played an important part in defining his particular preoccupations as a writer. For in many ways it was Haemstede's work as minister in the persecuted churches which can be said to have formed his distinctive view of church history and determined the conclusions he would draw from it.

In the canon of Protestant church history, Haemstede was certainly not the first in the field. Already some 40 years previously, Luther had laid the foundations of a distinctive Protestant view of church history, in terms which to a large extent guided and formed those who came after.[11] Luther's view of the historic past encapsulated some of the leading

---

[9] For the proclamation, see *Antwerpsch Archievenblad*, ed. P. Génard, II, no. 38, 353–5.

[10] This assumes Haemstede was still in Antwerp to record the deaths of Adriaen de Schilder and Heinryck de Kleermaker on 19 January. See note 29 below. For the identification of Emden as the place of publication see my *Emden and the Dutch Revolt* (Oxford, 1992), appendix no. 89. Previous writers have generally favoured Antwerp as the place of publication or left the question open, but the printing materials are unmistakably those of the Emden printer Gellius Ctematius.

[11] This paragraph follows substantially the excellent introduction to this subject in Kolb, *For All the Saints*, pp. 19–27. John M. Headley, *Luther's View of Church History* (New Haven, 1963) is the standard work.

themes of his theology. At the centre of Luther's interpretation of events stood a conviction that God and Satan were engaged in a continuous conflict.[12] The cornerstone of his historical perception was inevitably provided by the historical books of the Old Testament, which both Luther and Melanchthon interpreted as a continuing story of temptation to listen to the Devil's lies in various kinds of idolatry and apostasy. In this respect, as Peter Fraenkel puts it, 'the whole of sacred history appears as a series of ups and downs of true doctrine'.[13] Such a framework provided a template equally well-applied to the history of the post-apostolic church where the papacy emerged as the agency of the Devil. Nevertheless, for Luther as for other Protestant writers, the true Word of God was never truly submerged. Even the period of the papal tyranny was faintly illuminated by isolated individuals who continued to show obedience to the truth.

None of this was unique to Luther. For all Protestant writers, the history of the church took on a strongly providential tinge: in Luther's formulation, God had propelled the events of human life at all times. Evangelicals had no sense of a passive, inactive deity; rather God was constantly intervening to shape events.[14]

All these themes found their echo when Haemstede turned his hand to the new and distinctive form of Protestant martyrology. Even here Haemstede was not the first in the field: Haemstede's *Geschiedenisse der Martelaren* was published first in 1559, five years after the first partial editions of Foxe, Crespin and Rabus. In consequence it is inevitably somewhat derivative. All the martyrologists plundered each other's work quite shamelessly, and usually without acknowledgement, and Haemstede is no exception. His first edition makes extensive use of both the Latin and French editions of Crespin's *Livre des Martyrs*, and of the early parts of Ludwig Rabus's ongoing history of confession and martyrdom, the *Heyligen ausserwoehlten Gottes Zeugen*.[15] However it is undoubtedly the case that Haemstede's work profited by this delay. While early editions of Foxe and Crespin are tentative and partial, Haemstede's first edition evinces a striking maturity. Jean-François Gilmont, in a broad-ranging survey of the sixteenth-century martyrolo-

---

[12] Kolb, *For All the Saints*, p. 19. Heiko Oberman, *Luther Man between God and the Devil* (London, 1989).

[13] Peter Fraenkel, *Testimonia Patrum. The Function of the Patristic Argument in the Theology of Philip Melanchthon* (Geneva, 1961), quoted in Kolb, *For All the Saints*, p. 26.

[14] Compare Calvin in the *Institutes*, Book I, chap. 16: 'God's Providence governs all'. *Institutes of the Christian Religion*, ed. John T. McNeill (2 vols, Philadelphia, 1960), I. 197–210.

[15] J.-F. Gilmont, 'La genèse du martyrologe d'Adrien van Haemstede (1559)', *Revue d'Histoire Ecclésiastique*, 63 (1968), 379–414.

gies, rightly judges Haemstede's work the most complete and mature of the four at the time of first publication.[16]

Something of this may be discerned when one examines more closely the way in which Haemstede employs the materials he has borrowed from other writers. The contrast with Crespin is perhaps most striking and most illuminating, since the French compiler provided Haemstede's most important source. Haemstede clearly made extensive use of the two editions of Crespin's work which appeared in 1556: the first Latin edition, essentially a translation of the first two volumes published in 1554 and 1555 respectively, and the French *Troisième Partie*, a continuation of the earlier volumes containing new information which had come to Crespin subsequently.[17] Compared to Haemstede, Crespin is much more concerned to lay out a comprehensive array of his source materials: indeed, he sees this as an important guarantee of the veracity of the accounts he is presenting.[18] The result is that the work takes on at times a somewhat random quality: accounts are long or short depending on the quantity of material Crespin has to hand.[19] If this is true of Crespin, it is even more so of Ludwig Rabus, who made little attempt to edit, or even very much to organise, the materials which he collected into his expanding florilegium of martyrs' tales and confessions.[20] Haemstede is much more selective. The title of his work proclaims his intention to provide a coherent narrative made up of short summaries, 'op het kortste'.[21] Now admittedly brevity is often an extremely elastic concept in the hands of sixteenth-century religious writers, but an examination of the text reveals Haemstede to be in truth an effective and discerning editor.

This is immediately clear if one examines how Haemstede presents his short series of accounts relating to the Marian persecution in England. In essence these are lifted directly from Crespin's *Troisième partie* of 1556: Hamestede uses exactly the same eight individual histories that Crespin

---

[16] J.-F. Gilmont, 'Les martyrologes du XVIᵉ siècle', in Silvana Seidel Menchi (ed.), *Ketzerverfolgung im 16. und frühen 17. Jahrhundert* (Wolfenbütteler Forschungen, 51, 1992), p. 187.

[17] For the editions of Crespin see Gilmont, *Bibliographie 56/7* (Latin edition of 1556), 56/9 (troisième partie, 8°) 57/7 (16°). Haemstede's borrowings are documented in Gilmont, 'La genèse', 339–410.

[18] Gilmont, *Crespin*, p. 167.

[19] Thus the account of the martyrdom of the five students of Lyons (1551), well documented because of their close connections to Geneva, occupies a staggering 25 per cent of the space in the first edition (Gilmont, *Bibliographie 54/7*). David Watson, Chapter 3 in this volume.

[20] Kolb, *For All the Saints*, pp. 53–5.

[21] *De geschiedenisse ende doodt der vromer Martelaren de om het ghetuyghenisse des Evangeliums haer bloedt ghestort hebben, van den tijden Christi af, totten Jare M.D. Lix toe, by een vergadert op het kortste.*

has collected, sometimes following the French prototype word for word.[22] But not always, and in fact there are quite considerable changes to Crespin's text which arguably give Haemstede's account a greater force and internal coherence. Crespin's account of the English martyrs, principally Ridley, Latimer and Cranmer, appears to be based on those materials he had to hand in Geneva at the time of publication. They included long extracts from published and unpublished writings, presumably gathered up from contacts among the English exile congregation there.[23] Haemstede omits about 50 per cent of these original documents and adds instead two or three new paragraphs which highlight and contextualise the historical importance of the English persecution. Thus, in Haemstede's presentation, the reign of Edward VI becomes the golden age of the Christian community: 'There had been no land in which the evangelical teaching had been more truly preached, or Christian discipline better maintained'.[24] Seen in this context Mary, that cruel Jezebel, was inevitably a punishment of God for the unthankfulness of his people, an interpretation totally compatible, as we shall see, with Haemstede's general scheme of church history. And yet, Haemstede remarks, the fortitude of the English martyrs was all the more remarkable, because if they recanted they would have been allowed to go free. Here Haemstede is drawing an explicit contrast with the situation in the Netherlands, where a recanting heretic would have been spared the fire but still faced execution by the more humane method – beheading.[25] The new material adds up to no more than two or three hundred words, but the whole effect of Haemstede's editorial work is to knit the English persecution much more firmly into the seamless narrative of the suffering saints through all the ages. It is deft and effective.

This contextualising is all the more important because Haemstede is the first, indeed the only one of the four major Reformed martyrologists at this stage to present the modern persecutions as part of a complete scheme of church history extending back to the beginnings of the Christian church. This is an important point, and one on which I shall dwell, since it is fundamental to an understanding of the coherence of Haemstede's historical vision. The contrast with the other martyrologists is striking. Crespin, essentially concerned with identifying and expound-

---

[22] As in the case of his short account of the death of John Hooper. Haemstede, *Geschiedenisse*, pp. 362–3; Crespin, *Troisième partie*, pp. 542–3.

[23] Gilmont, *Crespin*, pp. 138–9.

[24] Haemstede, *Geschiedenisse*, p. 354.

[25] The development of the penal laws against heresy in the Netherlands is usefully summarised in the article by James Tracy, 'Heresy Law and centralization under Mary of Hungary: Conflict between the Council of Holland and the Central Government over the enforcement of Charles V's Placards', *ARG*, 73 (1982), 284–307.

ing the plight of sixteenth-century evangelicals, begins his account of the modern persecutions with the most important of the medieval forebears of the sixteenth-century evangelical martyrs, Jan Hus. John Foxe began the work which would evolve into the *Acts and Monuments* with a short Latin work devoted entirely to the English Lollards; the continuation volume of 1559, again in Latin, was similarly devoted to contemporary events.[26] Only the replanned and reorganised English edition of 1563, in which Foxe's work began to achieve its final and familiar shape, carries the story back into the medieval period, and then only to the year 1000. Ludwig Rabus's purpose was rather different, since he, influenced by Luther, proposed an orderly recital of the most significant events in the life of the church, rather than simply a compendium of martyrs' deaths. Rabus's haphazard sense of chronology and modest editorial interventions meant that the overall effect was much less orderly than his preface might have suggested; in any case the close attention to the martyrs of the biblical and patristic period contrasted with a total neglect of the medieval church.[27]

Only Haemstede offers a complete view of Christian persecutions, from the first biblical martyrs, Stephen, Paul and Simon Peter, through the early church to the victims of the medieval papacy. These sections of the work are comparatively short: the whole history of the church up to Wyclif occupies less than 44 pages, or 10 per cent of the work, but they are integral to his whole scheme. And Haemstede's proved to be an influential vision. The matter of Crespin's developing sense of historical purpose is dealt with elsewhere in this volume [Chapter 3], but it is surely significant in this context that he should add to the great folio of 1570 a new preface establishing the parallels between the sixteenth-century martyrs and those of the early church: a clear indication that Crespin had by now absorbed the central message of Haemstede's book. Grafted on to Crespin's work at this late stage, this sense of the continuum of church history was fundamental to Haemstede's agenda.[28]

This is a theme to which I shall shortly return, but first it is worth

---

[26] John Foxe, *Commentarii rerum in ecclesia gestarum* (Strasbourg: Rihel, 1554); John Foxe, *Rerum in ecclesia gestarum* (Basle: Brilinger and Oporinus, 1559). For details and lists of surviving copies see my 'The Latin Polemic of the Marian Exiles', in James Kirk (ed.), *Humanism and Reform: the Church in Europe, England and Scotland, 1400–1643* (Oxford, 1991), pp. 305–29.

[27] Kolb, *For All the Saints*, pp. 52–8.

[28] It is interesting too to speculate whether Foxe was aware of Haemstede's work when he devised his own more elaborate scheme for the definite *Acts and Monuments* of 1563. This possibility has not been discussed by previous writers on Foxe, but it is one I intend to address in a subsequent essay.

offering some preparatory remarks about Haemstede's method of composition. The *Geschiedenisse der Martelaren* appeared in the spring of
1559 with a title-page dated 18 March. The last events recorded in the
main text, the executions of Adriaen de Schilder and Heinryck de
Kleermaker, took place on 19 January, some eight weeks before.[29] Yet
the first edition of the martyrology is a substantial and well-produced
book, whose external features show little signs of haste: in terms of its
craftsmanship this was one of the finest books yet produced by the
rapidly growing Emden printing firm managed by Ctematius.[30] Given
that it is now certain that this work was published entirely in Emden, the
quality of the printing alone might indicate that the text was compiled,
and made available to the printer, over a period of months and years
before its final publication.[31] In fact, a certain amount of internal evidence would support such a theory. Haemstede, as I have indicated,
draws heavily on the earlier work of Rabus and Crespin, but not apparently the editions published immediately before 1559. The last section of
Rabus's great continuing work of which he makes use is that of 1556,
contemporaneous with the two Crespin editions on which he relies most
heavily. This would suggest that the bulk of the earlier sections was composed some time in 1557, a theory supported by his treatment of the
recent English martyrs, which relies on Crespin's published account of
1556 and makes no reference to the fundamental changes in the English
situation (notably the accession of Elizabeth) which had occurred since
this time and which predated by a few months the publication of
Haemstede's work. If this was the case Hamestede may well have composed much of the early part of his text during a trip back to Emden in
this year, in an interval of recuperation from his perilous duties in
Antwerp.[32] Both ministers of the Antwerp church availed themselves of
periods of leave in the exile mother church, and Emden would certainly
have provided more congenial conditions for writing than Antwerp,
where the ministers were forced regularly to move their place of resi-

---

[29] Haemstede, *Geschiedenisse*, pp. 444–7. At the last moment a further half-gathering is
added, which includes two further accounts, of the execution of Boutzon de Heu, put to
death in Brussels sometime in January 1559, and that of Cornelis Halewiin and Herman
Janssen, executed at Antwerp, 28 February. It is likely that this represents information
which came to Haemstede subsequent to his own departure, while he was already in
Emden.

[30] The output of Ctematius's printing-house is discussed in my *Emden and the Dutch
Revolt*. The six surviving copies of the first edition of the martyrology are listed on p. 275.

[31] The earlier assumption of Antwerp as a place of publication was largely due to the perceived impossibility of publishing so large and elegant a book anywhere else in so short a
space of time. Jelsma, *Haemstede*, pp. 281–2.

[32] Haemstede's presence in Emden is noted in the consistory minutes of 26 July 1557.
Kirchenratsprotokolle, ed. Schilling and Schreiber, p. 4.

dence to avoid the risk of detection. For the bookish Haemstede this was a considerable trial, since he had accumulated a large library which could not so easily be shifted.[33] The final, more contemporaneous sections would have been added after his return to his duties in Antwerp.

And it is these later sections which contain much of Hamestede's most original material, as well as some of the most effective and moving writing in the book. When it came to the turbulent events which tested and eventually almost destroyed the Antwerp church in 1557–59, Haemstede had no need of literary prototypes, since he experienced the pain and trauma of these particular persecutions at first hand. Indeed Haemstede the author is not afraid to recognise the presence of Haemstede the eye-witness and actor with a small measure of gentle self-advertisement. Take, for example, this exchange from the examination of Gilles Verdickt, a deacon of the Antwerp church arrested in 1558 while on a mission to comfort and reactivate the struggling small church in Brussels. Examined by the responsible local official Verdickt was charged with having preached illegally. 'Ah', he responded gamely, 'my preaching is not to compare with that which takes place in Antwerp. You should go there if you want to hear preaching. There they are doing it quite openly, so that everyone may judge their teaching.' The official then asked, 'who preaches there?' 'Adrianus van Haemstede', was Verdickt's reply.[34]

This exchange is worth quoting not only for Hamestede's shameless reference to his own ministry, but because it captures extremely effectively the tone of his writing in this narrative of contemporary events. In all these accounts, whether offered as third-person narratives or with snatches of reconstructed conversation as in this case, Haemstede is atmospherically entirely plausible; and to say that is not to offer an immediate judgement of the authenticity of exchanges of this nature. Where other historians have examined the factual base of these contemporary accounts, comparing them for instance with surviving official records of interrogations and executions, Haemstede's integrity as a chronicler of events has emerged largely unscathed.[35] But that is not to say that these narratives are wholly authentic in every particular. The suspicions of the modern historian are inevitably aroused by reading these beautifully crafted tales, not least because it is clear that Haemstede

---

[33] For the problems with his library see the letter of the Antwerp consistory to the church at Emden, February 1559, printed in *Brieven uit onderscheidene kerkelijke archieven*, ed. H.Q. Janssen and J.J. van Toorenenbergen (Werken der Marnix Vereeniging, 3rd ser., 2, 1878), pp. 63–5.

[34] Haemstede, *Geschiedenisse*, p. 425.

[35] H.T. Oberman, 'De Betrouwbaarheid der Martelaarsboeken van Crespin en Van-Haemstede', *NAK*, 4 (1907), 74–110.

is so strongly aware of both the literary and pedagogic potential of his writing. Reading his accounts of the deaths of, generally speaking, ordinary Antwerp citizens, one could not but be conscious of what skilful use the author makes of the natural dramatic potential of these tales. These stories contain some beautiful writing. There is a strong sense of narrative, of poignancy, plot twists and drama: most of the attributes of good story-telling are displayed in these stories. We sympathise very naturally with Arnold Diericksz, the simple rustic employed as courier between the secret churches and their friends abroad, who is arrested following a chance search of his baggage for other stolen goods – a search which reveals the incriminating letters which ultimately bring him to his death.[36] Carolus de Koninck's martyrdom becomes in Haemstede's hands the chronicle of a death foretold. Embarking in Emden on his way to the Netherlands de Koninck experiences a strange sensation of passing through a fire; the friend to whom he narrates this strange premonition in Groningen begs him not to continue on his journey. De Koninck reassures him: I must make this trip, but then no more. We of course know that he will never return, which adds to the sense of tragic heroism.[37]

Such devices undoubtedly heighten the dramatic and polemical weight of Haemstede's accounts: the serious purpose behind them is equally obvious. This is particularly so of the detailed reconstructions he offers of the interrogations of members of the Antwerp church, which contain much of the most serious theological discussion of this part of his work. As a historical source these accounts are not unproblematical. In the main body of his text Haemstede almost never provides a source or an explanation as to how an apparently verbatim account of a prison conversation came to his knowledge. The only elucidation of Haemstede's means of gathering his information comes in a brief address 'to the reader' at the end of the book.[38] Here Haemstede suggests, plausibly enough, that the longer confessions of faith were written by the prisoners themselves and then passed out to friends, and that family visitors were able to report the spirited defence put up by their loved ones when questioned by the local inquisitors and lay officials.[39] This may well be so – Hamestede was certainly on hand to receive such information – but it is evident that Haemstede's relation of these interrogations also had a clear

---

[36] Haemstede, *Geschiedenisse*, pp. 421–2.

[37] Ibid., pp. 417–19. Graham Greene uses a similar device with his whisky priest in *The Power and the Glory*.

[38] Haemstede, *Geschiedenisse*, p. 455.

[39] For family visitors see the account of the martyrdom of Anthonis Verdickt, Haemstede, *Geschiedenisse*, p. 444. Less plausibly, Haemstede also hints he might have had access to some of the official interrogation records. Even with Haemstede's contacts within Antwerp's ruling elite this seems unlikely.

teaching purpose. When arrested members of the Antwerp church defended their faith and conduct they spoke not only for themselves and their congregations, but also potentially for Hamestede's readers, who might one day find themselves undergoing a similar ordeal. In this respect the repeated debating triumphs of Haemstede's victims (and how frequently the monks and officials who pit their wits against them are forced to marvel at the theological brilliance of uneducated men)[40] have a clear didactic and inspirational purpose. To put it at its simplest, these martyrologies became a sort of specialist sixteenth-century conduct book. Future martyrs are themselves readers of martyrologies.

Viewed in this light the question of the authenticity or otherwise of these prison conversations becomes more troubling, and perhaps ultimately unfathomable. But perhaps too, in an investigation of Haemstede's purposes in writing his martyrology, it is also largely subsidiary: for what one has here is, if not in a modern sense always a true narrative, then certainly a revealing insight into the theological and political preoccupations of the men who led Dutch Calvinism during this formative decade of church building. The reader of Haemstede's narrative would be taught what to believe and how to respond to the most common charges levelled against them. On several occasions Haemstede includes fairly extensive confessions of faith or summaries of belief; the interrogations then offer a more lively and often appropriately simplified gloss on these fundamental doctrinal statements. It is worth quoting at length one such exchange, again from the examination of Gilles Verdickt, since this gives a good indication of what Haemstede is aiming at. Verdickt is first questioned by a secular official and interrogated on his sacramental beliefs:

> He questioned him first on the sacrament of the altar, to which Gilles replied that he recognised no such sacrament. 'So', said the officer, 'you are a profaner of the sacraments.' 'No, Sir', replied Gilles, 'it is your priests and monks who profane the sacraments, who have kept us and our forefathers in blindness and error, and led us to mute idols and damnation in Hell.'
>
> After this the priest of St. Goedele came to him, and later many other priests and monks with whom he conversed at length, especially over the sacrifice of the mass, through which they set at nought the unique sacrifice of Jesus Christ. He showed them that Christ cannot be offered up again for our sins or he must shed his blood again,

---

[40] Arnold Diericksz . . . 'witnessed with great confidence, confuting the false doctrines, the sacraments and the ceremonies of the papists with the help of the Holy spirit . . . They said, here was a countryman, who had never studied in any school, yet nevertheless the monks who were esteemed as learned men could not withstand him, but rather were confounded and put to shame'. Similar triumphs are recorded in the accounts of Carolus de Koninck and Gilles Verdickt. Haemstede, *Geschiedenisse*, pp. 418, 422, 426.

for without the shedding of blood there is no forgiveness of sins. . . . He questioned them for two days, bringing them into great confusion. . . . His other question was, what scriptural foundation they had for withholding the cup from the people in the communion. Here they advanced many pretexts which were all without foundation, and could not stand against Christ's explicit command, 'Drink this, all of you.'[41]

Doctrinal explication of this sort was inevitably one major component of Hamestede's account of these prison debates, and one can see in them a teaching tool in its way as effective as the better known and ubiquitous pedagogic weapon of all Protestant churches, the catechism. For just as with the catechism, but with a force heightened by the drama of the martyr's situation, the essential beliefs of the new Protestant congregations were simply expounded, as were the points at which the old church was deemed to be in error. These were the essentials of faith in the most direct sense: doctrines for which Haemstede's congregations were quite literally prepared to die.

This in a way expresses the generic purpose of the Protestant martyrology, a purpose which would be equally clear to readers of similar dramatic confrontations in Crespin's French or Foxe's English book. But some of Haemstede's preoccupations are much more particular to the circumstances of Dutch Calvinism in these early years of church-building. When Dutch Calvinists met together in secret congregations they acted against the explicit prohibition of the royal authority. Conventicles, as these small evangelical gatherings had become known, had been banned in the Netherlands from the first *placards* against the new teaching in the 1520s, and from 1529 it became a capital crime to attend such a meeting.[42] In addition to the obvious dangers of church membership Dutch evangelicals also had to defend themselves against a charge of wilful disobedience, and this was a matter of particular sensitivity in a land where Anabaptism, with its highly ambiguous attitude towards secular authority, had made a significant impact.[43] This issue, and the evangelical defence against such charges, was carefully ventilated in an exchange between Gilles Verdickt and the examining official:

The officer's most serious charge was that he had taken part in secret gatherings, which was against the king's command. Gilles said, 'Sir, is it not commanded to speak God's word? To call the people to

---

[41] Haemstede, *Geschiedenisse*, pp. 425–6.

[42] For the placards, *Corpus documentorum inquisitionis haereticae pravatis Neerlandicae*, ed. P. Fredericq (5 vols, Ghent/The Hague, 1889–1902), IV. 43–5, V. 1–5. Tracy, 'Heresy Law', pp. 288–90.

[43] Cornelis Krahn, *Dutch Anabaptism* (The Hague, 1968); James Stayer, *Anabaptists and the Sword* (Lawrence, KA, 1976).

repentence?' The officer replied, 'Preaching should take place in the church, other sorts of meetings cause disorder.' To which Gilles replied that what was good in the church could not be evil out of doors, and he could not believe that it was the king's intention to forbid God's word, but above all there was no suggestion of disorder in the community.[44]

Here one sees the relevance of Haemstede's constant references to the fidelity of the martyrs' teaching to the pure Word of scripture, and of the historical context which Haemstede provides for his contemporary narratives. For if arrested evangelicals had taught nothing but the unadulterated Word of scripture, how could a legitimate authority place them under legal constraint? Similarly, by placing the martyrs of Protestantism in a long context, Haemstede drives home the point that the true church has always been a suffering, and often a persecuted remnant, existing among a fallen people repeatedly seduced by the heathenish allure of false gods, pomp and idolatry. This is the lesson of the Old Testament, the early church, and of the medieval papacy, whose many corruptions Haemstede conveniently summarises in tabular form.[45] But the point is that such a remnant has always survived: even in the worst days of the triumphant papal supremacy God left a few true Christians so that the world would not be entirely like Sodom or Gomorrah.[46] With the bracing examples of Arnold of Brescia, Adelbertus Gallus and other brave enemies of Antichrist set before them, the Calvinists of Antwerp could congratulate themselves that they were the true inheritors of this tradition. In this context minority status becomes not the cause of despair but a vindication of righteousness.

This is the true lesson to be drawn from Haemstede's pathbreaking decision to place the sixteenth-century martyrs in a complete historical context. And this is the context in which early church martyrs such as Ptolemy and Lucius, or Petrus, tortured for his refusal to worship images, spoke directly to the modern experience. Others offered the further encouragement of evidence of divine favour through miraculous manifestations at the place of execution. Despite their claims to be offering an authentic narrative, all the martyrologists make some use of such motifs. In Haemstede these are more likely to be instances of divine retribution visited on the persecuting magistrate, while Crespin makes greater play of martyrs who speak to the crowd even after their tongue has been cut

---

[44] Haemstede, *Geschiedenisse*, pp. 426–7.

[45] 'D'artikelen der Papistiscer secten', ibid., pp. 41–2. The source of this pungent and telling list is not clear. Quite possibly it is, as Jelsma suggests, an original contribution of Haemstede's.

[46] Haemstede, *Geschiedenisse*, p. 36.

out.[47] Such miraculous manifestations clearly drew on a martyr tradition dating back to the early church, but in Foxe and Crespin such comparisons are necessarily implicit. By including his early historical sections Haemstede was in a position to include both modern miracles and these inspirational archetypes.[48]

The significance of these first introductory sections thus goes beyond the relatively small proportion of the volume's total length dedicated to the early church centuries. In distilling from the available sources a short but eminently coherent history of the Christian persecutions, Haemstede presents a wholly plausible context for his own suffering community, now clearly identified with the righteous martyrs through all the ages. This is even more the case if one considers these early sections in the context of the important exhortatory epistle which Haemstede attaches to the beginning of his volume. Addressed to the Lords, Regents, and Stadholders of the Dutch provinces, this foreword permits Haemstede both to extend the historical context, and to address one of his primary concerns in writing his book: calling the secular magistrate to a sense of his duty to protect the Christian community. To this end Haemstede sets before the modern rulers of the Netherlands the godly examples of the Old Testament kings and patriarchs: Moses, Abraham, Joshua and David, Josias and Ezekiel, all of whom called their people to repentance and away from the worship of false gods. The present-day magistrate should follow in their footsteps.[49]

But just as there are patriarchs and prophets, so the Old Testament is full of unjust rulers: 'So it has been from the beginning of the world and will be to the end, that the heedless world will persecute the children of light'.[50] A heedless people will fall into idolatry; the true preacher is left an isolated and persecuted figure. The Old Testament thus provides further obvious archetypes for the suffering Christians of Antwerp, not least in those righteous prophets and servants of God who refused to bow to unchristian commands. Haemstede here cites the significant examples of

---

[47] Although frequently practised in France (to prevent the condemned man stirring up the crowd gathered for his execution), this practice seems not to have been known in the Netherlands.

[48] Such as Romanus, the early church martyr, whose end was marked by several miracles. The first attempt to put him to death was thwarted when a miraculous shower doused the flames; at the second, successful, attempt Romanus praised God despite the removal of his tongue. Haemstede, *Geschiedenisse*, pp. 25–6. For the early church sources, see H. Delehaye, 'S. Romain, Martyr D'Antioche', *Analecta Bollandiana*, 50 (1932), 240–83.

[49] Haemstede, *Geschiedenisse*, sig. *ii^{r-v}.

[50] Haemstede, *Geschiedenisse*, sig. *iii^v.

Micah and Amos, those rough-hewn prophets who preached an uncom-
promising doctrine of sin and repentance to a heedless people, or Daniel,
whose fearless fidelity to the true God caused his precipitous fall from
favour at the court of King Nebuchadnezzar.[51] But there are ominous
lessons too for the magistrate in the fate of kings who strayed from the
paths of righteousness, for whom the severest punishments are reserved.
Haemstede here cites Saul, Hieroboam and Ahab, all of whom suffered
defeat and loss of their kingdoms for their wilful disobedience to God's
law. To Haemstede it was manifestly clear that 'those who follow the
tyranny of Pharaoh, disobey God's word, and persecute God's people,
will by God's hand be cast into the waters of corruption and be utterly
destroyed'.[52]

In some senses this evocation of biblical prototypes is largely conventional, but it is clear that Haemstede is offering a deeper lesson for those
who will go on to read the main text. This introduction, with its strong
sense of dialectic rhythm woven into the narrative, extends the lessons of
the early church back to the beginnings of history. Hamestede takes comfort in the repeated waves of history. The people of Israel are repeatedly
raised up and cast down; seen in this context the Christian centuries simply continue a timeless oscillation of sin and repentance.[53] In this way
Haemstede turns an essentially conventional Protestant understanding of
Old Testament history into something both intensely personal and
focused on the particular situation for which he is writing.

It is important not to lose sight of this when one recognises the more
specific purpose Hamestede has in mind with his introduction, addressed
as it is directly to the magistrates of the Netherlands. This section of the
work raises directly one of the central preoccupations of Haemstede's
ministry in Antwerp, and one which would ultimately bring about his fall
from grace within the Calvinist community. It is clear that Haemstede
believed strongly that his work in Antwerp, and by implication also his
martyrology, could be an instrument for winning the secular magistrate
to the support of the Gospel. This is the immediate purpose of the introduction, and it is a theme to which Haemstede returns at the end of the
work, in an exhortatory epistle addressed directly to the Antwerp
authorities. Now, of course, the context was rather different, since the
magistrates had already dramatically rejected and cast out Haemstede
and his congregation, a circumstance which accounts for the explicitly
prophetic tone: 'Oh Antwerp, Antwerp, it is also for you that God's word
is set forth, and you are called to repentance ... Your ill deeds cry out to

---

[51] Ibid., *iv^r.
[52] Haemstede, *Geschiedenisse*, sig. *v^r.
[53] Compare Luther: Kolb, *For All the Saints*, p. 26.

heaven. Widows and orphans are ground down, their goods taken from them, their men folk assaulted. And the blood of the martyrs flows over your streets.'[54]

But for Haemstede the chance of repentance still remained. 'I know that there are many of you who know that Christians are unjustly persecuted', he wrote in his foreword, setting before them the edifying examples of justices who had helped the innocent in the Old Testament.[55]

Haemstede's belief in the convertibility of the magistrate became one on the guiding principles of his ministry, and surfaced repeatedly in his account of the Antwerp martyrs. Some of the most important exchanges in Haemstede's account of the prison interviews are between arrested reformers and magistrates obviously troubled by the consequences of sending sincere and peaceable men to their deaths. Sometimes Haemstede makes explicit his sense of the distance between the magistrates and the policy they were required to enforce. Thus in his account of the examination of Carolus de Koninck:

> The authorities and the Council saw that he possessed an invincible foundation in the Holy Scripture, and some were persuaded in their consciences that he spoke the truth. Nevertheless, from fear of the bloodthirsty Religious, they said very different things when the monks were present than when they were alone with Carolus.

In the resolution of this narrative one troubled magistrate comes secretly to Carolus and offers to use his influence to secure him security and protection if he will recant. But de Koninck, Christ-like, resists this temptation.[56]

For all the discouraging evidence that the magistracy would ultimately enforce the law, whatever their own personal convictions, Haemstede never wavered from his belief in the ultimate convertibility of secular authority. And it was this conviction which ultimately led him to embark on a course of action which brought disastrous consequences both for himself and for his church. Distinguished writer though he undoubtedly was, Haemstede clearly found the constraints of life within a secret church difficult to tolerate. He was of a very different social background from his mainly artisan congregation, and found the strict discipline of Calvinist congregational life uncongenial. The congregation in Emden, which performed a sort of watching brief over the young Antwerp

---

[54] Haemstede, *Geschiedenisse*, p. 447. Compare Luke 13:34–5: 'Oh Jerusalem, Jerusalem, which killest the prophets, and stonest them that are sent unto thee . . . behold, your house is left unto you desolate.'

[55] Notably Abdiah (Obadiah), chamberlain of the idolater Ahab, who rescued 100 prophets from the wrath of Queen Jezebel. 1 Kgs 18:4. Haemstede, *Geschiedenisse*, sig. *iv*.

[56] Haemstede, *Geschiedenisse*, p. 418.

church, was forced to adjudicate a painful series of disputes in which the minister and his congregation found themselves at odds.[57] First the congregation complained that their minister would not confine his preaching to the official congregation, but insisted on addressing other gatherings of secret sympathisers. Since these groups would not submit themselves to the discipline and authority of the official congregation the affront to church order was clear, but it seems that with these so-called salon meetings Haemstede was making a genuine effort to reach out to social groups that would not yet feel comfortable within the formal structure of the secret church: the implication is clearly that these included contacts within Antwerp's ruling elite. These salon-meetings, which smacked too much of condoning Nicodemism for Haemstede's less flexible colleagues, were swiftly condemned, but the minister then alarmed the congregation further by proposing to preach publicly in defiance of all royal proclamations. Despite the obvious misgivings of the congregation Haemstede finally took the plunge, deluded that certain of the magistrates had privately indicated sympathy for such a course. The result was the very opposite of what Haemstede had intended. The embarrassed authorities were forced to instigate a more rigorous enforcement of the placards. The meeting place of the church was raided, and the records of the congregation seized. Its leading members sought safety in flight.

Haemstede's ministry never recovered from this fatal miscalculation. Although he was initially welcomed in the exile congregations to which he now retired, the resentments of his former Antwerp colleagues pursued him. Appointed minister of the newly re-founded London Dutch church, Haemstede never dispelled lingering doubts about his ability to live within the constraints imposed by the collective authority of consistorial fellowship. In London Haemstede was soon embroiled in new disputes, this time over his attitude to a small group of Mennonites who had settled in the city, and for whom Haemstede expressed a cautious fraternity.[58] Haemstede's rather lax expression of goodwill was not an issue which should necessarily have led to a breach, but it touched a raw nerve, and the minister compounded the offence by refusing to withdraw or apologise. Excommunicated for his disobedience, Haemstede first sought the mediation of his long-suffering friends in Emden, but their goodwill was finally dissipated when he made a dramatic and wholly counterproductive return to London to argue his cause. His final disgrace now

---

[57] These and the following events are described in my 'The Exile Churches and the Churches "Under the Cross": Antwerp and Emden during the Dutch Revolt', *JEH*, 38 (1987), 187–209. Jelsma, *Haemstede*, pp. 36–81.

[58] Andrew Pettegree, *Foreign Protestant Communities in Sixteenth-Century London* (Oxford, 1986), pp. 167–80. Jelsma, *Haemstede*, pp. 115–205.

inevitably followed, and Haemstede died soon after his second departure from London, abandoned by even his most patient supporters and still under sentence of excommunication.

This miserable end was all the more tragic because on the main point at issue, whether Anabaptists could be regarded as 'true brothers in Christ', Haemstede was not essentially unorthodox. In his martyrology Haemstede maintained a strict line against Anabaptist deviations, which are several times denounced.[59] More significantly Anabaptist martyrs, many of whom met their deaths in these years, sometimes in the same fire as members of the Antwerp Calvinist congregations, are studiously ignored in Haemstede's work.[60] One cannot avoid the conclusion that in his final conflict with the London church Haemstede was a victim more of his own stubbornness than fundamental differences of doctrine or principle. In this sense Haemstede, to borrow from Graham Greene, was more of an accidental heretic than a martyr for theological principle.

Perhaps it was a sense of this which persuaded the Dutch Reformed church to keep faith with Haemstede's book, which remained the fundamental chronicle of the emerging Dutch Calvinist church.[61] The imperfections of the author did not detract from the greatness of the book. And this is certainly a great book, distinguished not only by the circumstances of its composition, but by the clarity of its historical vision and its subtle, innovative integration of contemporary narrative and a continuous view of church history. Even if successive churches might have found Haemstede impossible as a colleague, it is still wholly appropriate that we should recognise his skill and distinction as a writer.

---

[59] For example, Haemstede, *Geschiedenisse*, p. 430 (Anthonis Verdickt). Cf. his opening admonition to the magistrates to promote the cause of the Gospel, since ignorance propagates the growth of sects. Ibid., sig. *iii*.

[60] Dutch anabaptist martyrs have their own martyrology, *Het Offer des Heeren* (1562). See Pijper, *Martelaarsbeken*, pp. 73–119.

[61] Second, revised edition published Vianen and Emden, 1565. Pettegree, *Emden*, appendix no. 145. H. de la Fontaine Verwey, 'Hendrik van Brederode en de drukkerijen van Vianen', *Het Boek*, 30 (1949–51), 17–18.

CHAPTER FIVE

David or Josiah? Old Testament Kings as Exemplars in Edwardian Religious Polemic

Christopher Bradshaw

Protestant writers in the reign of Edward VI (1547–53) never tired of pointing out to the king that his elevated position gave him certain biblically defined duties both to the spiritual health of his people and to his God. Polemicists regaled the young king with the examples of Old Testament monarchs – those beloved of God for their piety, and others accursed by the almighty for their false religion. The exemplars most often cited came from the historical books of the Old Testament that dealt most directly with the establishment and degeneration of the kingdoms of Israel and Judah: 2 Kings and 2 Chronicles, rich narrative journals which provided many role models to the king of England. Nor were such political uses of scriptural exemplars confined to writers of polemic. By the 1540s many of the Edwardian episcopacy were using the same examples to describe their desired model for reform. The question is, of course, what such exemplars were perceived to represent. How far for instance would a sixteenth-century English king be expected to model his character and religious policy on that of a Jewish king of the ancient world?

Among the Protestant writers of the sixteenth century, it was commonly held that the scriptures were an immutable source of truth, inspired as they were by the never changing God: 'The gospel is as yt Lorde is, everlasting'.[1] Such a belief held by polemicists such as John Bale and Robert Crowley, and by preachers and writers like Knox and Lever, was endorsed by the weighty sanction of the apostle Paul.[2] Had not Paul himself written that God was the same through all eternity, being the same yesterday, today and tomorrow?[3] If God was constant, then his historical reactions to mens' sins and virtues would be constant. It did not

---

[1] J. Bale, *A Dialoge or communycacyon to be had at table betwene two chyldren*, STC 1290 (London: R. Foster, 1549), sig. A3ᵛ.

[2] R. Kyle, 'John Knox And Apocalyptic Thought', *Sixteenth Century Journal*, 15, 4 (1984), 458, 459.

[3] Heb. 13:3.

seem strained or artificial to the printer and writer Robert Crowley, that he could describe the sins of Tudor England and God's reaction to them, using exactly the same words as Ezekiel had used to describe Israel centuries before.[4] This bore witness to the bibliocentric world view of these writers. But just as important is that the applicability of scriptural examples to contemporary events was greatly heightened; it had a didactic significance in the here and now, and was not merely a convenient analogy.

The fact that authors did not always give an extended explanation of the analogies they used means that the comprehensive nature of these biblical images is often lost on the modern audience. Often merely the name of an Old Testament king would be mentioned before Edward, and a lesson drawn from this example. But writers could use biblical imagery to convey broad allusions to their readers. A system of ideas could be encapsulated and conveyed through the utilisation of shared associative concepts.[5] Writers and preachers expected the king, and their other readers, to go back to the Bible and read about the exemplars they mentioned. Such exemplars suggested roles that a king should adopt, and others which he should avoid. Thus to be called Josiah was a compliment, since scripture admitted Josiah to have been a great reformer in the eyes of God. To be called Ahab was, in contrast, wholly unflattering since it conveyed a picture of religious vacillation, sanction of idolatry, and ultimately untimely death.[6] In other words, English Protestant writers addressed a biblical audience, one fully equipped to understand the significance of what may now appear to us as no more than passing allusions.

In most polemical works, and those of John Bale in particular, the identification of contemporary kings with those of the Old Testament was thus much more than just a compliment or an insult. It was an attempt to set a specific potentate within a Protestant scheme of history, placing him on one side of a historical divide between Christ and Antichrist. In its mature form Bale's history divided the whole of humanity along similar lines, as followers of the true church or followers of the false.[7] This often manifested itself as the battle waged by historical characters who had defended those doctrines the reformers considered to be

---

[4] Ezek. 34:1–4. Cited in R. Crowley, *The Way To Wealth Wherein Is Taught A Most Present Remedy For Sedition*, STC 6096 (London, 1550). Reprinted in *Select Works Of Robert Crowley*, ed. J.M. Cowper (Early English Text Society extra series, 15, 1872), p. 139.

[5] C. Hill, *The English Bible And The Seventeenth Century Revolution* (Oxford, 1993), pp. 51–7.

[6] See esp. 1 Kgs 18:21.

[7] J. Bale, *The Image Of Both Churches*, STC 1297 (London: R. Jugge, 1548). Reprinted in *Select Works Of Bishop Bale*, ed. Rev. H.C. Christmas (Parker Society, 1849).

their especial beliefs against their persecutors. Many of the rites or beliefs that the Protestants considered the most notable of Roman Catholic traits were assigned to the false church. Good and evil fought out a historical battle between these churches, in the persons of their adherents. Bale had no doubt that the Roman Catholic church was false, and that the church of the reformers was the true body of Christ. Just as Christ and Antichrist were antithetical forces, so the true and false churches were opposites, and Bale's writings are replete with contrasts meant to highlight this premise: light and dark, black and white, gold and dung are just a few of the many forms. The Roman Catholic claim to be the true church was based on a historically continuous tradition, an institutional unity that had begun with the apostles and had survived and developed unbroken to the sixteenth century. Bale argued that the undeniable existence of the Roman church in history did not prove it to be the true church. Only a body of believers united by biblically derived beliefs could be the church of Christ. Doctrine in this church did not develop outside the authority of scripture, as William Turner wrote in 1548: 'beleueth that the Holy Goste reueiled the messe to the fathers and not to thapostles. Either ye take violently awai thapostles fro Christes true church, or elles lye shafully in saying yt Christs church beleueth a thing, when as the principal members of Christ's church, neither do nor did'. (sic)[8]

In explaining the unity of the Roman Catholic church Bale admitted its historical heritage, but argued that the nature of this church was proved by its beliefs, not its longevity. The purpose of Bale's use of history was to show how the Roman Catholic church had reached the state it was in by the sixteenth century: history became a way of showing how error had become endemic in that organisation. Error was defined as unwritten verities – practices sanctified by church tradition, but not legitimised by the example of scripture. The process whereby error, the carrier of evil infections, could creep into the church was insidious. Evil was like a Trojan horse: what ostensibly seemed like a good idea, if not biblically verified, could usher all sorts of evil errors into the church. The best example of the cancerous possibilities of unwritten verities was the vow of celibacy, which Bale fumed against in book after book. At one time vows had been useful as guides that helped one to keep the Mosaic law. The sacrifice of Christ had abolished the need for the system of vows. The Christian was not justified before God by attempts to keep the law, but should rely on contrition and the mercy of God, through Christ, in order to gain his salvation; not, in other words, on his own ability to observe a vow. Humanity was incapable of keeping any of its promises, Bale wrote, and to place any trust in this inability was to court disaster. Peter had

---

[8] W. Turner, *The examinacion of the masse*, STC 24362 (London, 1548), sig. D7ʳ.

been damned by his vow not to deny Christ, because he had broken it, but he was saved by his repentance and the resultant mercy of the Lord.[9] Therefore to place oneself under a vow was to deny one's frailties as well as one's duty to God. Nowhere was this more true than in the vow of celibacy: 'Who can promise to perform miracles, and perform them at his pleasure, who can vow that his hear wyll nott growe nor that his nayles increse and fulfyll it in effecte? No more can they live chaste'(sic).[10] Celibacy was not advocated in scripture either. God's first commandment to man in Genesis was to take a wife, though Bale wisely omitted to comment on the trouble this ultimately caused Adam. So God did not approve of celibacy and would not help someone to maintain a celibate state by the help of his grace. Natural 'heats' showed that nature was also against celibacy. Man's will was no match for God and nature and those forced to live chaste were driven into immoral acts of fornication and adultery.

By these means the tradition of celibacy in the Catholic church had become a tradition of immorality and perversion, for the false sanctity attached to the estate of celibacy was what allowed the reality of the vow, the immoral act, to survive within the church. Saints who had been exemplary models of piety became for Bale the bearers of a historically continuous tradition in the Roman Catholic church, of spiritual error and evil acts. Saints were begotten in whoredom, Bale wrote. This extraordinary and depressing conspiracy theory allowed the polemicist to give his opponents a doctrinal unity in history which was the antithesis of what he perceived to be his own church's true doctrinal unity. Nor was this enemy an impotent foe. Bale identified the unity of Rome as evil, and evil was never inert but active. It was often enough for the false church to pervert true doctrine, to seduce the minds of men. Sometimes, however, evil went further than misleading by error. In the *Actes of the Votaryes*, Bale relates the meeting in AD 976 between the lobby for clerical celibacy led by St Dunstan and a Scottish bishop who argued cogently for clerical marriage. The Scottish bishop, being a man of godly persuasion, argued from the scriptures and therefore could not be trounced by the false arguments of Dunstan and his monks. In a rage the saint stormed out, but not before he had set the Devil to work on his behalf against his enemies. 'Sodenly', Bale writes; 'the joystes of the loft fayled, and they that were under it peryshed there'.[11]

Protestants were widely agreed that the Devil could work miracles,

---

[9] J. Bale, *The apologie of Johan Bale agaynst a ranke papyst*, STC 1274a (London: J. Daye, 1550?), sig. B3ʳ.

[10] Ibid., sig. B4ʳ.

[11] J. Bale, *Actes of the votaryes*, STC 1273 (London, 1551), Bk I, sigs. I7ᵛ–I8ʳ.

albeit false ones, in order to mislead the faithful into damnation.[12] There was a conviction therefore not just of the error of the false church but that its error was based upon the force of evil. Reformers were involved in a fight with Antichrist and there was to be no compromise. Central to the argument of Bale's *Image Of Both Churches* was the rhetorical question, could Christ associate with Antichrist or purity with corruption?[13] He knew the answer was no. Thus victory for the reformers had to be complete or not at all. This thought-scheme impregnated the polemical use of biblical imagery and goes some way to explain why they chose the Old Testament kings they did, with which to define the king's role. Josiah and Hezekiah were members of the true church in a way that Ahab and Ahaz never were, because they fulfilled the polemicists' vision of godly reform.

The most commonly quoted example was that of Josiah, the late seventh-century BC king of Judah and a zealous reformer.[14] The example recommended itself partly as an endorsement of reform by a king and his council when the king was still in his minority. Biblical authority answered the criticism of Gardiner, and others, that a council should implement reform only when the king was grown up. But to observe only this is to miss the main point writers were making. The fact is that all the positive exemplars, including Josiah, which the polemicists held up to Edward had one thing in common: they were iconoclasts. This was not a message the Protestants wanted Edward to overlook and thus they made it explicit. Bale, dedicating his *Apology agaynst a ranke papyst* (1550) to Edward, listed the destructive reforms of Jehu, Ezekias, Asa, Jehosaphat and Josiah. He ends his preface by drawing the lesson that: 'Sufficient are these most worthy examples of the scripture, to declare what the duty of a king is concerning the affairs of our Christian religion'.[15]

The evidence from polemical literature suggests that reformers were

---

[12] On this belief see W. Tyndale, 'The Four senses of Scripture', in *The Obedience Of A Christian Man*, STC 24446 (Antwerp, 1528). In *Doctrinal Treatises And Instructions To Different Portions Of The Holy Scripture* ed. H. Walter (Parker Society, 1848), p. 327. Also P. Nicolls, *The Copie of a letter*, STC 18575 (London, 1548), sig. D4ᵛ.

[13] J. Bale, *Image,* in *Select Works*, pp. 251–2.

[14] 2 Kgs 22: 23 and 2 Chronicles 34: 35. The use of Josiah as an exemplar proffered by the reformers to the young King Edward VI are numerous. A few examples not mentioned in this chapter include: 'Letter Of Francis Burgoyne, Calvinist Minister Of Cordigny To Calvin', Dec. 1550 in *Literary Remains Of King Edward The Sixth*, ed. J. Nichols (2 Vols, New York, 1966), I. clxix; J. Hooper, *Early Writings Of John Hooper*, ed. S. Carr (Parker Society, 1843), pp. 436–7. H. Latimer, *Sermons By Hugh Latimer*, ed. G.E. Corrie (Parker Society, 1844), pp. 175–8. J. Knox, *The Works of John Knox*, ed. D. Laing (6 Vols, Woodrow Society, 1846–64), IV. 398–9, 487–91.

[15] J. Bale, *The apology of Johan Bale agaynst a ranke papyst*, dedicatory preface; sig. A3ᵛ.

willing to take the comparison between Old Testament precedents and contemporary events very near to the logical conclusion the comparison demanded. Just as Josiah had reformed absolutely, so should Edward. In the words of Becon: 'He [Josiah] never stopped till he had reformed his whole realm'.[16] The very totality of the reform demanded betrayed the influence of biblical accounts of the suppression of idolatry by Old Testament kings, as it was meant to. Josiah had destroyed not only statues because they were idols, but had attacked any object associated with false worship: groves, altars, buildings, even creatures.[17] Many reformers baulked at killing idolators, the Edwardian writers were virtually unanimous in their agreement that the destruction of false worship must not include the murder of the idolators; but English Protestants' definition of what constituted idolatry could be as wide as that of the authors of the books of Kings and Chronicles.

The beginning of Edward's reign was accompanied by a huge upsurge in such polemical writing, as the advocates of evangelical reform moved swiftly in their attempt to take control over the religious agenda. If this was the nature of the advice being given to the Edwardian regime, then an understanding of the potential impact of such writings will affect any general judgements on the nature of the Edwardian project. There was nothing measured or moderate about the reforms being proposed here. Further, in proposing such radical action reformers were attempting to strike at the heart of the structure of Catholic devotional worship.

Eamon Duffy in his book *The Stripping of the Altars* has drawn attention to the fact that medieval religion in England functioned as a comprehensive whole: that the religious life of a community was propagated by the visible and tangible machinery of Catholic worship.[18] Protestants in the 1540s were well aware of this, it seems. The lists in polemicists' writings enumerate as abuses an exhaustive number of Catholic ceremonies and rites.[19] The inclusive nature of these lists showed an appreciation of the potency of visual imagery and ceremonial religion for the common

---

[16] T. Becon, *The Flower Of Godly Prayers*, STC 1719.5 (London: J. Daye, 1550]. Reprinted in *Prayers And Other Pieces By Thomas Becon*, ed. J. Ayre (Parker Society, 1848), preface.

[17] 2 Kgs 23.

[18] E. Duffy, *The Stripping of the Altars: Traditional Religion In England, 1400–1580* (London, 1992).

[19] J. Bale, *The Epistle exhortatorye of an Englishe Christiane*, STC 1291 (Antwerp: Widow of C. Ruremond, 1544), sig. C1ᵛ. Also T. Cranmer, *The Confutation Of Unwritten Verities* (1547?). Printed in *Miscellaneous Works And Letters Of Archbishop Cranmer*, ed. J. Cox (Parker Society, 1843), p. 63. The latter writes of all non-scriptural religious practice: 'Their idolatry beside, yea and also contrary to the Word of God, as invocation and praying to the Saints, worshipping of images and relics, with pilgrimages and offerings, and the sacrifice of the mass . . . and pardons to deliver men's souls from Purgatory; holy bread,

man. Reformers appreciated the attractions of medieval parish religion. In John Bale's *A dialogue or familiar talke betwene two neighbours*, a Catholic neighbour told his reforming colleague that: '[it] is a goodly sight to se the sweete images, well painted wyth fayre lightes afore them, a very good smel to feele the perfumes and odours, whe sir Iohn senceth' (sic).[20] The thing that strikes one about this passage is its emphasis on the senses of sight, smell and touch. Bale, distrustful of sensual reactions in religious matters, expressed it in typically two-church form as a seduction by error, but an understandable seduction all the same: 'The gorgeous, glittering apparelled woman', Bale wrote of the Catholic church, had led many astray, but, 'Take away the rites and ceremonies, the jewels and ornaments, the images and lights . . . and what is their Holy whorish church anymore?'.[21]

Such lists indicate the aim of sweeping away a whole system of popular religion. Reform was not adapting a system, but destroying it in favour of another, as two-church theory demanded, and as Josiah had done. Mixed reform, Hooper said in a Lenten sermon of 1550, was neither wholly good or wholly bad, but achieved the same as no reformation at all. He appealed to the king for full reform, citing Jehu as a warning. This king had compromised himself and the law of his God by only partially destroying idolatry and not utterly.[22]

Destruction in Edwardian England can thus be explained in part as what Dr Duffy has called it a 'sacrament of forgetfulness'. To remove all traces of Catholic ritual would deny to people the means of practising traditional piety.[23] It would also break what the reformers saw as the error of long term behavioural character, caused by Catholic ritual. Since childhood people had, by association, come to revere what they saw others honouring.[24] Robert Crowley told Miles Hogarde: 'You compt it no strange syght to se the sacramet honoured with deuine honour, because in your time it hath ben so honoured. In dede to the bodilie eie this sight is nothing strange because it is a continuall obiect and dayelye renued

---

holy water, ashes, palms, and other such baggage', such 'wicked *doctrines*', were both '*idolatries and heresies*' (my emphasis). Also worth noting is the similarity of such writing with the Edwardian injunctions of July 1547: 'Take away, utterly destroy all shrines . . . candlesticks, trindles or rolls of wax, pictures, paintings, and all other monuments of feigned miracles', in C. Buchanan (ed.), *Background Documents to Liturgical Revision 1547–9* (Bramcote: Grove Liturgical Pamphlets, 1983), p. 5.

[20] J. Bale, *A dialogue or familiar talke betwene two neighbours*, STC 10383 (London: J. Daye, 1554), sig. C5ʳ.

[21] J. Bale, *Image Of Both Churches. Select Works Of Bishop Bale*, pp. 511, 509.

[22] *The Early Writings of John Hooper*, ed. S. Carr (Parker Society, 1843), pp. 435–7.

[23] E. Duffy, *The Stripping of the Altars*, pp. 480–83.

[24] D. Freedburg, *The Power of Images* (Chicago, 1989), p. 5.

Image'(sic).[25] Destruction would end this pattern. Bale for one hoped that by eradicating the revered parts of Catholic worship, he would end the superstitions they had given rise to: 'For had there been no ceremonies', he wrote in 1543; 'neither had there been any superstitions . . . it will be easier to bring the one back, if the other remain'.[26] Just as King Ezekias had destroyed the brazen serpent wrought by Moses, so a king who reformed by iconoclasm, 'Took away the occasion with the superstition, lest they should rise again'.[27] Latimer had said much the same thing to the court in March 1549: 'Restore again the true ministry of the church, in case ye remove away all the monuments tokens and leavings of Papistry: for so long as any of them remaineth, so also the occasion of relapse into the abolished superstition of Antichrist'.[28] Far from being the unfortunate ideological offspring of a lunatic fringe, iconoclasm was part of the desire to build a new religious system of worship and was thereby central to the reform process itself. The attack on the devotional system of medieval religion in the reforms of 1547–49 was, Bale wrote, something that 'Chiefly pertaineth to religion'.[29]

The king, called Josiah by Cranmer at his coronation in 1547, had fulfilled the biblical exemplar suggested to him. Thomas Becon, writing after the death of Somerset, chose to remember his iconoclastic policy as his crowning glory: 'What shall I speak of that godly and mighty prince Edward, duke of Somerset, that in the time of his protectorship, did so banish idolatry out of this our realm, and bring in again true religion'.[30] What is interesting about this comment is its assumption that suppression of idolatry was not only an integral part of reform, but a prerequisite for any reform aiming at the restoration of true religion. It was an ordering of reform, discernible in the writings of Bale, Crowley and even Cranmer: 'The error of idolatry was so spread abroad that not only the unlearned people, but also the priests and teachers of the people . . . were corrupted . . . until three noble kings, Jehosaphat, Ezekias, and Josias, God's elect ministers, destroyed the same clearly, and reduced the people

---

[25] R. Crowley, *A Confutation of the mishapen aunswer to the ballade called the Abuse of ye blessed sacramet*, STC 6082 (London: J. Daye and W. Seres, 1548), sig. A7ᵛ.

[26] J. Bale, *Yet A Course At the romyshe foxe*, STC 1309 (Antwerp: A. Goinus, 1543), sig. A5ʳ.

[27] Ibid., sig. M6ʳ.

[28] H. Latimer, 'The Fourth Sermon Preached Sermon Before King Edward' 29 March 1549. In *Sermons By Hugh Latimer*, ed. G.E. Corrie (Parker Society, 1844), pp. 438-40.

[29] J. Bale, *An expostulation or complaynt agaynst the blasphemyes of a frantycke papyst of Hamshyre*, STC 1294 (London: J.Daye, 1552), sig. C2ᵛ.

[30] T. Becon, *A Comfortable Epistle To The Afflicted People of God*, STC 1716 (1554). *Prayers And Other Pieces By Thomas Becon*, ed. J. Ayre (Parker Society, 1844), p. 205.

from their feigned inventions unto the very commandements of God'.[31]
Most instructive of all is that it corresponded to Old Testament accounts,
where kings always destroyed idols and idolatry, *before* a return to the
law.[32] The consensus between Edwardian polemicists and the writers of
the Old Testament accounts seems to have been that any reform would
fail if idols were not first removed.

This should make us suspicious of some recent theories on the English
Reformation. The recent book by Dr Christopher Haigh, postulates that
Somerset's reforms of 1547–49 were proof of the protector's preoccupa-
tion with the war in Scotland. Building on the theories of M.L. Bush, Dr
Haigh sees the reforms in ceremonials as *ad hoc* reactions of a reluctant
government to the pressures of a minority of reformers.[33] Implicit in this
interpretation is the assumption that the reforms of 1547–49 were a
series of compromises that shirked the important issue of theological
change in favour of externals. Such ideas not only overlook Somerset's
active patronage of this minority, but infer that reform of religious practice was of secondary importance to theological reform, and here I think
the reformers would have disagreed with him.[34]

As early as 1548 the reformer and polemicist William Turner, physi-
cian in Somerset's household, recognised that a reform process was
under way and wrote of what he considered its direction to be. The time
of persecuting those who professed the truth, under the Six Articles,
was over, for it was the king's 'Intent and purpose at the beginning of
his reign to purge and cleanse the church of all abuses and enormi-
ties . . . [to] examine and try with the touchstone of God's Word'.[35] The
reformers were well aware of the central role played by the king in state-
motivated reform. The specific role they repeatedly gave Edward as an
image-breaker was not because the issue was held to be a matter of indif-
ference, but because it was believed to be vital. If Josiah taught anything
by way of example, it was that the purification of religious practice and
the return to true religion were inseparable.

---

[31] T. Cranmer, 'Homily On Good Works', In *Miscellaneous Works And Letters Of
Archbishop Cranmer* ed. J. Cox (Parker Society, orig. ser. 1846), p. 145.

[32] Especially 2 Kgs 23:24, Josiah put away 'Images and idols, that he might perform the
words of the Law'.

[33] C. Haigh, *English Reformations* (Oxford, 1993), p. 170. On the February 1548 ban on
images: 'Somerset had blundered into a total ban on images in London and he had got away
with it.'

[34] On the patronage links between the inner circle of Somerset and the polemicists see my
M.Litt. dissertation *Aspects Of Edwardian Religious Polemic* (St Andrews, 1993), app. I.

[35] W. Turner, *A Newe dialogue Wherein is contayned the examinatio of the Messe*, STC
24363 (London: Daye and Seres, 1548) sig. A7ᵛ–8ʳ.

Another problem with this view is its division of ceremony and theology into separate compartments. Polemical Protestant writing does not draw the hard and fast distinctions between destruction of idols and the abolition of theological error that modern scholars seem to. For instance, John Bale's definition of an idol could include statues, but also the vow of celibacy. Just as statues led us from spirituality to sensuality, so the spiritual intent of the vow, a theological idea, had become a disguise for extramarital sex and sodomy. In effect the vow was an idol, since it offered an approximation to the truth, while in fact it was nothing less than the vehicle that perpetuated sin – a sin cloaked in seeming virtue. Theologically, the error of vows was that they placed their trust in the power of the human will to keep them, rather than in the redemptive power of God's grace. However, the effect was described as idolatry: 'By this vow, thou becomest of God's creature, a idol of thine own'.[36] The point was, where did the idol end, and the theological error begin? Often ceremonies were described as both heresies and idolatries. What polemicists were saying was that idolatry itself was merely theological error enacted. The medieval church had put its theology into the medium of visual imagery. Therefore error was not abstract, but a tangible entity. If this were indeed the case, what would be the use of reforming ideas, until the visual opposition to these ideas had been rooted out? Perhaps the best example of this was the mass, which reconciled visual imagery and a theological article of belief in one rite. As a result transubstantiation was often termed the 'idol of the altar' by Protestants and denigrated in the same terms as an image because of its theological claims.[37] Luke Shepherd is the best example of this type of criticism.

The rhetoric of corruption used to criticise the mass, and all supposed idols, bespoke the conviction that to reformers idols were not mere reminders of error. Idols were embodiments of false doctrine, because somehow they had become imbued with the corruption of the doctrines they represented. Thus in a way Dr Duffy's explanation of the reasons for iconoclasm are not comprehensive enough, at least to explain the reaction of the Protestant polemicists to popular religion. There was a violence in polemicists' writings which suggests that more than a sacrament of forgetfulness fuelled the image-breaking. Bale, on his seemingly never-ending hunt for Roman error, gives a clue on this score. Describing his

---

[36] J. Bale, *The apologie of Johan Bale agaynst a ranke papyst* sig. B3ʳ.

[37] T. Hancock, 'The Autobiography of Thomas Hancock: Minister Of Poole', in *Narratives Of The Days Of The Reformation*, ed. J.G. Nichols (Camden Society, Old series, 77, 1859), p. 73, 'The idol of the altar'. Also on the mass as corruption, an atrophic charm, and juxtaposed with sexual imagery, see L. Shepherd, *Upchering Of The Mass*, STC 17360 (London: J. Daye, 1548).

visit to a Hampshire church in September 1550 he related his horror at discovering papist ceremonial in a parish church. Just as bad was the surviving statuary. However, this imagery had been removed from the church and stored in the steeple and belfry. The images were out of sight and, to an extent, out of mind. But to Bale the point was that images 'Should not only be removed out of the churches of England and Ireland, but also that they should be defaced, mangled and utterly destroyed for their abominations'.[38]

The destruction wrought on idols by Josiah had been of comparative thoroughness and vehemence. 2 Chronicles tells of graven images and groves 'stamped into powder', or 'He made dust of them'.[39] In 1 Kings 23 the vessels of Baal are burnt in purificatory fire and the ashes scattered. Altars were stamped to powder and the dust thrown to the wind. The accounts are quite clear that this had been a purging of contaminants. Corruption of theological error had somehow impregnated every particle of the idols' matter. Such filthiness demanded utter destruction. The term 'purge' is used both in the Old Testament account and when Bale praised Edward's reforms in 1552, both Josiah and Edward, he writes, having purged their respective Judahs.[40] Bale compared the unclean nature of idols to excrement. In *A dialogue or familiar Talke*, written in 1554, Nicholas, the personification of the orthodox English Catholic, tells his fervent reformist neighbour Oliver that since images were ever wont to make the church pleasing to the eye this was sufficient reason to keep them in the churches; during the late king's reign the deprivation of church interiors meant that the church had looked like 'an old barn'. Stung by this reply Oliver angrily retorts that to furnish God's house with idols was analogous to a man invading Nicholas's house and 'Paint[ing] the walls with dong or with maser scourings . . . no more' he said, 'do the si [sic] image makers please God but provoketh his anger'.[41] The statues of Roman saints were described elsewhere as '*Stercoreos Deos* (dungy gods)',[42] and were held by Protestant writers to be embodiments of the inherent perversion of Roman Catholic doctrine. Bale described Roman priests wallowing in the theology of prayers for the dead as pigs wallowing in their dung, who had deserted the clean river

---

[38] J. Bale, *Expostulation or complaynt agaynst the blasphemyes of a franticke Papyst of Hamshyre* I° sig. C2ʳ.

[39] 2 Chr. 34:4 and 2 Kgs 23:6,12.

[40] J. Bale, *Expostulation or complaynt agaynst the blasphemies of a frantycke papyst . . .*, preface, sig. A2ʳ.

[41] J. Bale, *A Dialogue or Familiar talke*, sig. C5ʳ–C5ᵛ.

[42] J. Bale, 'Eulogy On Edward The Sixth', (1557), in *Literary Remains Of King Edward The Sixth*, I. cciii.

for the noxious mud.[43] In the votaries the historical error of the Catholic clergy is described as 'Their own vile donge' which would be cast in their faces.[44] A marginal note to Malachi 2:3 would have drawn readers attention to the spiritual nature of such earthy imagery, for the verse described Israel's sins as defecation. The use of such metaphors was to suggest that false doctrine, like defiled matter, could contaminate: those who worshipped dungy gods were likely to smell bad. Certainly they could not be pure as all true Christians should be. Ridley was only one of many who compared the idols of Catholic ceremonial to sexual depravity and defilement, the involvement of the worshipper and the false god in the partnership of illicit practice: 'Idols being *meretrices*, *id est*, whores, for that the worshipping of them is called in the prophets fornication and adultery. [They] ought to be banished and especially out of the churches where the spiritual fornication hath been most committed'.[45] This comparison was reiterated in the 1547 Book Of Homilies. The true church could have nothing to do with idols.

He who supped with the Devil could never find a spoon sufficiently long to escape the corruptions of the association. Those who were contaminated were swiftly perverted, becoming like their idols. Bale applied the direct lesson of the Old Testament when he wrote that idolators became idols. Describing the recantation of Tolwyn, vicar of St Antony's in London, in December 1541 Bale attributes Tolwyn's failure to be faithful, at least in part, to the pernicious influence of idols in the church of St Antony's. The church was named after a statue of Saint Antony: 'A prophane and beastlye idoll and so are all they that stande up in tabernacles within hys templeth' (sic). Tolwyn had been at the greatest risk as pastor of the evil place: 'To be the vycereget or represent the persone of such an idoll is non other (I suppose) than to be an idoll in dede ... Wherefore I wish the said poore man [Tolwyn] no longer to be under soche tyttles and offyces as cane not be used without daunger of sowle' (sic).[46] Bale added that to continue doing so was to be a part of Antichrist. Idols in other words took over the worshipper's individual identity in favour of their own ideology. The pope, Bale wrote, had become the biggest idol of all – the great Baal Peoz of Rome, the embodiment of the perversive force of idolatry and its attendant sexual corruption. In using this example, once again Bale had drawn the precedent for

---

[43] J. Bale, *An answere to a papystycall exhortacyon pretendyng to auoyde false doctryne*, *STC* 1274a (Antwerp: S. Mierdman, c.1548), sig. A8ᵛ.

[44] J. Bale, *Actes of the votaryes*, sig. B1ʳ.

[45] N. Ridley, 'A Treatise On The Worship Of Images', in *The Works Of Nicholas Ridley*, ed. Rev. H.C. Christmas (Parker Society, 1841) p. 87.

[46] J. Bale, *Yet a course at the romyshe foxe*, Iᵒ sig. B7ʳ–B7ᵛ.

the metaphor from the Old Testament accounts.[47]

Error as a corruptant was pursued into the metaphor of the church as a body. Hooper wrote of the need to 'purge and cleanse the soul, from all unwholesome and contageous disease, and sickness of sin'.[48] This idea was further expanded in the 1547 Homilies that likened error to a corrupt and bitter humour infecting a person's body.[49] It is worth remembering in this context that the prescribed way to cure evil humours and impurities was with a purge. The terminology is strongly reminiscent of the Old Testament accounts. This biblically grounded viewpoint concerning contamination may explain why reformers tried to root idols not only out of the churches, but out of private homes as well.[50]

All over Protestant Europe, evangelicals in the first phases of reform were obsessed with what they perceived to be corruptions in Catholic worship. Reformation was necessarily seen as a process of purification, and the removal or eradication of the idolatrous form of worship a first priority in the building of a new evangelical polity. From what we have seen of the way that evangelical writers urged Somerset and his colleagues to Reformation, English Protestant authors were as conscious of this as any of their continental brethren. The removal of Catholic imagery was not a subsidiary concern, nor even secondary to the wider process of theological reconstruction. The reforms of Protector Somerset, far from being an intermediary period before proper reform, were part of a recognised process, connected with the later theological changes. The Old Testament kings had shown the way to purify and then return the law to the realm. Far from deconstructing Reformation perhaps it is time to reintroduce a degree of historical determinism to the Edwardian Reformation once more, or at least to view the period through the biblical construct that the Protestants believed themselves to be pursuing.[51] It is clear that Protestant writers and preachers did not see their actions as *ad hoc* reactions. How far this was true of their patrons is a point of discussion. Certainly the formulators of religious change, Cranmer, Latimer, Hooper and Ridley, all used the same exemplars when suggest-

---

[47] *Expostulation*, sig. A2ᵛ.

[48] J. Hooper, 'Sermons Upon The Ten Commandements', in *The Early Writings Of John Hooper*, p. 286.

[49] R.B. Bond (ed.), *Certain Sermons Or Homilies (1547) And A Homily Against Disobedience And Wilfull Rebellion (1563)* (Toronto, 1987), p. 6.

[50] On an instance of Protestant perceptions of Catholic practices surviving in the home see W. Baldwin, *Beware the Cat; The First English Novel*, intro., and ed. W.A. Ringler and M. Flachmann (California, 1988), pp. 38–9.

[51] Dr Haigh claims that the English Reformation has to be deconstructed. While this is true overall, it is not applicable to the determinism of the polemicists' world view. See C. Haigh, *English Reformations* (Oxford, 1992), p. 14.

ing roles to the young king. Margaret Aston tells us that Edward himself penned verses against idolatry, which he gave to his uncle.[52] The iconoclastic nature of reform legislation suggests that the reform initiative, if not the king himself, had accepted the biblical role that court preachers and polemicists had so often proffered to Edward.

---

[52] M. Aston, *England's Iconoclasts* (Oxford, 1988), p. 275.

CHAPTER SIX

Calvinism and the Dutch Israel Thesis

Paul Regan

We used to think it strange and wondrous when we read those stories in Holy Scripture which talk about the towns of Jersualem, Samaria and Bethel, which were besieged by their enemies in such a way that they were forced to eat unnatural foods like dogs, cats, rats, horses and children. With even greater amazement, we then read about the liberation of these towns, considering this to be an exceptional miracle and wonderwork of the Lord (as it in truth was). Yet the Lord has now placed us in such a century, that we can live through and see with our own eyes these very same things. We regard these things with no less wonder and because of this believe that the Lord's hand has not been shortened and is no lesser in power and miracles than in the Old Testament. Indeed, as we look over this period and its affairs, we are forced [to conclude] that He is the same unchanging God, who has always stayed the same and that He carries out today just the same wonderful punishments and just the same wonderful deliverances according to His justice and mercy.[1]

The lines above are taken from a pamphlet produced in the immediate aftermath of the relief of Leiden on 3 October 1574. The epic nature of the siege and the spectacular manner in which the city was relieved[2] had moved the writer, Jan Fruytiers, to look afresh at familiar scriptural stories. What had hitherto seemed strange and unreal had come alive in his own time, prompting him to claim that the God who had delivered Jerusalem from the hands of the Assyrians had also brought about the relief of Leiden. As his account of the siege unfolded, Fruytiers kept on drawing parallels between contemporary and scriptural events, the impli-

---

[1] Taken from the preface to the *Corte Beschryvinghe vande strenghe Belegheringhe ende wonderbaerlicke Verloßinghe der Stadt Leyden in Holland* (Delft, 1574), pp. 3–4. The work, attributed to Jan Fruytiers, appears in the Knuttel collection of pamphlets: W.P.C. Knuttel, *Catalogus van de pamfletten-verzameling berustende in de koninklijke bibliotheek* (9 vols, The Hague, 1889–1920), I. no. 226 (hereafter referred to as K 226: *Corte Beschryvinghe* . . .).

[2] The classic account of the siege and relief of Leiden is Robert Fruin's, 'Het beleg en ontzet der stad Leiden in 1574' in P.J. Blok, P.L. Muller et al (eds), *Robert Fruin's Verspreide Geschriften* (10 vols, The Hague, 1900–05), II. 385–490. Fruin's essay first appeared in 1874.

cation being that the Netherlandish rebels were, in some sense, latter-day Israelites under the protection and guidance of the Lord.[3]

Jan Fruytiers was neither the first nor the last Netherlandish Calvinist to draw comparisons between his own age and the experience of the Old Testament Jews. Between the mid-1500s and the end of the eighteenth century, Hebraic imagery and Israelite parallels abound in the literature of Netherlandish Reformed Protestantism. Since 1945, these parallels and the use of Hebraic imagery have attracted much attention from historians.[4] In spite of all the attention, though, historians have by no means reached a consensus about all aspects of the subject. The century from 1550 to 1650, the first hundred years of Netherlandish Reformed Protestantism, remains the main area of disagreement. The debate centres not upon the source for the Israelite parallels, which was clearly the biblical culture which developed in the wake of Protestantism,[5] but upon what Reformed Protestants in the Low Countries understood by the parallels they drew with the Israelites. Were the parallels an expression of a Calvinist sense of national identity, a belief that the Netherlanders were a New Israel, a chosen people like the Israelites of old? Or were the parallels tied up with a theocratic vision of the state, expressing a Calvinist view of the place of the Reformed church within the United Provinces? Perhaps, instead, the parallels were simply a turn of phrase natural to writers raised in a biblical culture, amounting to nothing more than insubstantial rhetoric?

A surprising feature of many of the works which have tried to answer these questions has been the absence of a clear chronological framework. The omission is surprising because the significance of the parallels clearly depends upon which period is studied.[6] Between 1550 and 1650, both

---

[3] K 226: *Corte Beschryvinghe*, pp. 12, 23, 27, 30.

[4] The most significant studies have been: H. Smitskamp, *Calvinistisch nationaal besef van Nederland vóór het midden der 17de eeuw* (The Hague, 1947), pp. 13–19; G. Groenhuis, *De Predikanten. De sociale positie van de gereformeerde predikanten der Verenigde Nederlanden voor ñ1700* (Groningen, 1977), pp. 77–107; C. Huisman, *Neerlands Israël. Het natiebesef der traditioneel-gereformeerden in de achtiende eeuw* (Dordrecht, 1983); S. Schama, *The Embarrassment of Riches. An Interpretation of Dutch Culture in the Golden Age* (London, 1987), pp. 51–125, esp. 93–125; G.J. Schutte, *Het Calvinistisch Nederland* (Utrecht, 1988).

[5] For this see Smitskamp, *Calvinistisch nationaal besef*, pp. 16–17 and Schama, *The Embarrassment of Riches*, pp. 94–5.

[6] Something of a rough chronology is present in the work of Gerrit Groenhuis. He begins with the simple parallels found in the sixteenth-century Beggar songs, moves on to the more elaborate parallels in the first half of the seventeenth century and finally to a 'form of identification' in the 1660s and 1670s. See Groenhuis, *De Predikanten*, pp. 77–107 and 'Calvinism and National Consciousness: the Dutch Republic as the New Israel' in A.C. Duke and C.A. Tamse (eds), *Britain and the Netherlands*, VII (The Hague, 1981), 118–33. Schama's interest lay in establishing the influence of Hebraic imagery during what he called

the Reformed church and the political state of the Low Countries under-
went great changes. In the 1550s, Reformed Protestants constituted a
tiny proportion of what was still an overwhelmingly Catholic population; in the 1570s, they were leading participants in a bitter civil war;
from the 1590s to 1620, the Reformed were an influential, though
divided, body in the emerging Dutch republic; and after 1620, they dominated the establishment of an increasingly self-confident European
power. If the significance of the Israelite parallels depended upon how
Reformed Protestants viewed the state in which they lived and upon
what they considered the role of the Reformed church to be within that
state, then the importance of placing the Israelite parallels within a
chronological framework becomes clear. In this chapter, the emphasis
falls upon the period from the 1540s to the 1580s because it was during
these years, the first five decades of Netherlandish Reformed
Protestantism, that the basic characteristics of the Dutch Reformed
church and the nature of its relationship with both the magistrates and
the international Reformed movement were established.

As was the case elsewhere, Reformed Protestants in the Low Countries
began to see their predicament in a biblical light from early on in their
existence.[7] In the De Christlicke Ordinancie, for example, printed in
1554, Marten Microen, minister of the former Dutch church in London,
sent his greetings to those whom he termed the lovers of eternal salvation and truth, 'among all lands and peoples, which at the present time,
lie in the Egyptian darkness of the false gods under the power of the
Roman Pharaoh'.[8] The use to which the Old Testament stories, in partic-

---

'the formative period of the Dutch Republic's history – between 1580 and 1660' and not
with the stages by which parallels developed: The Embarrassment of Riches, p. 96. A concern for greater chronological rigour is evident in a number of works from the 1980s,
though not always explicitly so. See S. Groenveld, 'Natie en nationaal gevoel in de
zestiende-eeuwse Nederlanden', Het Nederlands Archievenblad, 84 (1980), 372–87, 381
and Verlopend getij. De Nederlandse republiek en de Engelse Burgeroorlog 1640–1646
(Dieren, 1984), 61–2; M. Ultee, 'The Riches of the Dutch Seventeenth Century', The
Seventeenth Century, 3 (1988), 223–42, 226; and A.Th. Van Deursen, 'Simon Schama: de
band met de zeventiende eeuw' in his De eeuw in ons hart. Negenentwintig opstellen over
geschiedenis, geschiedschrijving en geschiedbeleving (Franeker, 1991), pp. 193–201.

[7] By the mid-1550s a number of Dutch translations of the Old and New Testaments had
already been published, as well as at least two separate translations of the Psalms. Further
translations of the Bible and the Book of Psalms were to be produced in the 1550s and
1560s. See C.C. De Bruin, De Staten bijbel en zijn voorgangers (Leiden, 1937) and W.F.
Dankbaar, 'Het Calvinistisch volkskarakter in het geestelijk lied, bepaaldelijk in Valerius'
"Nederlandsche Gedenck-Clanck" ' in his Hoogtepunten uit het Nederlandsche Calvinisme
in de zestiende eeuw (Haarlem, 1946), pp. 162–89, 163.

[8] De Christlicke Ordinancie der Nederlantscher Ghemeinten Christi die vanden
Christelicken Prince Co. Edewaerdt. den VI. in 't iaer 1550 te Londen inghestelt was
... Doer Marten Microen, ed. W.F. Dankbaar (originally published London, 1554;
reprint. The Hague, 1956), p. 35.

ular, were put varied greatly, the long history of Israel in the Old Testament making it possible for ministers to adopt as parallels whichever stage of Jewish history seemed most appropriate to their circumstances. Note the remark by the minister Petrus Dathenus in a letter to his colleague Godfridius Wingius in April 1561: 'We too have our burden to bear, although to you it may seem otherwise; in truth you are the overseer of a people sighing under the Egyptian load, I preside over a people in the wilderness, free from the yoke of tyrants, but querulous, inflexible, arrogant and murmuring.'[9] As well as describing their situation, the Old Testament analogies also fulfilled other functions for the Reformed. Like the martyrologies, but in a much more superficial manner, the analogies helped the suffering believers to make sense of their pain by identifying their cause with the cause of God's people throughout history.

In other works, the Old Testament characters were deployed more as models for the readers to imitate. This is the case with the address to the rulers in the Netherlands which appears at the beginning of the first Dutch martyrology, Adriaan van Haemstede's *De Geschiedenisse ende den doodt der vromer Martelaren . . .* , published in March 1559.[10] Haemstede called upon the rulers in the Low Countries to reform the church and to cease persecuting the Reformed. He set before the rulers the example of Hezekiah:

> But, in particular, we have a fine example for all the authorities of our time in King Hezekiah because as it was in his time with the Chosen People of the Lord in Israel, so it is today with Christians. They made images, they followed foreign gods condemned by God's Word, they burnt incense before the metal serpent, the true religion had been cast out and the Lord's Temple had been shut. But this pious Prince destroyed the images, turned over the high places and the groves, broke the metal serpent that Moses had made, opened the House of the Lord and established the true religion again.[11]

In the few examples which exist for the period before the Revolt, there is no indication that Reformed ministers understood the parallels to be part of a sustained metaphor; rather, they were simply a way of describing their situation in a manner which was comprehensible to all.

With the advent of the Revolt, Israelite parallels began to appear in a greater variety of sources. After the winter of 1565–66, the production of

---

[9] *Ecclesiae Londino-Batavae Archivum*, ed. J.H. Hessels (3 vols, Cambridge, 1889–97), II. 154–6. The passage was originally in Latin; translation by Hessels.

[10] A. Haemstede, *De Geschiedenisse ende den doodt der vromer Martelaren, die om het ghetuyghenisse des Euangeliums haer bloedt ghestort hebben, van de tijden Christi af, totten Jare M.D.LIX toe, by een vergadert op het kortste* (Emden, 1559).

[11] Haemstede, *De Geschiedenisse*, opening address.

pamphlets, songs and prints increased greatly and, with the exception of a few lean years, was to remain high for the rest of the sixteenth century.[12] It is no surprise, therefore, to find that it is from this point that Israelite parallels begin to appear in pamphlets and songs and not just in the works and correspondence of Reformed ministers. As early as the summer of 1567, one songwriter was referring to the Beggars as 'Israel's exiles' and claiming that, in spite of the collapse of Reformed support in the spring of 1567, the Beggar cause would ultimately triumph:

> Herewith we take our leave, honourable friends,
> And, to conclude, we hope still
> To rise like Israel from shame,
> And see Pope Leo brought to ruin:
> Although, at the moment, we are playing
> A foolish game in Babylon,
> 'Twas also the same with Israel.[13]

In 1574, one pamphlet writer, writing after the capture of Middelburg in Zeeland and a victorious naval engagement, drew attention to the fate of the Egyptians in the Red Sea: 'You have here, dear reader, the story and honourable account that happened no less than to the Children of Israel when Pharaoh and his proud host were drowned in the Red Sea . . . ' The writer took this as a demonstration of 'the paternal care and power for His people' which God had always shown.[14] Biblical examples also continued to be used by writers in an attempt to win over opponents to the cause of the Revolt. The author of the pamphlet, the *Vermaninghe aen die gemeyne Capiteynen ende Krijchsknechten in Nederlandt*, published on 1 April 1568, tried to persuade native soldiers serving under Alba to join the rebel side by comparing the situation of the Reformed church to that of Jerusalem under threat from the Assyrian armies sent by Sennacherib. The soldiers were warned that the Lord would hold not only Philip II and Alba responsible for the evil inflicted upon his church but also the common soldiers themselves. The angel of the Lord's destruction of the Assyrian army outside Jerusalem was used as an illustration of the fate that would befall them should they continue to serve Philip and Alba, who were designated respectively as

---

[12] See C.E. Harline, *Pamphlets, Printing, and Political Culture in the Early Dutch Republic* (Dordrecht, 1987), pp. 3–10.

[13] *Het Geuzenliedboek. Naar de oude drukken*, ed. E.T. Kuiper and P. Leendertz (2 vols, Zutphen, 1924–25), I. no. 27. See also song number 83 (1573) in vol. 1.

[14] *De waerachtige Geschiedenisse des Schipcrijchs ende het innemen der Stadt Middelborch geschiet in Zeelandt* (Dordrecht, 1574), fos A3ᵛ and A2ᵛ. The pamphlet was catalogued by J.F. Van Someren, *Pamfletten niet voorkomende in afzonderlijk gedrukte catalogi der verzamelingen in andere openbare Nederlandsche bibliotheken* (2 vols, Utrecht, 1915–22), I. no. 61.

Sennacherib and Rapsake, Sennacherib's captain.[15]

It would be premature to conclude from all these examples, though, that there was a widespread sense of a Dutch Israel by the mid-1570s. The nature of the changes brought about by the Revolt ought, in themselves, to suggest caution. Before 1565, the letters, doctrinal tracts, devotional works and the Dutch martyrology were almost exclusively written by and for members of the Reformed churches. It is clear, then, that whenever the writers used Old Testament imagery, they were applying it just to the Reformed. After 1565, and especially from 1567, when the Reformed churches became closely identified with the cause of the Revolt, matters became more problematic. The problem lies in determining how far, if at all, we can speak of the thousands of songs, pamphlets and prints produced from the later 1560s, as being Calvinist.[16] The character of these later works was very different from those produced before 1565 because the later works were, in the main, political propaganda, written not so much to build up the community of believers as to justify and strengthen the cause of those fighting against Brussels and Spain. To the extent that the Calvinists were the principal supporters of the rebel cause, then the propaganda can be described as Calvinist, but there is no warrant for treating the pamphlets, songs and other works which appear during the first part of the Revolt, from 1565 to the 1580s, as works which best express the sixteenth-century Calvinist understanding of the world. To do so would be to run the risk of mistaking rhetoric for the experience and doctrine of Reformed Protestants.

The principal statement of faith of the Netherlandish Reformed church was the so-called Belgic Confession of Faith which was drawn up in the earliest years of the Netherlandish Reformed movement. Article 27 of the Confession states that 'this holy Church [the universal church] is not confined, bound or limited to a certain place or to certain persons, but is spread and dispersed over the whole world; and yet is joined and united with heart and will, by the power of faith, in one and the same spirit'.[17] The belief expressed in this article is clearly at odds with any notion of a national Israel, something which was made clear 24 years later by the prominent Calvinist, Philip van Marnix van Sint Aldegonde.

---

[15] *Vermaninghe aen die gemeyne Capiteynen ende Krijchsknechten* (1568), fols 9^v–13^r, catalogued in J.K. Van der Wulp, *Catalogus van de tractaten, pamfletten, enz. over de geschiedenis van Nederland, aanwezig in de bibliotheek van Isaac Meulman* (3 vols, Amsterdam, 1866–68), I. no. 187.

[16] See W.F. Dankbaar, 'Het Calvinisch volkskarakter', pp. 166–9 and Kuiper, *Het Geuzenliedboek*, pp. xx–xxiii.

[17] *Reformed Confessions of the Sixteenth Century*, ed. A.C. Cochrane (London, 1966), pp. 185–219, 209.

In October 1585, not long after the fall of Antwerp, Marnix tried to draw some comfort from the disaster. In words which recall the Belgic Confession, he wrote:

> We know that the Church of God is not tied down to particular places or seats: it is Catholic, that is to say Universal, not Alexandrian, nor Roman, nor Belgic ... We should not refer to ourselves by such terms as 'the Church of the Lord', or 'the children of Abraham' or 'the family of Israel': for God can create children of Abraham out of stones . . .[18]

According to these two statements, separated by a quarter century, it was the church, made up of people from all nations, which constituted the new Israel.

In the mid-1500s, this belief in the universality of the church was not an abstract doctrine but an ever-present reality for Reformed Protestants throughout Europe. The Belgic Confession was, in itself, ample testimony to the international nature of Calvinism in this period. The Confession, composed in 1559, was modelled on the French Confession of Faith, and was printed in northern France in 1561. Guy de Bray, the author of the Confession, and those who helped him draw up the work were keen to secure the approval of Geneva for the Confession.[19] De Bray himself was much travelled, having spent some years on the exile circuit in England, France and the Swiss Confederation and having acted as chaplain to the Duke of Sedan.[20] The internationality of the Reformed movement in this period is nowhere more evident than in the various confessions, church orders and martyrologies produced in these years, all of which bear the marks of mutual inspiration and influence. Haemstede's Dutch martyrology, for example, is remarkable for the low proportion of martyrs from the Low Countries; only just over a quarter of the accounts concern native martyrs. Most of the rest came from France but contemporary examples were drawn from a number of other European countries.[21] Another illustration of the international nature of

---

[18] Philips van Marnix van St. Aldegonde. Godsdienstige en Kerkelijke Geschriften, J.J. Van Toorenenbergen (The Hague, 1878), pp. 61–74, 66–7. Translation by Dr Gillian Lewis.

[19] Approval was withheld in 1559 but was given to a later, revised confession. Cochrane, Reformed Confessions, pp. 185, 187.

[20] P.M. Crew, Calvinist Preaching and Iconoclasm in the Netherlands 1544–1569 (Cambridge, 1978), p. 40.

[21] Van Haemstede, De Geschiedenisse, preface; J.F. Gilmont, 'La genèse du martyrologe d'Adrien van Haemstede (1559)', Revue d'histoire écclesiastique, 63 (1968), 379–414; J.F. Gilmont, 'Un instrument de propagande religieuse: les martyrologes du XVIe siècle', Bronnen voor de religieuze geschiedenis van België, Middeleeuwen en Moderne Tijden (1968), pp. 378–88.

Netherlandish Reformed Protestantism is provided by the varied background of Reformed ministers, most of whom spent much time abroad before working in the Netherlands.[22] The register of students studying at the Geneva Academy from 1559, for example, includes the names of a number of ministers who later became prominent in the Netherlands Reformed church.[23]

The ties between the Reformed churches were strengthened even more once conflict broke out in France and the Low Countries. Sympathy for suffering fellow believers as well as self-interest helped perpetuate into the later sixteenth century the universal outlook of mid-sixteenth-century Calvinists. Support for other Reformed churches took various forms: fast days were held with prayers being said for brethren in other countries; collections were taken and the money distributed to congregations and individuals considered in special need; and, in their wills, more wealthy Calvinists left behind legacies and donations for Calvinists from other countries.[24] The most visible sign of assistance, though, was the military and political help which Reformed Protestants rendered to each other from the 1560s. Military forces from France, Germany and England, constituted mainly or entirely of Protestants, were sent to provide help to the rebels in the Netherlands in 1568, 1572, 1574, 1578 and 1585–86.[25] Moreover, throughout the 1570s and 1580s, volunteers from France, England and Scotland fought alongside local troops against the Spanish.[26]

In the songs and pamphlets produced from the later 1560s, Netherlandish concerns predominate but many writers do reveal an awareness of events taking place elsewhere and of the common European nature of the struggle against Spain.[27] A prime example is the *Corte Beschryvinghe* of 1574, which was quoted at the beginning of the chapter. The pamphleteer repeatedly uses the events of the siege to demonstrate God's providential care for his people. 'For the same hand', he wrote after describing the relief of the city, 'that defeated his enemies there [Jersualem] and delivered His People, has undoubtedly done the same here'.[28] What the writer understood by the term 'God's people' is

---

[22] Crew, *Calvinist Preaching*, pp. 40–41.

[23] *Calvinism in Europe 1540–1610*, ed. A.C. Duke, G. Lewis and A. Pettegree (Manchester, 1992), pp. 219–23.

[24] Duke, Lewis and Pettegree, *Calvinism in Europe*, pp. 211–16.

[25] G. Parker, *The Dutch Revolt* (rev. edn, Harmondsworth, Middlesex, 1985), pp. 109–10, 137, 164, 192–4 and 217–18.

[26] Parker, *The Dutch Revolt*, pp. 148–9.

[27] See Kuiper, *Het Geuzenliedboek*, I. nos 106 (1575), 112 (1576) and II. 146 (1588), 149 (1590).

[28] K 226: *Corte Beschryvinghe*, 27.

revealed in the preface. If we were to read through the chronicles, he wrote, we would find few periods in which there have been as many sieges as in the last two years. Those of Haarlem and Middelburg are well known but the same has also happened in France, at La Rochelle, 'Sommiers' and Sancerre. At Sancerre, the inhabitants were besieged for many months and were forced to eat not only animals but shoeleather and parchments.[29] That Jan Fruytiers, the author of this work, was thinking of an universal rather than a national Israel is further evident from a song which appears at the end of the pamphlet:

> Do you not know that the Vineyard of the Lord
> Is the House of Israel which you persecute and torment?
> . . . .
> Prophets have found, Martyrs have testified
> That the blood of Christians is the seed of the Churches:
> Haven't you learnt from all the miracles
> Which God has done in Germany and in England?
> How wonderfully that He, to strengthen His Word
> Has aided Piedmont, Scotland and France.
> Tell me: How's it going with your Triumvirate?
> What is Alba the bloodhound bringing against God's Word
> The hand which we saw slay Henry and Francis
> Shall, undoubtedly, sort out the lying Charles?
> How will the Council of Trent or the League of Bayonne help
> Yes, what shall the unparalleled Parisian murder bring about
> Do you still not see that you resist Christ
> When you hang and murder His followers?[30]

The references to events elsewhere in Europe show that, for this writer, the 'House of Israel' was the church of God throughout the world. The international origins of Reformed Protestantism and the confessional nature of the conflicts in Western Europe after 1559 suggest that, during the first phase of Netherlandish Reformed Protestantism, this song-writer's vision of the church was the dominant understanding of the New Israel. The reminders of the church universal were too frequent and too pervasive for anyone in the Netherlands to have formulated a notion of a national Israel before the 1590s.

As well as the international nature of Reformed Protestantism in the sixteenth century, there were also circumstances peculiar to the Low Countries which militated against the development of a national conception of the New Israel. To begin with, the nature and position of the Reformed church in the sixteenth-century Low Countries were not such

---

[29] K 226: *Corte Beschryvinghe*, 4.
[30] K 226: *Corte Beschryvinghe*, 33.

as to favour the notion of a Dutch Israel.[31] With the exception of a brief period in 1566–67, a reformation on a scale comparable to that seen in England, Germany and Scandinavia, did not even begin to take place in the Low Countries until 1572 in the provinces of Holland and Zeeland and, in other parts of the Netherlands, from 1577–80. The long years of persecution left an enduring mark upon Netherlandish Reformed Protestantism. Like all reformers in the sixteenth century, the Reformed Protestants in the Low Countries sought, in the first place, to reform the church rather than to create a separate confession but the opposition of the authorities to any reform of the church along Protestant lines compelled Reformed Protestants to develop their own forms of church organisation and practice. The forms of church government, doctrine and practice which they developed were Calvinist in nature with two principal characteristics: a presbyterian form of church government and an exclusive conception of church membership.

The significance of this development, the adoption of a Calvinist church order and discipline after long years of persecution, became apparent after 1572 when the rebels seized control of large parts of Holland and Zeeland and soon brought to an end the public exercise of Catholicism. With the collapse of Catholicism throughout most of Holland and Zeeland, the Reformed church was presented with the opportunity of establishing itself as a national, comprehensive church on the Lutheran and Anglican models. Most Reformed ministers, though, remained wedded to the more sectarian conception of the church which had developed in the years of persecution and exile. They envisaged a church which regulated itself, free from the interference of the magistrates, through the hierarchy of consistories, classes and synods. Furthermore, they hoped to maintain the pure, exclusive church which had developed before 1572. By contrast, most magistrates wanted a church which was both subject to their control in such matters as the appointment of ministers and was open to all members of society. The tension between these two different conceptions of the church

---

[31] The interpretation of the Reformed church in the Netherlands which appears here is based largely on the following works: J.J. Woltjer, 'De politieke betekenis van de Emdense Synode' in D. Nauta, J.P. Van Dooren and O.J. De Jong (eds) *De synode van Emden 1571–1971* (Kampen, 1971), pp. 22–49; A.Th. Van Deursen, *Plain Lives in a Golden Age* (originally published in Dutch 1978–81; English translation: Cambridge, 1991), pp. 260–79; A.C. Duke, 'The Ambivalent Face of Calvinism in the Netherlands, 1561–1618' in his *Reformation and Revolt in the Low Countries* (the essay originally appeared in 1985; London, 1990), pp. 269–93; J.J. Woltjer, 'De religieuze situatie in de eerste jaren van de Republiek' in *Ketters en papen onder Filips II* (exhibition catalogue: Utrecht, 1986), pp. 94–105; and J.J. Woltjer, 'De plaats van de calvinisten in de Nederlandse samenleving', *De zeventiende eeuw*, 10 (1994), 3–23.

brought about a series of disputes which lasted until the synod of Dordt
in 1618–19. During these disputes, the relationship between church and
state was gradually defined.

On some points, the Reformed church was compelled to change its
position. The old Catholic church had fulfilled a number of public roles,
such as baptisms, marriages and burial ceremonies and had been concerned with the welfare of the population as a whole. After 1572, when it
replaced the Catholic church as the dominant confession in Holland and
Zeeland, the Reformed church was forced to reconsider its view of those
people, by far the overwhelming majority of those living in the two
provinces, who were not members of the their church. The Reformed
attitude to those outside their church was evident in the case of infant
baptism. Initially, there was much reluctance to baptise children whose
parents were not members of the church but in 1578, at the national
synod of Dordrecht, the Reformed church took the decision to offer baptism to all children, irrespective of the profession or Christian affiliation
of the parents. In response to the question of whether ministers should
baptise the children of Catholics, excommunicants and whoremongers,
the synod replied in the affirmative, 'because baptism is the rightful due
of children belonging to the covenant, and it is certain, that these children
are not outside the covenant.' Baptism was offered because the children
were part of the New Israel or the new covenant and as such were entitled to baptism because 'baptism is a general witness of the covenant of
God'.[32] From this perspective, then, all Netherlanders were considered to
belong to the New Israel and to be subject to the new covenant which
God had made with mankind through Christ. For this reason, Caspar
Grevinchoven, a Reformed minister in the late sixteenth and early seventeenth centuries, could compare Catholics to the children of Israel in
Samaria, who, in the time of Rehoboam, fell away and were expelled
from the house of David. The New Israel, though, was not a national
entity but the whole of Christendom.[33]

By virtue of its dominant position, then, the Reformed church took
over many of the public roles which had hitherto been fulfilled by the
Catholic church, thus moderating its sectarian character. On other matters, though, the Reformed church retained the structures and practices
which it had developed before 1572. On the crucial question of membership, the Reformed church refused to blur the distinction between membership of the church and membership of society. A Netherlander was

---

[32] A.Th. Van Deursen, *Bavianen en Slijkgeuzen. Kerk en kerkvolk ten tijde van Maurits
en Oldenbarnevelt* (Franeker, 1991), pp. 136–7. The translation of the first quotation was
made by Maarten Ultee and appears in Van Deursen, *Plain Lives in a Golden Age*, p. 264.

[33] Van Deursen, *Bavianen en Slijkgeuzen*, p. 139.

not a member of the Reformed church by virtue of his birth and was under no legal obligation to attend services in the Reformed church. If someone wished to become a member of the Reformed church, he or she had to submit to an examination of their faith by the *classis* and the congregation. Once they became members, they were subject to consistorial discipline. Although everyone was permitted to attend a Reformed service, only members of the Reformed church were admitted to the Lord's Table. Principally because of this determination to maintain the pure character of the church, the Reformed church grew only slowly in the provinces of Holland and Zeeland. By 1587, the Reformed church still commanded the allegiance of less than a tenth of the population of Holland. Even by 1620, almost 50 years after the rebels first gained a foothold in the northern Netherlands, only 20 per cent of the population of the republic were members of the Reformed church.[34] The minority position of the Netherlandish Reformed church and its continuing sectarian character in the sixteenth century would seem to preclude any simple identification between the Dutch and Israel. It seems improbable that a church which set itself apart from the rest of society should construct a notion by which all Netherlanders were deemed to constitute a chosen people.

A second point of contrast between the sixteenth-century Netherlands and other European countries was the absence of a strong sense of national identity. The most fundamental shift in historiographical thinking about the sixteenth-century Low Countries since 1945 has been the abandonment of the belief that the Revolt was a 'national' struggle for independence against Spanish tyranny. The contrary view, that Netherlandish patriotic sentiment, such as it was, arose during the Revolt has become the standard view. What now appears to have been a more important force in sixteenth-century Netherlandish society was particularism, the sense of attachment to city or province which usually overrode any sense of a common fatherland.[35] It is true that Reformed Protestants, by constructing a general Netherlandish church with a com-

---

[34] A. Duke and R.L. Jones, 'Towards a Reformed Polity in Holland, 1572–78' in Duke, *Reformation and Revolt*, pp. 199–226, 199; and Woltjer, 'De plaats van de calvinisten', p. 3.

[35] The most important studies of the Revolt published since 1945 have been J.W. Smit, 'The Netherlands Revolution' in R. Foster and J.P. Greene (eds) *Preconditions of Revolution in Early Modern Europe* (Baltimore, 1970), pp. 19–54; J. Woltjer, 'De vredemakers', *Tijdschrift voor geschiedenis*, 89 (1976), 299–321; and H. Schilling, 'Der Aufstand der Niederlande: Bürgerliche Revolution oder Elitenkonflikt?' in H.-U. Wehler (ed.), *200 Jahre amerikanische Revolution und moderne Revolutionsforschung* (Göttingen, 1976), pp. 177–231. On patriotic sentiment specifically see Groenveld, 'Natie en nationaal gevoel', passim.

mon body of doctrine and a common organisation, did much to encourage the development of supra-provincial sentiment, but the forces of particularism proved too strong for them to overcome completely.[36] The strength of provincial identities is evident in the correspondence and synodal resolutions of the Reformed church. In August 1571, the exile Reformed community in Cologne wrote to William of Orange to inform him that a general synod would be held shortly. The community noted though, that the 'Holland nation' declined to come and stated that it would be better if the synod were held 'without any of the Netherlandish nations being absent'.[37] What makes the sixteenth-century Low Countries distinctive was not so much the strength of provincial loyalties, which was a feature of all European countries in this period, as the weakness of a counterbalancing national identity. In those areas of fifteenth- and sixteenth-century Europe where the myth of a special destiny did develop, namely fifteenth-century Florence and sixteenth-century Germany, France and England, one common factor which emerges was a well-developed sense of national identity.[38] Without doubt, the weakness of such a sense in the Low Countries during the 1540s to the 1580s would have hindered considerably the development of the idea of a common Netherlandish Israel.

During the 1540s to the 1580s, then, it seems clear that the Hebraic imagery used by Netherlandish Calvinists did not refer to an exclusively national conception of the New Israel. The international nature of Reformed Protestantism, the sectarian character of Netherlandish Calvinism and the weakness of supra-provincial sentiment in the Low Countries all obstructed the formation of an Israelite myth. Parallels with Israel were drawn by Netherlandish Calvinists but, on closer inspection, these parallels either turn out to be of an incidental character, as with Dathenus's letter of 1561, or appear to refer to a universal understanding of Israel. The possibility that some Reformed Protestants did formulate, or at least deploy in propaganda, a more national understand-

---

[36] See A. Pettegree, *Emden and the Dutch Revolt. Exile and the Development of Reformed Protestantism* (Oxford, 1992), pp. 244–7.

[37] *Brieven uit onderscheidene Kerkelijke Archieven*, ed. J.J. Van Toorenenbergen, series 3, vol. 5, pt 1 (Utrecht, 1882), 3–6.

[38] See D. Weinstein, 'Millenarianism in a Civic Setting: the Savonarola Movement in Florence' in S.L. Thrupp (ed.), *Millennial Dreams in Action. Essays in Comparative History* (The Hague, 1962), pp. 187–203; G. Strauss, 'The Course of German History: the Lutheran Interpretation' in A. Molho and J.A. Tedeschi (eds), *Renaissance Studies in honor of Hans Baron* (Illinois, 1971), pp. 663–86; and M. Yardeni, *La Conscience Nationale en France Pendant les Guerres de Religion (1559–1598)* (Paris and Louvain, 1971), pp. 34–5; W. Haller, *Foxe's Book of Martyrs and the Elect Nation* (originally published 1963; Bedford Historical Series, London, 1967).

ing of Israel cannot, however, be ruled out altogether. Since 1945, Reformation historians have accorded much more attention to the 'pluriform' character of Reformed Protestantism in the sixteenth-century Netherlands, acknowledging that the triumph of orthodox Calvinism in the Reformed church was not complete until the later 1500s.[39] Some Reformed Protestants, especially in the northern Netherlands, held a more inclusive conception of church membership and a more Erastian understanding of church–state relations. They were more willing to accommodate the Lutherans, less willing to distinguish between membership of the church and membership of civil society and more inclined to favour magisterial authority in disciplinary matters.[40] The intellectual obstacles towards the formation of a Dutch Israel myth would thus appear to be much less marked for this strand of Reformed Protestantism than for the Calvinists because of their desire to create a more 'national' church.[41]

In this respect, it is significant how frequently Israelite parallels appear in the work of one such Reformed Protestant, Laurens Jacobsz Reael.[42] The parallels appear in some of the songs which Reael produced during the years 1571–74.[43] In 1573, for example, when Reael was still in exile in Emden, he wrote a song whose beginning was modelled on Psalm 137, 'By the Rivers of Babylon'. Like the psalm, the song begins with the exile recalling his homeland:

> As we sat down by the rivers to the east,
> Thinking of all that was lost
> And of you, O Zion, our home in the Netherlands.[44]

---

[39] See esp. W. Nijenhuis, 'Variants within Dutch Calvinism in the sixteenth century', *Acta Historiae Neerlandicae*, 12 (1979), 48–64 and, for a different view, Van Deursen, *Plain Lives*, pp. 260–61.

[40] The variety of opinions within Netherlandish Reformed Protestantism became evident in 1566–67, during discussions with the Lutherans and in 1570–71, when the Reformed churches tried to gather support in Germany to establish a synodal form of church government. See Pettegree, *Emden*, pp. 82–4, 178–82; Woltjer, 'De plaats van de Calvinisten', pp. 10–14; and Woltjer, 'De politieke betekenis van de Emdense Synode', pp. 22–49.

[41] It is unlikely, of course, that these more heterodox Reformed Protestants would formulate a notion of an *elect* nation. Rather, the emphasis is upon the possibilities arising from their desire to build up a more national church.

[42] For Reael's views see Pettegree, *Emden*, pp. 179–80. For further evidence of his broad conception of Protestantism see his 'Een nieu Liedeken' in Kuiper, *Het Geuzenliedboek*, I. no. 42.

[43] The main published collection of beggar songs lists ten songs which are believed to have been produced by Reael, spanning the years 1571–74: Kuiper, *Het Geuzenliedboek*, II. 397.

[44] Kuiper, *Het Geuzenliedboek*, I. no. 83.

In this case, Reael was thinking just of those Netherlanders who had been forced, mainly for religious reasons, to flee from their homelands, but elsewhere the meaning of the phrases which he uses is less clear. In one song from 1571, Reael called upon those who had stayed behind in the Low Countries to 'Fly, fly from Babel, my Chosen People'; in another song from the same year, he speaks of the 'Christian Nation'.[45] The context of these lines does not suggest that Reael was affirming a belief in the election of a Netherlandish nation. Reael's main purpose in these songs was to persuade his compatriots to reject Rome and all her works, to which end he drew imaginatively upon scriptural imagery. For example, the source for his exhortation to flee from Babylon ('Babel') was not an Old Testament passage but Revelation 17–18, in particular, 18:4, where a voice from heaven urges the people of God to come out from Babylon: the emphasis here was clearly religious.[46] Whilst it would be wrong to treat these songs as an expression of a belief in the notion of a Dutch Israel, Reael's free use of biblical imagery remains significant for the way in which it is tied, more closely than was the case elsewhere, to the conception of a people and country.

With the establishment of the Dutch Republic during the late sixteenth and early seventeenth centuries, conditions gradually became more favourable for the development of the idea of a Dutch Israel among Reformed Protestants. Over the course of the first half of the seventeenth century, the Reformed church lost much of its earlier exclusiveness as it attracted more members from both the magistracy and the population at large. Furthermore, the Dordt settlement of 1618–19 gave the Reformed church a more secure position in the Dutch state and encouraged Calvinists to turn outwards more to the society around them. Through these changes, the Dutch Reformed church took on much more of the character of a national rather than a sectarian church. At the same time, the waning influence of the Swiss and French Reformed churches and the destruction of the Reformed churches in Bohemia and the Palatinate after 1620 would have tended to heighten the sense of distinctiveness of Dutch Calvinists. This development would have been further assisted by the contrasting economic and political fortunes of the Dutch Republic and other European states during this period. By the mid-1600s, both the changing character of the Reformed church and the increasing strength and self-confidence of the Dutch Republic, would have made it easier for some Dutch Calvinists to formulate a notion of a Dutch Israel. It is pre-

---

[45] Kuiper, *Het Geuzenliedboek*, I. nos 41 and 42.

[46] In another song, Reael also reveals an awareness of the international nature of the struggle against Spain, a fact which supports the view that Reael was not expressing a belief in the election of a Netherlandish nation. Kuiper, *Het Geuzenliedboek*, I. no. 52 (1572).

sumably for these reasons that, during the mid-1600s, some Reformed ministers began not only to draw parallels between the republic and Israel, but to assert that the Dutch Republic was a New Israel.[47]

---

[47] See Groenhuis, 'Calvinism and National Consciousness', pp. 122–4. Further research also needs to be done on the possible influence of Heinrich Bullinger's covenantal theology on the development of an Israelite myth in the seventeenth-century Dutch Republic. On Bullinger generally see J. Wayne Baker, *Heinrich Bullinger and the Covenant. The other Reformed Tradition* (Ohio, 1980) and A.J. Van't Hooft, *De theologie van Heinrich Bullinger in betrekking tot de Nederlandsche Reformatie* (Amsterdam, 1888).

CHAPTER SEVEN

The Protestant Interpretation of History in Ireland: the Case of James Ussher's *Discourse*

Ute Lotz-Heumann

From the perspective of central Europe the Irish Reformation was a late event. Although a political reformation had, as in England, taken place under Henry VIII, the process of confession-building,[1] of creating a distinctly Protestant church, began only in the last decade of the sixteenth century and gained momentum at the beginning of the seventeenth century.[2] This process can be called a 'second reformation'.[3] It was, however, a second reformation mainly in a chronological sense, not in the strict sense of the word as it is used in German historiography to describe a Calvinist 'reformation of life' after a Lutheran 'reformation of doctrine'.[4] In contrast to Germany, the 'first reformation' in Ireland was basically a legal and administrative act, whereas the 'Second Reformation' of the late sixteenth and early seventeenth centuries aimed at a reformation of doctrine and life.[5]

However, the Protestant Reformation in Ireland shared important characteristics of the second reformations in the German Empire. First,

---

[1] On the concept of confession-building see E.W. Zeeden, *Konfessionsbildung: Studien zur Reformation, Gegenreformation und katholischen Reform* (Stuttgart, 1985).

[2] The standard history of the church of Ireland in this period is Alan Ford, *The Protestant Reformation in Ireland, 1590–1641* (Frankfurt/Bern/New York/Paris, 1987).

[3] See Ford, *The Protestant Reformation*, pp. 16, 287; Helga Robinson-Hammerstein, 'Review of Ford, *The Protestant Reformation*', *JEH*, 37 (1986), 470–74; Heinz Schilling, 'Literaturbericht "Konfessionsbildung" und "Konfessionalisierung"', *Geschichte in Wissenschaft und Unterricht*, 41 (1991), 447–63.

[4] On the concept of the second reformation in German historiography see Heinz Schilling, (ed.), *Die reformierte Konfessionalisierung in Deutschland – Das Problem der 'Zweiten Reformation'* (Gütersloh, 1986). An English translation of Schilling's article 'Die "Zweite Reformation" als Kategorie der Geschichtswissenschaft' in this book (pp. 387–437) appeared in English as 'The Second Reformation – Problems and Issues' in Heinz Schilling, *Religion, Political Culture and the Emergence of Early Modern Society: Essays in German and Dutch History* (Leiden/New York/Cologne, 1992), pp. 247–301.

[5] During the reign of Edward VI the Protestant Reformation did not have a lasting impact on Irish society. See Brendan Bradshaw, 'The Edwardian Reformation in Ireland, 1547–53', *Archivium Hibernicum*, 34 (1976–77), 83–99.

its 'reformation of doctrine', accomplished by the formulation of the Irish Articles of 1615, was markedly Calvinist.[6] Second, the Irish Reformation was a pure 'reformation from above', lacking any kind of popular support. It was initiated by the prince and embraced only by a ruling elite in state and church. But the situation in Ireland was different and more complex in that this ruling elite was a colonial elite, the so-called New English, Protestant immigrants since the accession of Elizabeth I. This late Protestant Reformation in Ireland was almost immediately confronted with a vigorous Tridentine Catholic movement that competed for the religious allegiance of the majority of the Irish people. Thus Protestant and Catholic confession-building were parallel processes in Ireland as they were perhaps nowhere else in Europe, and this created a particularly tense and problematic situation. During the last decades of the sixteenth and the first decades of the seventeenth century the church of Ireland appears to have quickly lost the battle for the conversion of the Irish people and then to have felt constantly threatened by the activities of Tridentine Catholicism.

By the middle of the seventeenth century it was clear that the official state religion was a minority confession.[7] The *cuius regio eius religio* principle had not succeeded, or rather, this Europe-wide 'mechanism' was never really set in motion because in the sixteenth century the English state in Ireland was so weak that it was not able to assist Protestant confession-building. As is obvious in England, state-building had to precede confession-building in order to enable the secular power to assist in establishing the new confession and in gradually converting the people.[8] In Ireland, on the other hand, the close connection and identification of the Protestant church with the English state, its officials and its colonisation projects, which culminated in the plantation of Ulster in the early seventeenth century, did more harm than good to the Protestant cause because the activities of the English state were resented by the majority of the population. Whereas in other European countries 'confessionalisation', the close relationship between state-building and confession-building, furthered integration and the development of a unified identity, the confessionalisation of Irish society resulted in confrontation and opposition.[9]

---

[6] See Ford, *The Protestant Reformation*, pp. 194–201; R.B. Knox, *James Ussher: Archbishop of Armagh* (Cardiff, 1967), pp. 16–20.

[7] See K.S. Bottigheimer, 'The Failure of the Reformation in Ireland: Une Question Bien Posée', *JEH*, 36 (1985), 196–207.

[8] The latest work that stresses the slowness of the conversion of the English people to Protestantism and the decisive role of the state in this process is Eamon Duffy, *The Stripping of the Altars: Traditional Religion in England, c. 1400–c. 1580* (London, 1992).

[9] On the concept of confessionalisation in German historiography see Wolfgang

By the standards of the sixteenth and early seventeenth centuries, the medieval heritage of Ireland made possible an exceptional split between confessional and political identities among the so-called Old English, descendants of Anglo-Normans who had settled in Ireland after the Norman conquest of the twelfth century. The native inhabitants of Ireland, the Gaelic Irish, who were traditional opponents of English intervention in Ireland, were Catholics and therefore also its confessional opponents. However, the Old English, the majority of whom were town-dwellers, were loyal supporters of the English crown and considered themselves upholders of English culture in Ireland. On the whole they kept aloof from the Gaelic Irish. The majority of the Old English went through a complicated phase of identity development in the second half of the sixteenth century, which resulted in a dual identity. Instead of becoming Protestants as was expected of subjects of the English crown, they embraced Tridentine Catholicism though remained politically loyal to the British monarchy.[10]

Thus the confessionalisation of Irish society was decisively shaped by two characteristics: first, by the specific way Ireland experienced early modern state-building, that is, through colonisation; and second, by Ireland's medieval history of an ethnically split population, resulting in the dual identity of the Old English.

Because Ireland's Reformation and colonial confessionalisation were relatively late processes, confessional interpretations of history, which had been formulated in Germany during the Lutheran Reformation of the first half of the sixteenth century, were not developed in Ireland until the seventeenth century. The first major attempt at forging a Protestant interpretation of history for Ireland was made by James Ussher, the

---

Reinhard, 'Reformation, Counter-Reformation, and the Early Modern State: A Reassessment', *CHR*, 75 (1989), 383–404; Heinz Schilling, 'Confessionalization in the Empire: Religious and Societal Change in Germany between 1555 and 1620' in Schilling, *Religion*, pp. 205–45.

[10] This involved an estrangement from the English government because of the influx of Protestant New English officeholders and culminated in the idea of a defence of ancient liberties, including the Catholic faith, against encroachments by the government and the newcomers. See C. Lennon, *The Lords of Dublin in the Age of Reformation* (Dublin, 1989); C. Lennon, 'The Counter-Reformation in Ireland, 1542–1641' in C. Brady and R. Gillespie (eds), *Natives and Newcomers: Essays on the Making of Irish Colonial Society 1534–1641* (Dublin, 1986), pp. 75–92, 221–4, 242–3. The identity development of the Old English can be regarded as another parallel to the German second reformation, where towns defended their liberties and traditional rights, among which they counted their Lutheran faith, against their Calvinist princes. See for example the case study on Lippe and Lemgo in Heinz Schilling, *Konfessionskonflikt und Staatsbildung: Eine Fallstudie über das Verhältnis von religiösem und sozialem Wandel in der Frühneuzeit am Beispiel der Grafschaft Lippe* (Gütersloh, 1981).

famous scholar and archbishop of Armagh,[11] in his *Discourse of the Religion Anciently Professed by the Irish and British* of 1622.[12]

Ussher did not belong to the majority group in the church of Ireland, the New English. On the contrary, Ussher belonged to a minority of the Old English who conformed to the state religion. His own family had split along confessional lines at the end of the sixteenth century. His paternal uncle, Henry Ussher, had been the Protestant archbishop of Armagh from 1595 to 1613.[13] His maternal uncle, Richard Stanihurst, converted to Catholicism and emigrated to the Spanish Netherlands in the early 1580s.[14] Because of Ussher's extraordinary family background his interpretation of Irish history is very interesting for the historian who wants to trace the development and interaction of ethnic, political and religious identities in the upheaval of the sixteenth and seventeenth centuries.[15]

Before writing his treatise on the Irish church, Ussher had already published a general Protestant church history in 1613.[16] He proceeded from the standard Protestant scheme of history, which had first been formulated in the Empire in the first half of the sixteenth century by Sleidan and by Flacius Illyricus in the *Magdeburg Centuries* and had been introduced to England by writers like John Bale and John Foxe. According to this

---

[11] There are only two recent articles on Ussher: Hugh Trevor-Roper 'James Ussher, Archbishop of Armagh' in his *Catholics, Anglicans and Puritans* (Chicago, 1988), pp. 120–65; J. Leerssen, 'Archbishop Ussher and Gaelic Culture', *Studia Hibernica*, 22–3 (1982–83), 50–58. The standard but slender biography is Knox, *James Ussher*. See also *DNB*, 20 (London, 1921–22, reprint: 1973), 64–72.

[12] The *Discourse* appeared first as an addition to Sir Christopher Sibthorp's *A Friendly Advertisement to the Pretended Catholickes of Ireland*, STC 22522 (Dublin, 1622). Its first separate edition, which will be quoted here, was published in London in 1631 (*STC* 24549). For rather short remarks on the *Discourse* see Knox, *James Ussher*, pp. 107, 159; Ford, *The Protestant Reformation*, pp. 221–2; Trevor-Roper, 'James Ussher', p. 136.

[13] On Henry Ussher see *DNB*, 20, (London, 1921–22, reprint. 1973), 62–3.

[14] On Stanihurst see C. Lennon, *Richard Stanihurst, The Dubliner, 1547–1618: A Biography with a Stanihurst Text 'On Ireland's Past'* (Dublin, 1981).

[15] The identity of the Protestant Old English as a minority within its ethnic group on the one hand and within its confessional group, the church of Ireland, on the other hand has so far not been studied by historians of early modern Ireland. See the short remark by C. Brady: 'Those native-born lawyers, churchmen and administrators who did conform found themselves to be part of a tiny minority, increasingly isolated and without influence in their own community'. 'The Decline of the Irish Kingdom' in Mark Greengrass (ed.), *Conquest and Coalescence: The Shaping of the State in Early Modern Europe* (London/New York/Melbourne/Auckland, 1991), pp. 94–115, here p. 109.

[16] *Gravissimae Quaestionis, de Christianarum Ecclesiarum, Continua Successione Historica Explicatio*, STC 24551 (1613). In this work Ussher treated only the period until 1371. He never published the last part which was to cover the time up to the Reformation. See Ford, *The Protestant Reformation*, p. 221; Knox, *James Ussher*, pp. 106–9; Trevor-Roper, 'James Ussher', pp. 135–6.

Protestant chronology the church was uncorrupted for about six hundred years after Christ. Then Antichrist gradually began to stir and consequently corruption crept into the church. Finally in the eleventh century, the millennium, the thousand years during which Antichrist was bound, came to an end. He was let loose, and this resulted in the tyranny of the papacy and the complete corruption of the church. During the late Middle Ages the true church was kept up only by small groups of believers, such as the Waldensians. The Protestant church of the sixteenth century had regained the purity of the early church.

In the *Discourse* Ussher also adhered closely to this time-frame, concentrating on the early history of the Irish church until the twelfth century. First, there was the 'golden age' of the early Celtic church. Ussher stressed that this church had been beneficial to the whole of Christianity, for it was in early medieval Ireland where 'the knowledge both of the Scriptures and of all other good learning was preserved in that inundation of barbarisme, wherewith the whole West was in a manner overwhelmed'.[17] Then 'in this Countrey, as well as in others, corruptions did creep in little by little, before the Divell was let loose to procure that seduction which prevailed so generally in these last times'.[18]

Ussher attempted to show that the church of St Patrick believed in essentially the same doctrines as the Protestant church of Ireland of his own time. By constructing an ancient predecessor for the church of Ireland and thereby giving Protestantism in Ireland an indigenous history, he tried to remove its stigma as a 'new English heresy'. In the prefatory epistle addressed to Sir Christopher Sibthorp he stated his thesis that 'the religion professed by the ancient Bishops, Priests, Monks, and other Christians in this land, was for substance the very same with that which now by publike authoritie is maintained therein, against the forraine doctrin brought in thither in later times by the Bishop of Romes followers'.[19]

The *Discourse* is written in thematical, not chronological order and therefore appears more like a theological treatise than a historical narrative. It is divided into 11 chapters, each of which is concerned with a particular subject, mostly points of controversy with the Catholic church, for example, the Bible, purgatory, transubstantiation, marriage and divorce, the controversy between Rome and the Celtic churches about the calculation of the date of Easter, and the temporal power of the pope. Only some parts of the *Discourse*, such as the chapters on the controversy about Easter, are chronological narratives.

Ussher was a meticulous and diligent scholar, as is obvious in the

---

[17] *Discourse*, chap. VI, p. 55.
[18] *Discourse*, The Epistle, A2 ᵛ.
[19] *Discourse*, The Epistle, A3 ʳ.

Discourse. Most of the treatise is an accumulation of quotations from early Christian authors, particularly Bede, with only some commentaries or interpretations from the author himself. In accordance with his view of history he accepted only 'the ancienter lives of our Saints (. . . as have beene written before the time of Sathans loosing . . .)'[20] as sources as the later ones had, according to Ussher, been falsified by monks and friars.

Ussher presented all the facts known to him, even if this harmed his own argument. Consequently he sometimes ran into problems while trying to prove the alleged purity and independence from Rome during the early Irish church. For example, he found it difficult to explain away the fact that St Patrick, in whose time, according to the Protestant interpretation, the Irish church was wholly independent of Rome, had advised that unresolved questions be referred to Rome. Ussher played this down by writing:

> if I my selfe had lived in his daies, for the resolution of a doubtful question I should as willingly have listened to the judgement of the Church of *Rome*, . . . ; so reverend an estimation have I of the integritie of that Church, as it stood in those good daies. But that St. *Patrick* was of opinion, that the Church of *Rome* was sure ever afterward to continue in that good estate, . . . , that it should never erre in judgment, . . . ; that will I never beleeve.[21]

On the whole Ussher's style and method were thus not calculated to make the *Discourse* a work with great popular appeal.

The following analysis of the *Discourse* concentrates on three aspects of this treatise: first, the intended audience; second, the internal contradictions of the argumentation, which reveal a conflict between religion and ethnicity; and third, the political aspect, that is, the status of Ireland as a kingdom under the English crown.

In view of the complicated population situation in Ireland, the first important question regarding the *Discourse* is which group or groups Ussher wanted to address with his version of Protestant history. In the prefatory epistle Ussher made it clear that he did not want to 'preach to the converted'. His work was not meant for Protestants in Ireland. On the contrary, Ussher expressed his hope that the *Discourse* might be an instrument to convert Irish Catholics. He wrote:

---

[20] *Discourse*, chap. III, p. 27; see The Epistle, A2 ᵛ.

[21] *Discourse*, chap. VIII, p. 87. Similarly, Ussher admitted that '*Ireland had beene of old defiled with the Pelagian heresie*', *Discourse*, chap. VIII, p. 92; see chap. II, p. 19; although Pelagius had in very important aspects held opposite views to Calvinism and thus to the church of Ireland, Pelagius had denied Predestination and asserted free will. (See Trevor-Roper, 'James Ussher', p. 144.) He tried, however, to 'limit the damage' by referring to 'Sedulius and Claudius, two of our most famous Divines' (*Discourse*, chap. II, p. 16) who resisted the teachings of Pelagius.

> if unto the authorities drawn out of Scriptures and Fathers . . . a true discoverie were added of that Religion which anciently was professed in this Kingdome; it might prove a speciall motive to induce my poore country-men to consider a little better of the old and true way from whence they have hitherto been mis-ledd.[22]

On the other hand Ussher seems to have been sceptical as to whether his treatise was appearing soon enough to convince Catholics in Ireland of the truth of Protestantism. His later remarks in the epistle remind one of similar statements by other Protestant clergymen, who, despairing of the possibility of converting the inhabitants of Ireland, used the doctrine of predestination to explain their recalcitrance:[23]

> Yet on the one side, that saying in the Gospel runneth much in my minde; *If they heare not Moses and the Prophets, neyther will they be perswaded, though one rose from the dead*: and on the other, that heavie iudgement mentioned by the Apostle; *because they received not the love of the truth, that they might bee saved, God shall send them strong delusion, that they should beleeve lyes*. The woefull experience whereof, wee may see daily before our eyes in this poore nation.[24]

This ambiguity in Ussher's attitude may reflect the situation in which the church of Ireland found itself in the early seventeenth century. There was on the one hand still a general hope of a breakthrough for Protestantism in Ireland. But on the other hand everyday experiences left Protestant clergymen more and more disillusioned and despairing.

Having excluded the New English Protestants as his audience for the *Discourse*, Ussher did not state explicitly whether he wanted to address the Old English or the Gaelic Irish or both. However, several features of the *Discourse* suggest that Ussher's arguments were meant to influence his own people, the Old English, rather than the Gaelic Irish.

First, the *Discourse* is written in English, which is a clear indication that Ussher intended his work for an Old English audience. If he wanted to address the literate Gaelic Irish, he would either have had to use their native language or Latin.

Second, and more important, is Ussher's use of sources. Quite often he

---

[22] *Discourse*, The Epistle, A2 ʳ⁻ᵛ.

[23] See for example the remarks by Richard Olmstead quoted in Ford, *The Protestant Reformation*: 'it is possible that [if] men living under a powerful ministry of the word . . . shut their ears to it, resist the motions of the blessed spirit, that that curse may be set upon man's soul . . . which our saviour set upon the fig tree, *Never fruit grow on thee hereafter* . . . ' (p. 211) and 'Oh the woes that belong to such, and you the poor natives of this kingdom, what will become of your poor souls misted in the darkness of superstition by those locusts come out of the bottomless pit, the priests and Jesuits . . . ' (p. 213).

[24] *Discourse*, The Epistle, A2 ᵛ.

referred to Gerald of Wales[25] as a reliable and acceptable source about conditions in Ireland.[26] The Gaelic Irish would certainly have resented this as Gerald of Wales expressed strong feelings of cultural superiority. However, Gerald's work was well-known and accepted among the Old English.[27] Similarly, Ussher used the testimony of a fourteenth-century Anglo-Norman archbishop of Armagh, Richard Fitzralph, in his attack on the mendicant friars, who were very popular and highly esteemed in Gaelic Ireland.[28]

Third, Ussher explicitly put his work in the context of all the Stuart dominions by entitling it *A Discourse of the Religion Anciently Professed by the Irish and British* and by using examples and quotations from all Celtic regions of the British Isles. He stated in the epistle:

> the name of *Scoti* in those elder times . . . was common to the inhab-itants of the *greater* and the *lesser* Scotland . . . that is to say, of *Ireland*, . . . The religion doubtlesse received by both, was the selfe same; and differed little or nothing from that which was maintained by their neighbours the *Britons*.[29]

Such favouring of the idea of 'British unity', even if it was, as in this case, on a religious rather than a political level, could only appeal to the Old English, who were loyal to the Stuart kings and their multinational king-dom. It would have had little appeal for the traditionally independent Gaelic Irish.

It becomes even clearer that Ussher was aiming at the Old English when we compare his work with the historical treatise of another Old Englishman in the first half of the seventeenth century: Geoffrey Keating, a secular priest in Munster. In his *History of Ireland* (*Foras Feasa ar Éirinn*), written around 1634,[30] Keating fashioned a Catholic

---

[25] Gerald of Wales was a member of one of the leading Norman families involved in the conquest of Ireland. He wrote a treatise entitled *Topographia Hibernica* in 1187 and a his-tory of the conquest of Ireland (*Expugnatio Hibernica*). See F.J. Dimock (ed.), *Giraldi Cambrensis Opera*, 5, Rolls Series (London, 1867); T. Wright (ed.), *The Historical Works of Giraldus Cambrensis* (London, 1863, reprint. New York 1968). On the reception of Giraldus Cambrensis among writers about Ireland in the sixteenth and seventeenth cen-turies see W.R. Jones 'Giraldus Redivivus – English Historians, Irish Apologists, and the Works of Gerald of Wales', *Eire–Ireland*, 9 (1974), 3–20.

[26] See *Discourse*, chap. III, p. 22; chap. V, pp. 51, 54; chap. XI, pp. 118, 125.

[27] See Jones, 'Giraldus Redivivus', p. 10.

[28] See *Discourse*, chap. VI, pp. 59–60. On the importance of the mendicant orders in Gaelic Ireland well into the seventeenth century see A. Clarke 'Colonial Identity in Early Seventeenth-Century Ireland' in T.W. Moody (ed.), *Nationality and the Pursuit of National Independence*, Historical Studies 11 (Belfast, 1978), 57–71, here p. 66.

[29] *Discourse*, The Epistle, A3 ʳ⁻ᵛ.

[30] The standard edition of Keating's work is D.Comyn and P.S. Dinneen (eds), *Foras Feasa ar Éirinn: The History of Ireland* (4 vols, London, 1902–14).

interpretation of Irish history which tried to suit the Gaelic Irish as well as the Old English historical experience.[31] In order to address the Gaelic Irish he avoided or explicitly rejected strategies for reaching the Old English. Keating wrote his *History* in Gaelic, and in his introduction he attacked Gerald of Wales and other Old English authors who treated the Gaelic Irish unfavourably, stressing that he wanted to 'set the records straight' against such authors.[32] Further, in contrast to Ussher, Keating rejected 'the revival of the so-called British History'[33] in England by drawing attention to 'the status of the Stuarts' Irish patrimony as an ancient kingdom, prior in origin, indeed, to the kingdoms of Scotland and England'.[34]

Ussher himself made it absolutely clear towards the end of his *Discourse*, in chapter XI, that he wanted to address only the Old English. In this chapter, in which he discussed the temporal power of the pope and his right to absolve subjects from their oath of allegiance, he turned explicitly against the Gaelic Irish, represented by the Gaelic lord Philip O'Sullivan Beare.[35] Ussher defended the loyal Catholic Old English, who had not taken part in the Nine Years' War, against O'Sullivan Beare. He wrote:

> But now cometh forth *O Sullevan* againe, and like a little furie flyeth upon the *English–Irish* Priests of his owne religion, which in the late rebellion of the Earle of *Tirone* did *not deny* . . . that it is lawfull for them of the *Romish* Religion, to . . . fight for their Soveraigne and fellow-subjects that are of another profession, against those of their own religion that trayterously rebell against their Prince and Country.[36]

On the last page of his treatise he then stated that his only hope of converting anybody in Ireland to Protestantism was directed towards the politically loyal Old English; the Gaelic Irish were implicitly regarded as 'lost' – to the king, the country and the faith. Ussher wrote about the Old

---

[31] On Keating see B. Bradshaw 'Geoffrey Keating: Apologist of Irish Ireland' in B. Bradshaw, A. Hadfield and W. Maley (eds), *Representing Ireland: Literature and the Origins of Conflict, 1534–1660* (Cambridge, 1993), pp. 166–90; B. Cunningham, 'Seventeenth-Century Interpretations of the Past: The Case of Geoffrey Keating', *Irish Historical Studies*, 25 (1986), 116–28; B. Cunningham, 'Geoffrey Keating's *Eochair Sgiath An Aifrinn* and the Catholic Reformation in Ireland' in W.J. Sheils and D. Wood (eds), *The Churches, Ireland and the Irish*, SCH 25 (Oxford/New York, 1989), 133–43.

[32] See Jones, *Giraldus Redivivus*, pp. 15–16.

[33] Bradshaw, 'Geoffrey Keating', p. 171.

[34] Bradshaw, 'Geoffrey Keating', p. 171.

[35] O'Sullivan Beare lived in Spain and wrote a history of Catholic Ireland under Queen Elizabeth, published in Lisbon in 1621. See *Historiae Catholicae Iberniae Compendium* ed. M. Kelly (Dublin, 1850); M.J. Byrne (ed.), *Ireland Under Elizabeth: Chapters Towards a History of Ireland in the Reign of Elizabeth* (Dublin, 1903).

[36] *Discourse*, chap. XI, p. 128.

English: 'I am in good hope, that their loyall mindes will so farre distaste that evill lesson, which those great *Rabbies* of theirs would have them learne [that is, to give up their allegiance to the English king], that it will teach them to unlearne another bad lesson, wherewith they have beene most miserably deluded [that is, Catholicism]'.[37]

The next problem that needs to be discussed is why Archbishop Ussher's attempt to construct a Protestant interpretation of history for the Old English did not fully succeed. This brings to light an identity conflict between religion and ethnicity. Ussher's problem was that the general Protestant historical time frame could not be convincingly connected with the history of the Old English.

The majority of the Old English, above all the urban population, had kept apart from the Gaelic Irish ever since they came to Ireland and had looked down upon the Gaelic church and Gaelic culture in general. Under these circumstances, would the Old English want to consider themselves heir to the Celtic church, which they had always held in low esteem and to which they had always felt superior? How could Ussher's references to 'the religion of our Ancestors'[38] or '*our ancient Monkes*'[39] then appeal to the Old English? In this respect Ussher's line of argumentation could hardly convince the Old English.

One of the most important turning points in the general Protestant interpretation of history was the loosing of Antichrist in the eleventh century, which had, in the Protestants' view, resulted in the corruption of the church. In the *Discourse* Ussher described in detail how the Roman liturgy was introduced into Ireland with the help of the English, that is, Anglo-Norman, church in the course of the twelfth century. This is very problematic for Ussher's general argument, for the introduction of Roman forms of worship into the Irish church, that is, the beginning of Antichrist's work, coincided with the coming of the Anglo-Normans, the ancestors of the Old English, into that island.[40] To state it plainly: if Ussher had really made the last step and explicitly connected the general

[37] *Discourse*, chap. XI, p. 132.

[38] *Discourse*, The Epistle, A3 ʳ.

[39] *Discourse*, chap. VI, p. 54.

[40] The ecclesiastical reforms in Ireland began before the Norman conquest of 1169/70 and were to some extent independent of it. There were several synods before the conquest, for example, Cashel 1101, Raith Bresail 1111, Kells 1152; see K.S Bottigheimer, *Ireland and the Irish* (New York, 1982), p. 63; M. Richter, *Medieval Ireland: The Enduring Tradition* (New York, 1988), pp. 126–9. This was known in the seventeenth century and Geoffrey Keating explicitly referred to it in order to stress that the Irish church was not in need of reform from outside; see Bradshaw, 'Geoffrey Keating', p. 175. However, in the papal bull *Laudabiliter* the English king was commissioned to implement ecclesiastical reforms in Ireland. See *Irish Historical Documents 1172–1922* ed. E. Curtis and R.B. McDowell (1943, reprint. London/New York 1968), pp. 17–18. The changes towards the

Protestant historical chronology with the history of his own people, he would have had to say that the Old English helped Antichrist to gain control over the Irish church. This was the identity conflict in which Ussher as a Protestant Old Englishman found himself and which he could not successfully resolve.[41] Consequently, his language was noticeably 'neutral' when he described the consequences of the Norman invasion in Ireland, and he struggled not to connect them directly with the Protestant interpretation of history. He wrote:

> Lastly, the worke [which had been begun by Gilbert and St Malachy] was brought to perfection, when *Christianus* Bishop of Lismore, as Legate to the Pope, was President in the Councell of *Cashell* [of 1171–72]: wherein ... a generall act [was] established, that *all divine offices ... should from thenceforth be handled in all parts of Ireland, according as the Church of England did observe them.* The statutes of which Councell were confirmed by the Regall *authoritie* of King *Henry* the *second*; ... And thus late was it, before the *Romane* use was fully settled in this Kingdome.[42]

Ussher's problems can again be highlighted by comparing his treatise with other confessional interpretations of history. In Wales the Bishop of St David's, Richard Davies, constructed a Protestant identity for the Welsh in his preface to the Welsh edition of the New Testament of 1567.[43] Davies accepted the same general Protestant framework of history that Ussher did, with the early Welsh church as a pure and uncorrupted church, the Protestant precedent. But according to Davies's interpretation, the Welsh were forced by the Saxons to accept the Roman faith. Davies's account thus struck a successful blow 'at those who insisted that Protestantism was something English and alien ... by showing that Romish religion, far from being in the national tradition of the Welsh, was something degrading imposed upon them by their enemies'.[44] Ussher was at a grave disadvantage here. It was impossible for

---

Roman order were reinforced after the Norman conquest, for example, in the second synod of Cashel in 1171/72. Moreover, Ussher's main source for the period of the Norman conquest, Gerald of Wales, did of course stress the role of the Anglo-Normans in this 'reform' of the Gaelic church.

[41] For similar remarks on this dilemma in Ussher's line of argumentation see B. Cunningham,'The Culture and Ideology of Irish Franciscan Historians at Louvain 1607–1650' in C. Brady (ed.), *Ideology and the Historians*, Historical Studies 17 (Dublin, 1991), pp. 11–30, 222–7, here pp. 11–12; Trevor-Roper, 'James Ussher', pp. 147–8.

[42] *Discourse*, chap. IV, p. 33.

[43] See P.R. Roberts, 'The Union with England and the Identity of "Anglican" Wales', *TRHS*, 22 (1972), 49–70, here 67; G. Williams, *Reformation Views of Church History* (London 1970), p. 63.

[44] G. Williams, 'Some Protestant Views of Early British Church History' in his *Welsh Reformation Essays* (Cardiff, 1967), pp. 207–19, here p. 213; see Roberts, 'The Union with England', p. 67.

him to argue that the Old English had been forced to accept the Roman order. On the contrary, he had to cope with the fact that they had brought it with them to Ireland and had helped to impose it on the Gaelic church in Ireland.

This comparison with Wales also makes clear that a Protestant interpretation of history catering exclusively to the needs of the Gaelic Irish might have been very convincing. It could have argued that, although some corruption crept in, the Celtic church remained essentially pure and retained its independence from Rome until it was forced to succumb to Rome by the Anglo-Norman conquest. However, such an interpretation would have thrown a very bad light on England and the English kings, especially as Ireland lacked the uniquely close relationship which Wales had with the Tudors. Therefore it could probably have been formulated only in an Ireland independent of England.

As it was, a persuasive interpretation of history for the Gaelic Irish was never developed by the church of Ireland. The Protestant church had problems in two decisive areas. First, it made very slow progress with printing in the Gaelic vernacular. Second, by the early seventeenth century there were few Gaelic-speaking clergymen left in the church of Ireland who might have written tracts in the vernacular or 'spread the message' by their teaching and preaching. Certainly by the middle of the seventeenth century the church of Ireland had lost its battle for the religious allegiance of the Gaelic Irish and had 'retreated', catering almost exclusively to the New English.[45]

The last point involves Ussher's discussion of the political aspect of his problem, that is, the temporal power of the pope and the pope's power to absolve subjects from their allegiance to the king. This was a very important question in Ireland in the sixteenth and seventeenth centuries, and Ussher devoted his entire last chapter to the issue. Here he tried to think and write 'in compartments', cutting this secular question off from the rest of the treatise and using only secular arguments, for example, that the English crown had acquired its rights over Ireland by the military conquest of the twelfth century and 'divers hundreds of yeares possession'.[46] In this way he seems to have adapted to the outlook of the Catholic majority of his own population group. For the Old English in Ireland, similar to the English Catholics, insisted that they could completely separate their secular loyalty to the English monarch from their confessional allegiance to the pope. However, in an age in which religion and society, church and state were so closely intertwined

---

[45] See Ford, *The Protestant Reformation.*
[46] *Discourse*, chap. XI, p. 118.

it was difficult to convince anybody of this claim.[47]

In spite of Ussher's effort to separate the religious and the secular, his problems with the Norman conquest in Ireland surfaced again. First, he cited Gerald of Wales with regard to the acts 'confirmed in the Nationall Synod held at *Cashell*: . . . *For it is fit and most meet, that as Ireland by Gods appointment hath gotten a Lord and a KING from England; so also they should from thence receive a better forme of living'.*[48] He thus explicitly appealed to an Old English feeling of cultural superiority and their idea of a cultural mission to the Gaelic Irish, which was still vibrant in the early seventeenth century.[49] However, shortly afterwards he cited Gerald again on the confirmation of the bull *Laudabiliter* by Pope Alexander III, inserting after '*Apostolicall authority*': '(for so was it in those dayes of darknesse esteemed to bee)'.[50] Ussher's overall problem remained. Henry II, and thus the Old English, first came into the possession of Ireland by papal agreement and this happened at a time that sixteenth- and seventeenth-century Protestants considered to be 'the time of the papal Antichrist'.

Nevertheless, from the point of view of the Old English this chapter on the rights of the English kings over Ireland is certainly the most conclusive and convincing in the *Discourse*. By proving at great length that Ireland was a kingdom under the English crown from the days of King Henry II, Ussher appealed to Old English nationalism and loyalty. He wrote: 'it maketh something for the honour of my Country (to which, I confesse, I am very much devoted)'.[51] In this respect his treatise could certainly appeal to the Old English – but only to the Old English.

---

[47] Under the circumstances of the sixteenth and seventeenth centuries, when the unity of a state was only regarded as secure if political and confessional identities went together, the English crown had to be suspicious of Old English Catholics. Even if they professed political loyalty, the fact remained that the pope had already absolved the English monarchy's Catholic subjects from their oath of allegiance under Elizabeth I. James I made this very clear to a delegation of Old English in 1614: 'Surely I have good reason for saying you are only half-subjects of mine. For you give your soul to the pope, and to me only the body, . . . Strive henceforth to become good subjects, that you may have *cor unum et viam unam*, and then I shall respect you all alike.' Quoted in A. Clarke and R.D. Edwards, 'Pacification, Plantation, and the Catholic Question, 1603–23' in T.W. Moody, F.X. Martin and F.J. Byrne (eds), *A New History of Ireland. Early Modern Ireland 1534–1691* (Oxford, 1976, reprint 1978), pp. 187–232, here p. 217.

[48] *Discourse*, chap. XI, p. 125. At this point Ussher mentioned only the political acts of the synod of Cashel and chose to ignore the fact that Giraldus Cambrensis also meant the ecclesiastical influence of the Anglo-Normans. See Curtis and McDowell (eds), *Irish Historical Documents*, pp. 18–19.

[49] This notion now worked in the context of Tridentine Catholicism. See Clarke, 'Colonial Identity', pp. 70–71.

[50] *Discourse*, chap. XI, pp. 125–6.

[51] *Discourse*, chap. XI, p. 128.

Anybody who wanted to construct an interpretation of history accept-able to the Gaelic Irish had to deny that the pope intended to give Ireland to Henry II. Accordingly, O'Sullivan Beare in his history of Ireland claimed that the pope only wanted the English king to collect St Peter's pence.[52] And the Old Englishman Geoffrey Keating, who tried to address both population groups, fashioned a complicated *translatio imperii* from the Gaelic high kingship to the English crown with papal authorisation in an attempt to make the Norman conquest acceptable to the Gaelic Irish.[53]

It is clear that in his *Discourse of the Religion Anciently Professed by the Irish and British* Archbishop Ussher adapted to Ireland the standard Protestant scheme of history. By proving that the early Celtic church was the predecessor of the church of Ireland, he tried to give Protestantism in Ireland a historical justification.

Further, Ussher intended his *Discourse* as a means of converting Catholics. It became clear, for example, from his use of language and sources that he saw his own population group, the Old English, the majority of whom had become Reformed Catholics by the end of the six-teenth century, as his audience for the *Discourse*.

Finally, we have seen that it proved very difficult for Ussher to con-struct a Protestant history and identity for the Old English. An identity conflict between confession and ethnicity emerged as the specific histori-cal experience of the Old English clashed with the standard Protestant historical chronology. The Protestant Old Englishman James Ussher faced an intellectual dilemma, which he could not resolve without deny-ing either his ethnic or his confessional identity. In his text he therefore tried not to connect too closely the two clashing events – the Anglo-Norman conquest of Ireland and the beginning of the reign of Antichrist after the millennium in Protestant history.

Moreover, it was comparatively easy for Archbishop Ussher to appeal to the Old English on the political side of the question, that is, the status of Ireland as a kingdom and the sovereignty of the English kings over Ireland. However, contrary to Ussher's hopes, for the Old English in Ireland in the seventeenth century this did not automatically mean that they also followed the English king's lead in religion.[54]

---

[52] O'Sullivan Beare made the following note on the clause 'et illius terrae populus te hon-orifice recipiat et sicut dominum veneretur' in Pope Adrian IV's bull *Laudabiliter*: 'Sicut Dominum venerentur, id est, ut principem dignum magno honore, non Dominum Iberniae, sed praefectum causa colligendi tributi ecclesiastici', *Historiae Catholicae Iberniae Compendium*, p. 64.

[53] See Bradshaw, 'Geoffrey Keating', pp. 174–5.

[54] I am grateful to Professor Karl S. Bottigheimer and Dr Jane Dawson for their helpful comments on this chapter.

CHAPTER EIGHT

Let the Fiancées Beware: Luther, the Lawyers and Betrothal in Sixteenth-Century Saxony

Pamela Biel

This chapter is about the process of beginning a marriage. As Beatrice Gottlieb has remarked, in a comment that applies as much to the Reformation as to the centuries which preceded it, marriages in the Middle Ages were processes which took place over a period of time.[1] The beginning stage of this process was generally espousal, or betrothal, and many people regarded this stage as being of paramount importance. Martin Luther, for example, attempted to refashion betrothal as something acceptable and healthy for Christian society. His opinions, however, were not accepted wholly by either the jurists or legislators of his day, although they exerted a powerful influence on the marriage ordinances produced by the churches and governments of the Protestant territories and in the writings of the jurists. These conflicts, and the consensus that eventually emerged among the theologians, jurists and legislators of the day, demonstrate a changing understanding of betrothal and marriage, two of the building blocks of social organisation which, in turn, display part of the new self-understanding of society in sixteenth-century Saxony as a whole, as compared to medieval times.

The Medieval Traditions: Gratian and Lombard

Before taking a close look at two of the defining medieval theories of betrothal it is worth mentioning that the consent of the participants was regarded as being of paramount importance both for marriage and for betrothal throughout the medieval period. Canon law required the consent of participants alone for the conclusion of a valid engagement.[2] Pope

---

[1] Beatrice Gottlieb, 'The Meaning of Clandestine Marriage' in Robert Wharton and Tamara K. Hareven (eds), *Family and Sexuality in French History* (Philadelphia, 1980), p.49.

[2] Even today, canon law has a relatively open attitude towards engagements, requiring the presence of two witnesses and a priest for a valid betrothal. *Can.* 1071,1: 'Matrimonii promissio sive unilateralis, sive bilateralis sue sponsalitia, irrita est proutroque foro nisi facta fuerti per scripturam subsignatam a patribus et vel a parocho aut loci Ordinario, vel a duobus saltem testibus.'

Alexander III, who reigned from 1159 to 1181, and who was perhaps the strongest voice for the consent theory, laboured long and hard to make consent alone the basis of betrothal and marriage. Charles Donahue, and in his wake Georges Duby and Jack Goody, have proposed several reasons why the consent theory ultimately triumphed over the theory of parental permission in the Middle Ages.[3] Be that as it may, in the period directly preceding the Reformation, the general agreement was that two people could become engaged by the act of consenting to this fact just as they could be married in the same way.

Gratian's *Decretals*, that wide-ranging collection of opinions, interpretations, legislation and miscellany compiled in the eleventh century, assembled a number of opinions on the subject of betrothal from which the compiler attempted to propose a coherent legal understanding of the concept.[4] By dint of the omnivorous nature of Gratian's compilation, his work had acquired by the twelfth century the status of a standard source for interpretations of the law as well as for the development of new legislation. The most thorough description of betrothal, which Gratian calls *desponsatio*, occurs in the second part of his collection, case number 27.

A person who has promised chastity but has become engaged to a woman has eliminated the earlier vow with the later. If this woman then becomes engaged to another and marries this second person, the first man may demand her back. Here we first need to ask whether a liaison is possible for those who have sworn vows. Second we should know whether it is possible for betrothed people to break off engagements and marry others.[5]

The second point is clearly more important for the present discussion as the first chiefly concerns the nature of vows of chastity. According to what may be a later interpolation, but which nonetheless appears as part of the solution to this case, betrothal was a separate category, somewhere between being completely unattached and being fully married and it

---

[3] Charles Donahue, 'The Policy of Alexander the Third's Consent Theory of Marriage', in Stephan Kuttner (ed.), *Proceedings of the Fourth International Congress of Medieval Canon Law* (Vatican City, 1976), pp. 251–81. Georges Duby, *Medieval Marriage: Two Models from Twelfth Century France* (trans. Elborg Forster, Baltimore, 1978) and Jack Goody, *The Development of the Family and Marriage in Europe* (Cambridge, 1983) enlarge on the thesis that Donahue presents.

[4] *Corpus Iuris Canonici: Pars Prior – Decretum Magistri Gratiani*, ed. Aemilius Friedberg (Graz, 1959, reprint of the 1879 Leipzig edn). Hereafter: Gratian, *Corpus Iuris*, with the Friedberg column number in square brackets.

[5] 'Quidam votum castitatis habens disponsavit sibi uxorem; illa priori condicioni renuncians, transtulit se ad alium, et nupsit illi; ille, cui prius desponsata fuerat, repitit eam. (Qu.I) Hic primum queritur, an cougium possit esse inter uouentes? (Qu.II) Secundo, an liceat, sponsae a sponso recedere, et alii nubere?' Ibid. [1046].

involved an agreement between the two parties.[6] Gratian carefully separated betrothal from sexual congress: 'Thus they are called united by
engagement in faith, even when between them there has been no sexual
contact.'[7] This same separation did not apply to marriage, thus indicat-
ing the fundamental difference between betrothal and marriage.[8]

On the one hand, then, engagement had some of the effects of marriage. Following the Old Testament (Deuteronomy 22:25), Gratian
noted that the penalty for sex with the fiancée of another was death and
that a brother may not take his dead brother's betrothed in marriage. In
both of these cases the Old Testament law and the church's laws treated a
betrothed couple as if they were already married. Yet Gratian also mar-
shalled at least two other cases in which betrothal does not have the same
effect as marriage. For example he allowed an engaged girl to enter a
monastary if she wanted to, while a married woman could only do so if
her husband also took vows.[9] Engagement and marriage had quite a bit
in common, it is true, but they were not the same thing, primarily because
the latter was a sacrament while the former was not.

The diction in the previous example – Gratian referred to a girl,
puella, and not a woman, *femina* – indicates that Gratian does not see
betrothal as a fully developed state. Rather for him it was a necessary
precursor to marriage. He noted that betrothed people could be called
united (*coniuges*), but that they were still not married.[10] Three times, citing the impeachable authorities of Ambrose and Jerome, Gratian
asserted that 'In engagment the union is initiated, not completed: when
union is begun the couple get the name of united, not when the girl and
the man know each other';[11] 'Marriage is consummated in coming

---

[6] ' "A prima fide disponsationis coniuges appellantur", citing Isidor of Seville in the body
of the item.' Ibid., 27.2.6 [1064]. See also Willibald Plöchl, *Das Eherecht des Magisters
Gratianus* (Leipzig, 1935), p. 35.

[7] 'Coniuges verius appellantur a prima disponsationis fide, quamvis adhuc inter eos
ignoretur coniugalis concubitus.' Gratian, *Corpus Iuris*, 27.2.6 [1064].

[8] He makes it clear in case 10 that marriage, *'nuptiae'*, results in children. Ibid., 27.2.10
[1065]. This does not, however, rule out the possibility that a woman could produce a child
without sexual intercourse. Mary, who according to the report of the evangelist regarding
her conversation with the angel at the annunciation (Luke 1:34) had not had sex, had nevertheless borne a child. In this case, so beloved in the medieval and Reformation periods,
marriage, and even procreation, did not necessarily involve carnal knowledge.

[9] 'Desponsata puella non prohibetur monasterium eligere: Desponsatam puellam non
licet parentibus alii viro tradere; tamen monasterium sibi licet eligere.' Ibid., 27.2.27 [1071]
See also case 28.

[10] Ibid., 27.2.38 [1074].

[11] 'In desponsatione coniugium initiatur: Cum initiatur coniugium, coniugii nomen
asciscitur, non cum puella viri admixtione cognoscitur.' Gratian's further comment to this
is: 'Ecce, quod in desponsatione coniugium initiatur, non perfecitur'. Ibid., 27.2.35 [1073].

together',[12] and, finally, 'Matrimony is initiated in the contract of engagement, perfected in sexual congress'.[13] Later Gratian, in his summation of a number of headings, noted that 'engagement is a pact which represents the expression of a desire for a future act, it is not the act in the present'.[14] Thus betrothal was for Gratian an indication of potential and a statement of intention regarding a future act.

Peter Lombard proposed a slightly different and some might say more subtle explanation of betrothal in Book IV of his *Sentences*, the standard medieval theology textbook.[15] Many scholars consider Lombard the leading representative of the Gallic approach to marriage, an approach which influenced subsequent papal legislation on the subject and which differed, as we shall see, from Gratian's approach. Where Gratian separated betrothal, marriage and consummation such that betrothal was a strong statement of intention or a promise but was not, ultimately, binding, Lombard conceptualised matters differently.

Lombard divided engagement into two categories, present and future engagements. For Lombard, future engagements were the opportunity for regulation of administrative matters while present engagements formed a more binding relationship. Rudolf Sohm noted that the division of engagement into two categories or types does not appear in other, older sources for canon or church law, and thus is something that may be considered original in Lombard's thought.[16]

This configuration of present and future engagements as different sorts of beginnings to marriage appears in Book IV of the *Sentences*. In the twenty-eighth distinction Lombard considered whether engagement and marriage can actually be separated from one another since canon law considered consent alone constitutive of marriage and engagement certainly involves consent. Lombard separated promises for future action from promises of present action in the following way. A promise for a future marriage does not rule out the possibility that one or both of the participants, for some legitimate ground, may deny the promise. If they do, the promise must either be annulled or broken but, as no marriage

---

[12] 'Coniunctorum permixto matrimonium perfecit.' Ibid., 27.2.36 [1073].

[13] 'Matrimonium sponsali conventione initiatur, conmixione perfecitur'. Ibid., 27.2.37 [1073].

[14] 'Ex his omnibus apparet, sponsas coniuges appellari spe futurum, non re presentium . . . ' Ibid., 27.2.45 [1076].

[15] Petrus Lombardus, *Sententiae in IV. Libris Distinctae* 2 (Books 3 and 4) (Grottaferrata, 1981) (hereafter: Lombard, *Sentences* and page number).

[16] Rudolf Sohm, *Das Recht der Eheschliessung aus dem deutschen und canonistischen Recht geschichtlich entwickelt* (Weimar, 1875), p. 111. This is one of the few points that Sohm makes where Emil Friedberg, his ever-ready combatant, does not object. See Emil Friedberg, *Verlobung und Trauung* (Leipzig, 1876).

has taken place, the possibility that the two people separate and legitimately marry others remains open.[17] Had a marriage taken place – as might seem to be the case from the giving of mutual assent to become engaged – no such breaking of the vow would be possible since an irrevocable sacrament would have been performed.[18]

A promise to marry in the present tense, however, particularly if accompanied by the usual aspects of matrimony such as sexual intercourse or the consequent production of children, indeed constituted a valid marriage for Lombard.[19] Betrothal, for Lombard and with him the medieval tradition more or less complete, came in two categories: present betrothal, which is tantamount to marriage, and future betrothal, a looser and more contingent arrangement. This position became, in the course of the twelfth and thirteenth centuries, the standard teaching of the church.

It is therefore clear, then, that in its dominant teaching, the medieval church separated the Justinianic dictum that consent made a marriage from the further Roman requirement of like consent from the parents, guardians or tutors before an engagement could be considered binding. Two people could become engaged by mutual consent. Nobody else need be present, save God, who was, in any case, hard to avoid.

Luther on Betrothal

From his first comments on the subject to his last, Luther emphatically rejected both Gratian and the Italian tradition and Lombard and the Gallic tradition, and his rejection was typical of the attitude of Protestant theologians in general. In *Von Ehesachen*[20] he rejected the fundamental distinction between promises in the future and promises in the present.[21] His first objection to the distinction is linguistic: in sixteenth-century

---

[17] 'Qui promittit, nondum facit; qui ergo promisit se in uxorem ducturum aliquam, nondum eam duxit uxorem; et quae spopdit se nupturam, nondum nupsit . . . Item, si ex quo iurant, mox efficiuntur coniuges, tunc hanc rem efficiunt quando iurant se facturos.' Lombard, *Sentences*, p. 432.

[18] 'Ideo dico quia coniugium tunc non fuit, sed futurum promittitur. Si vero ille post uxorem duxit et illa marito nupsit, coniugium utrinque fuit, et non potest dissolvi.' Ibid., p. 432. Marriage was accepted as having sacramental importance even before it was included in the official list of seven sacraments at the Fourth Lateran Council in 1215.

[19] 'Non autem sic est quando iuramentum coniugii praesentis consensus attestatione firmatur, quia post talem consensum, si quis alii se copulaverit, etiam si prolem procreaverit, irritum debet fieri, et ipse ad priorem copulam revocari.' Ibid., p. 432.

[20] This tract was published in 1530 and it represents Luther's response to the confusion regarding matrimony in the Protestant territories as well as conflict with lawyers regarding certain points at which canon law as incompatible with certain Protestant teachings. *WA* XXX. 205–48.

[21] Luther refers to the distinction as a *lauter narren spiel*, p. 211.

German, as in the language as it is currently spoken, the present tense is often used to indicate future time. Luther noted:

> No German speaker indicates a future engagement when he says 'I want to have or take you [in marriage].' Nobody says 'I shall want to have you [as a wife]' as they try to confuse us with 'accipiam te'. Actually in German 'accipio te' is 'I want to have or take you [in marriage].' Indeed I don't really know myself how a man or maid in German could or should express a future engagement.[22]

In simple linguistic terms, therefore, ostensibly the German language does not allow people to express the distinction between present and future engagements.[23]

Luther further rejected the medieval view of betrothal when he noted that legal engagements, that is, those made publicly with the consent of parents, were as binding and had as necessary consequences all those of a marriage.[24] If marriage was indissoluble, then so are promises to marry; sexual intercourse with someone other than one's affianced is adultery,[25] and, although sexual intercourse with the betrothed before the wedding is not looked upon favourably, it is not the same thing as fornication. Consent for Luther, as for many of his medieval predecessors, makes a marriage. Such consent is valid the moment it is spoken and it can be neither delayed nor made conditional.[26]

Luther accepted the canonistic teaching on betrothal in one aspect alone: the question of conditional engagements. If such a thing as a future betrothal exists, it comes about because the consent of the relevant parties – the two affianced and their parents or legal guardians – has been made dependent on some condition which can only be realised in the future. Luther referred to engagements made 'for the future or conditionally', which indicates that the two categories are in his mind synony-

---

[22] 'Darumb redet kein Deutsch mensch von zu kunnfftigem verlöbnis, wenn er spricht "Ich will dich haben" odder "nemen". Denn man spricht nicht "ich werde dich haben", wie sie gaugkeln mit dem "Accipiam te", sondern "Accipio te" heisst eigentlich auff Deudtsch "Ich wil dich nemen" odder "haben" . . . Ja ich wüste selbs nicht wol, wie ein knecht odder magd solten odder kundten ynn Deuscher sprach per verba de futuro sich verloben.' Luther, *Von Ehesachen*, pp. 211–12.

[23] Adolf von Scheurl takes some care to point out that at this juncture Luther had fundamentally misunderstood the medieval tradition which at no time suggested that the use of the present or future tense alone dictated the status of an engagement. *Die Entwicklung des kirchlichen Eheschliessungsrechts* (Erlangen, 1877), p. 99.

[24] 'Es ist eben so wol ein Ehe nach dem offentlichen verlöbnis als nach der hochzeit.' Luther, *Von Ehesachen*, p. 231.

[25] Ibid., p. 229.

[26] See also: Roland Kirstein, *Die Entwicklung der Sponsalienlehre und der Lehre vom Eheschluß in der deutschen protestantischen Eherechtslehre bis zu J.H. Böhmer* (Bonn, 1966), p. 29.

mous.[27] The conditional nature of a promise to marry, even if the condition is unrelated to temporal sequence (for example, 'I will marry you if you contribute 100 guilders to our household'), separates it from the unconditional and permanent consent which characterises a present betrothal. For Luther, therefore, betrothal without conditions had a significance of magnificent proportions for those intimately involved in the act.

Magnificent proportions but equally significant difficulties. People cannot simply decide that they will marry: they must ensure that they have their parents' permission, and they must make the agreement public. Of course, according to Luther's system, once they have done this they are effectively married. There was no scope in Luther's conception of betrothal for the couple to change their minds and back out at this juncture. They had undergone an essential change: they may not discuss marriage with others and if either has sex with a third party it is adultery. Unless specific conditions were made explicit at the time of the agreement, done is done: let the fiancées beware! Luther's subsequent composition of a marriage ceremony notwithstanding, according to *Von Ehesachen*, betrothal could not be logically separated from consummation of a marriage.

This fact created substantial problems for the jurists and legislators in Protestant territories who sought to prescribe coherent policies regarding the inception and consummation of marriage. Simply put, Luther's teaching, however theologically sound, created legal chaos and could have threatened the society of his day with something approaching anarchy, had it ever actually been applied in the form in which it is presented in this tract. The threatened anarchy did not only come from the fact that according to Luther betrothals and thus marriages can be made utterly without recourse to church or civic authorities – an anathema in an age which believed that there could scarcely be too much control over individuals. In spite of the opening of his marriage book, in which he claimed to wish to respect local customs and laws,[28] Luther's understanding of

---

[27] 'Das lies ich wol verba de futuro heissen, wenn ein conditio, anhang odder auszug da bey gesetzt würde, Als ich wil dich haben, wo du mir wilt zu gut zwey odder ein iar harren, Item: ich wil dich haben, so du mir hundert gulden mit bringest, Item: so deine oder meine eltern wollen, und der gleichen, Inn solchen worten wird der wille nicht frey dar gegeben, sondern auffgeschoben und an etwas verbunden, das ynn seiner macht nicht stehet, Und darumb er auch damit zugleich bekennt, das ers itzt noch nicht thun konne, und sein will noch nicht frey sey, darumb bindet auch solch verlöbnis nicht als per verba de presenti.' Luther, *Von Ehesachen*, p. 212.

[28] 'So manch land So manch sitte, sagt das gemeine sprich wort. Dem nach weil die hochzeit und ehestand ein welltlich geschefft ist, gebürt uns geistlichen odder kichendienern nichts darynn zu ordenen odder regiren, Sunder lassen einer iglichen Stad und land hierynn yhren brauch und gewonheit, wie sie gehen. Ein Traubüchlein für die einfältigen Pfarrherr,' WA XXX/3. 74.

engagement and marriage flew in the face of Saxon custom from the later Middle Ages and his own day. The legal difficulties, which I shall consider first, come on two distinct fronts. Both involve matters of consistency which, although reputedly the bugbear of little minds, is indeed the elixir of life for most legal systems.

Marriage, and with it betrothal, had been understood by earlier jurists either on the model of a sacrament or on the model of a contract. Luther attempted to combine both understandings. Like a contract, Luther's betrothals were only valid if parental permission had been granted. Like a sacrament, once the promise was made, it conferred an irrevocable change on the individuals involved. Roman lawyers had combined marriage and betrothal and treated both as parts of a contract. Canon lawyers had treated betrothal as a contract and marriage as a sacrament. Luther wanted to have his contract and make it a sacrament too.

The second difficulty in Luther's presentation is that his understanding of betrothal made marriage, or at least the formal, public and ecclesiastical ceremony of matrimony, appear irrelevant, which was certainly not his intention. Although he appears to separate the two, logically there could be no distinction, as made clear above. What exactly could marriage add that engagement had not already provided?

The Protestant Legal Tradition: Kling and Beust

The writings of Lutheran jurists from the later sixteenth century reflect the painful position in which Luther had placed them. Most could not use Luther's teachings alone to construct laws regarding betrothal on account of the reasons mentioned above. Yet few were willing to remain with the (consistent) formulations of canon law since these depended on an idea of sacramentality, not to mention papal authority, to which most were unwilling to consent. I shall now examine two legal writers from Saxony with an eye to the way that they dealt with the creation of a particularly Protestant idea of espousal. In general, the jurists seem to want to preserve more of canon law than Luther had, while at the same time they sought to incorporate certain distinctively Protestant ideas into their legal constructs.

Melchior Kling (1504/5–71) is an excellent example of how one person tried to exclude internecine strife from the legal picture and create an objective, 'non-confessional' marriage law. Following his receipt of the doctorate in both laws (*utriusque doctoris iuris*) in 1536 from the university at Wittenberg, he was active both as an academic and as a political figure. His career was dotted by successful mediations between disputing members of the nobility (including, on one occasion, the Electoral Prince

Friedrich) as well as promotions to ever higher offices, including the position of professor of law at his *alma mater*, which he achieved shortly
after being granted his doctorate. His first work following this honour
presents the way that canon law incorporated various points of Roman
imperial law.[29] His goal in this first book, as the title suggests, was to
show how canon law represented a continuation of imperial law, not a
break with it. In his slightly later work, which is of interest to the present
discussion, Kling recognised that there have been new developments,
particularly in the area of marriage law, but he refused to address confessional issues specifically. The establishment of a particularly Protestant
understanding of engagement or marriage was not at stake for Kling;
rather his work was in the service of a legally coherent set of guidelines
for betrothal, marriage and divorce.

This tract, *Matrimonialium Causarum Tractatus,* appeared in 1553
and was frequently cited by legal thinkers for the next hundred years.[30]
In it Kling distinguished between two types of betrothals, those sworn
and those not. The sworn betrothals, provided they were constructed in
such a way as not to violate the basic premises of marriage and were concluded in a timely manner, were in principle indissoluble.[31] Promises
which were not made by oath, which included those sealed with a gift,
those made by children as well as all those which specify a future condition before the consummation of the marriage can be more easily dis-
solved.[32] Thus Kling adopted the parameters of Luther's concept of
betrothal in his idea of sworn engagements.

But he adopted these parameters with some important differences.
Primarily Kling gained ground by his introduction of the category of
sworn engagements as a particular category of engagements, and secon-
darily he differed from Luther in what exactly he meant by the consent of
the participants. By focusing on the swearing of an engagement, Kling
eliminated the awkward question of the sacramental nature of betrothal.
What makes this sort of engagement binding such that the participants
may not conclude such an agreement with other people is the act of
swearing a solemn oath, not something inherent in betrothal itself. Kling
in this way pushed the issue of sacramentality to one side: betrothal is a
contract enforced by the swearing of an oath.

---

[29] *Explicatio et Continuatio Titulorum Iuris Civilis, & Canonici* (Frankfurt, 1549).

[30] Melchior Kling, *Matrimonialium Causarum Tractatus, Methodico ordine scriptus*
(Frankfurt, 1553). An example of its continued popularity nearly a century after its first
appearance is the repeated citation of the work in the 1672 dissertation from Helmstedt by
Hulderich Eyben, 'Praeses/Antonius Bobes, Respondens *De Origine, Progressu, Usu et
Autoritate Juris Canonico in Terris Protestantium*'.

[31] Ibid., fo.1[v].

[32] Ibid., fo.3[r].

Kling also differed from Luther on the issue of consent. For Kling consent made a marriage, but he did not separate consent wholly from action and intention. People who were espoused have begun their marriages: sexual intercourse and/or the intention to be married consummate the union.[33] First, people consented to be betrothed, then they consented to be married and these were, for Kling, two distinct kinds of consent.[34] Unlike Luther, Kling perceived engagement as a necessary state in the building of a marriage, but it was not marriage itself.

Although the description of the two types of consent sounds a good deal like Gratian's description of betrothal as the beginning but not the completion of matrimony, Kling retained Lombard's distinction between present and future engagement, and he had, moreover, the temerity to brush off Luther's linguistic objections to this distinction.[35] Future promises, when not sworn, were easier to dissolve than those made in the present tense. They expressed an intention to do an act but, as Lombard also indicated, they did not accomplish the act itself. In particular, Kling believed this category of engagement appropriate for children or for those not immediately able to carry out their desire to marry. This category of promise implies the anticipation of a long interlude between the promise to marry and the inception of the marriage itself.[36] In those cases where a future engagement was followed by copulation, provided no coercion was involved, the future promise automatically converts into a present promise.[37]

Present engagements, save in the case just mentioned, did not necessarily involve sexual intercourse. Kling noted that not even marriage depends on sex, as is proven by the case of Mary and Joseph, who,

---

[33] Sexual intercourse alone cannot seal a union unless it meets certain conditions which have to do with the intention of the participants: the partners must join bodies and minds at the same time, neither may be coerced into the act, the act must be done *honestate* (that is, not with a prostitute), it must be done with the intention to marry this particular partner (that is, neither partner may be already married or promised to another), the partners must be of the opposite sexes such that the man is lord and master of the woman, and the act cannot arise from any gross error or misperception on either side (that is, when one partner sleeps with the other thinking that it is a third party, or that the partner is healthy when he or she is sick, etc.). Ibid., fo.4ᵛ.

[34] Ibid., fo.6ᵛ.

[35] ' . . . proterit idem in Germanica lingua intelligere. Saepe enim fit, quod adolescentes differunt ibi inteogantur vel a puella, vel ab eius cognatis, quid sit facturus, an velit eam ducere.' Ibid., fo.1ʳ.

[36] Not surprisingly, Luther's opinion was that the wedding should take place as soon as possible after betrothal. In a commentary made at table in June 1532, Luther said, 'Meum concilium semper est, ut factis sponsalibus quam citissime properetur ad nuptios. Differre enim periculosum est per calumniatores, quos subornat Satan, et utriusque amici plerumque incipiunt, quod non conducit.' *TR*, 3, 212 (no. 3179s).

[37] Ibid., fo.2ᵛ.

according to Mary's testimony, did not copulate before the birth of their child and yet who were married. Present engagement, Kling explained, gave the woman all the privileges and risks of being a wife, and was created by both parties consenting to engagement.[38] In fact, by the time he was done with his description, Kling had taken the logical step Luther seemed unwilling or unable to take. 'It is thus clear,' he commented, 'that by present engagements matrimony, living together, being consorts, being wed are meant. These here are all synonyms.'[39] Having thus made the problem of present engagements disappear, Kling moved on to other matters.

The issue of parental consent to marriage shows Kling at his mediating best. Civil law, by which he meant imperial Roman law, required the consent of parents, while canon law does not. In his day, as Kling noted, there was considerable difference of opinion on this matter, with the *theologi* on the side of civil law with the *canonisti* on the side of church law.[40] After considering all the various possible combinations – no parental consent but the couple were happy and the parents did not object to the union after the fact; no parental consent but the couple wished to separate and the parents did not object; no parental consent and the couple were happy but the parents objected, and so on – Kling noted that there are Old Testament examples both for allowing such 'unconsented' marriages and for separating couples who marry without parental consent. Kling closed the section without providing a concrete answer to this difficult question. There was no clear legal or theological weight on one side or the other and thus Kling did not feel compelled to take a firm position.

Where one might be inclined to attribute such fence-sitting on what Luther, at least, took to be a crucial matter, to the unwillingness of a member of the first generation of Protestant lawyers to commit himself to a particular position, the same cannot be supposed of Joachim von Beust (1522–94), the author of an extremely influential book on engagement and marriage.[41] Although this book had lawyers, judges and notaries as

---

[38] 'Sponsalia de praesenti dicuntur, quando de praesentibus nuptiis dispositive tractantur, Et contrahentes per verba de praesenti consentiunt.' Ibid., fo.3ʳ.

[39] 'Et sic patet, quod sponsalia de praesenti dicuntur matrimonium, connubium, coniungium, consortium, & nuptiae. Sunt enim haec synonyma.' Ibid., fo.4ʳ.

[40] Kling, fo. 33ᵛ.

[41] Ioachimus à Beust, *Tractatus de Sponsalibus et Matrimoniis ad Praxin Forensem Accommodatus* (Wittenberg, 1586). This was reprinted in what may have been an illegal copy, with expansions made by Ioannis Ruhelii, in 1588 in Wittenberg. Another reprint with substantial changes and additions was published without a date in Leipzig under the title *Tractatus connubiorum – Juris consultorum: Joachmi a Beust, Conradi Mauseri, Johannes Schneidwini, Basilii Monneri, Melchioris Klingii, Francisci Hottomanni*. Such reprints attest to the popularity of the original tract. All citations in what follows are from the 1586 edition, which is paginated.

its chief audience – Beust gave examples of how to word various types of appeals made to various courts – the work was also cited with some regularity in academic dissertations.[42] Beust's commitment both to Protestantism as a theological position and to a distinctly Protestant marriage law can be seen both in his biography, which can be said to culminate in this respect with his activities as an adviser to the Electoral Prince of Saxony and his participation in the general visitation of the Saxon churches (when he was 70 years old), and in his legal work which included a preface by Melanchthon in the second part of the book, and frequent citations of Luther as well as Protestant lawyers. In spite of these facts and what we shall see are definite developments in a distinctly Protestant understanding of betrothal, Beust cannot be said to have jettisoned all the characteristics of the medieval tradition.

The existence of two types of betrothal can, to a certain extent, be seen as the point at which two traditions collide. Like Kling, Beust noted that canon law recognised two distinct categories of engagement, those in the present and those in the future, although he noted that present engagements seemed to be more or less the same thing as marriage.[43] Luther's objection that there was no linguistic difference between the two types of engagements was dismissed more or less with a wave of the hand,[44] although, as a good jurist, Beust also noted that all parties would be better served if people would not only express their intentions to each other clearly, but would also take the time to get witnesses and, when doubt or ambiguity remained, swear attesting oaths to their intentions or actions.

For Beust, however, the problem was not that the category of present and future engagements tended to meld, but rather that he had difficulties holding the category of engagements as such apart from that of marriage. This trend is evident in his discussion of the abandonment, in which the proposed remedies and waiting periods are the same as those

---

[42] For example, those produced in Helmstedt at the end of the century: see Henricus Albrectus *Disputatio L. De Donationibus Inter Virum et Uxorem: de Divortiis & repudiis: soluto matrimonium, quem admodem dos petatur ex ff. & c.* (Helmstedt, 1586); Hieremias Setzerus and Joannes Gablerus, *Disputatio Duae in quibus Materia Sponsiorum & Nuptiarum, Paulo plenius examinata est* (Frankfurt, 1593); and Joannes Barterus, Johannes Bock and Ioannes Horn, *Disputatio de sponsalibus, Nuptiis et Divortiis* (Helmstedt, 159?).

[43] 'De iure enim civili sponsalia appellantur, quae sunt promissiones de futuro matrimonio contrahendo, quae de iure canonico sponsalia de futuro appellantur, sed Ius canonicum addit sponsalia de praesenti, quae de iure civili matrimonium seu nuptiae dicuntur. . . . Huiusmodi enim sponsalia, vere sunt matrimonium licet copula carnalis non intervenit.' Beust, *Tractatus*, p. 12.

[44] 'Concedit tamen sponsalia de futuro dici posse, si adiiciatur aliqua conditio.' Beust, p. 13.

of an abandoned spouse,[45] as it is when he considered the effects of future engagements. In the latter section, Beust limited himself to those engagements 'when a person promises or contracts an engagement, not when that person can be said to have contracted the engagement itself but where the promise [to contract the engagement at a later time] is made'.[46] The effects of such a promise for a future engagement included the giving of a marriage gift, the establishment of a relationship of consanguinity for members of the families on each side, the assumption that a marriage would take place barring the discovery of impediments, and, should sexual intercourse between the partners occur, the presumption of a consummated marriage.[47] With the exception of the third condition, all of these effects were the effects of marriage.

Indeed, the dividing line between espousal and matrimony was thin and seems to have been the matter of sexual intercourse. Like Luther, Beust tried to preserve a distinction between engagement and marriage. He did so by taking the step neither Luther nor the theologians or jurists of the Middle Ages were evidently willing to take: he made marriage depend not on consent but on sex. As one of the four effects of betrothal Beust listed the possibility that if an engagement is followed by sexual intercourse it became a marriage. Beust solved the problem which Luther's presentation of betrothal had bequeathed the tradition, but at the expense of two concepts which medieval thinkers held dear: consent and not sex as the basis of marriage and the difference between future and present betrothals.

Saxon Ordinances on Betrothal

Following 1521 changes gradually swept across the German-speaking lands as civic and territorial leaders took over legislation on marriage which the church had formerly controlled. The changes in local legislation as a rule followed one of two impulses: they came about because a newly converted Lutheran prince had arranged a visitation which made clear to all that changes were necessary, or when the prince secularised – that is appropriated – property that formerly belonged to the church and was therefore required to offer his new territories some means of administration. The ordinances examined here were thus formulated more or less at the same time as Kling, Beust and their generation of lawyers were

---

[45] Cf. Beust, pp. 90–99 with pp. 156–7.

[46] 'Etsi ille qui promisit velle sponsalia contrahere, non dicatur propterea sponsalia contraxisse, sed tantum promisse.' Beust, p. 109.

[47] Beust, pp. 110–11.

formulating the new Protestant academic approach to marriage law. These collections of church legislation are primarily from both parts of Saxony, although on occasion rules from other territories were invoked when they help to make a point clear.[48]

Most of the sixteenth-century legislation on betrothal and marriage is to be found in the church ordinances of the period. This does not, however, mean that the civil government did not participate in the writing of these rules. The twentieth-century separation of church and state would have been incomprehensible to the people of the sixteenth century. Rather, as innumerable theologians of the period insisted, marriage and betrothal were matters which linked the divine and human realms.

Given the usual reasons for writing the new legislation about marriage, one could expect that politicians and pastors, lawyers and theologians would want to take part in the composition of this legislation. This was indeed the case and was stated both explicitly in some cases and reflected implicitly in the contents of others. A typical example is the church ordinance written in 1583 for the court at Wintzingeroda in the Grafschaft Hohenstein: the ordinance was signed by and appeared according to the authority of two noblemen, Friedrich von Wintzingeroda and Hans Friedrich von Wintzingeroda, two jurists, Jeremiah Richelm and Wolfgang Höher and two pastors, Conrad Schneegans, the pastor of Ohmveld, and Andreas Wacker, the pastor at Wintzingeroda.[49]

The influence of such a mixed group of authors on the regulations concerning betrothal and marriage was evident also in the various sources on which the ordinances draw. The Celle ordinance of 1545 explained a particular prohibition by referring to 'divine, imperial and all other laws', a formulation which appeared frequently.[50] Several ordinances exhibited a thorough familiarity with Roman imperial law – the 1586 consistory ordinance for the Grafschaft of Mansfeld cites the Justinianic Digest and the Codex explicitly[51] – and many others make references to canon law. A particularly beloved source for marriage laws was, of course, the Bible, especially Leviticus 18 on the matter of prohibited degrees and the fourth commandment with regard to parental permission for betrothal or marriage. Luther was often cited, as was Melanchthon.[52]

---

[48] The sampling is hardly representative of all the various legislations produced in sixteenth-century Saxony, but rather reflects the selection made by Emil Sehling for the first two of his volumes of Protestant church ordinances. *Die evangelischen Kirchenordnungen des 16. Jahrhunderts* ed. Emil Sehling (vols 1–8 and 11–15, Leipzig, 1902–13/Tübingen, 1955 ff.).

[49] Ibid., I. 2, doc. 43.

[50] 'götlicher, kaiserlicher und alle andere gesetz', ibid., I. 2, doc. 28, p. 292.

[51] Ibid., doc. 40, p. 206.

[52] Luther's '*seligen buchlein*', by which the authors usually mean *Von Ehesachen* comes up with some frequency as in ibid., doc. 84, p. 417 et passim.

The 1580 Magdeburg consistory ordinance also suggested that the works of Melchior Kling and Erasmus Sacerius were also helpful interpreters of divine and natural law.[53]

In addition to displaying the wide range of intellectual interests of the composers of sixteenth-century Protestant marriage legislation, these ordinances also offered a distinct hierarchy of valuation for their source material. In spite of the claim made by many of the ordinances that divine, natural and positive law agreed, their use of these sources suggests that the legislators knew how to resolve inconsistencies when they arose. Above all, divine law, as it appears in the Old and New Testaments, had priority. The justification for revising the rules governing prohibited degrees of marriage is often to bring Roman or canon law into conformity with Leviticus, just as any allowance for divorce could be made to fit with New Testament prohibitions of the same. In general, Luther was the next highest court of appeal where no straightforward appeal to scriptures could be made.[54] Following Luther, the writers of these ordinances then appealed to Roman law as the positive expression of natural law. Although canon law did not have a particularly high standing in the marriage regulations, it was nonetheless cited with some frequency and just as frequently contradicted.[55]

Saxon legislators had definite expectations as to what steps were necessary to constitute a valid marriage. Betrothal was by all accounts a necessary step, one part of the multi-step process which included the following elements: the promise to marry, the announcement of the promise in the church, the church wedding (often called the *kirchgang*), and, finally, cohabitation and sexual intercourse. This order, while not always respected by the participants, was taken to be of great importance by the legislators. The 1548 Merseburg Instructions specified that for three weeks after the notification of intention to marry announcements of the impending union should be made by the pastor.[56] An earlier version of this document, printed in 1545, also stressed a threefold reading of the banns and elaborated that people should investigate the backgrounds and characters of their intended spouses since it was a source of 'big trouble' when difficulties were discovered after the promises were

---

[53] Ibid., I. 2, doc. 84, p. 417. Erasmus Sacerius was the general superintendent for the Grafschaft of Mansfeld between 1553 and 1559. He is responsible for a number of church ordinances and suggestions regarding ecclesiastical matters published during the period around the Peace of Augsburg.

[54] For an example, see ibid., doc. 40; p. 206.

[55] Gratian and the canonists are often contradicted on the matter of consent alone without parental permission being required for the construction of legitimate marriage vows.

[56] Sehling, *Die evangelischen Kirchenordnungen*, I. 2, doc. 6, p. 35.

made and the process of getting married was under way.[57] The 1580 ordinance published under the authority of August of Saxony does not say how often the banns are to be read, but forbids pastors to marry couples in advance of this announcement.[58] What is new and significant here is that the ordinances all make clear that if engagement is not properly announced then no legally binding wedding may take place. While previous custom had required the reading of the banns, this ceremony had not earlier had any bearing on the validity of the future marriage.

Contrary to Luther's teaching on the matter, which, for all practical effects, united betrothal with marriage and thus with either copulation or cohabitation, many of the church ordinances explicitly separated the two. The 1580 Saxon ordinance notes that people who slept together before the church wedding were to be subject to civil punishment, including jailing.[59] This, the ordinance continued, was to be the case even if no pregnancy occurred, or if the act was only discovered after the wedding had taken place. At the very least, in such cases, the bride could not wear the traditional crown of flowers at her wedding, while at the very most both parties were threatened with jail. Erfurt's 1583 ordinance took a dim view of those cases where, as one ordinance put it, the 'baptism of a child happens at the same time or right after the wedding'.[60] The ordinance counted such behaviour as an offence against good morals and threatened the perpetrators with fines or imprisonment.

Things were not, however, as uniform or consistent across Saxony as one might hope. It seems, rather, that the earlier marriage ordinances tended to uphold Luther's position on espousal in part. The 1556 marriage ordinance from Dresden, for example, seemed to consider betrothal tantamout to marriage. When a person slept with someone other than his fiancée he was to be punished for adultery.[61] Other ordinaces suggested strong punishment for those who tried to break their engagements by having sex with someone other than their betrothed.

While some of the Saxon ordinances differed from Luther in the separation of betrothal and sex, all argued with Luther that parental permission was absolutely necessary for the conclusion of a valid engagement. The 1545 Merseburger Articles stated: 'Equally, nobody should become engaged before his parents know about it; this is the ruling of divine,

---

[57] *Grosse muhe*, ibid., doc. 5, p. 27.

[58] Ibid., doc. 40, p. 386.

[59] Ibid., I. 1, doc. 40, p. 386.

[60] 'Die kinderteufe oft mit oder bald nach der Hochzeit geschehe', ibid., I. 2, doc. 75, p. 373.

[61] 'Darumb sol der Theter als ein ehebrecher gestrafft werden mit der publica poenitentia und durch weltliche oberheit und sold die versunung mit der ersten verlubnuss versucht werden.' Ibid., I. 1, doc. 32, p. 343.

natural, Imperial law and the ordinances of the Elector and prince and it is not be be overstepped. Whoever does so should be thoroughly punished'.[62] The same year the consistory regulations from Meissen made the same point regarding engagements: promises to marry made without prior consent of the parents were 'without power and do not bind'. Even if the parents were sure to agree, the children were still required to ask before they promised.[63] The bishop of Naumburg-Zeitz threatened bodily punishment for those children who did not respect their parents and especially those who expressed this disrespect by making promises to marry without parental permission.[64] The territory of Anhalt's 1572 ordinance, clearly drawing directly upon Luther's work, described a secret engagement as one which takes place without the knowledge and permission of the parents and explicitly forbad such arrangements.[65] These examples could be multiplied: every marriage ordinance that considered the subject of betrothals – and almost all did – forbad children to make promises to marry without consulting their parents.

Here one should mention that the requirement that children consult with their parents before entering into a betrothal was not limited to under-age children: only rarely did the marriage ordinances indicate that there was any difference between children who had attained their majority and those who had not. The 1556 ordinance from Dresden specified that even children who had attained their majority might not marry without permission of their parents,[66] while the 1580 ordinance issued by Herzog August allowed parents to disinherit children who had become engaged without permission or who married against their parents' will.[67]

The Saxon ordinances required more than just parental permission for a betrothal to be considered valid. As the previous discussion of the reading of the engagement announcement made clear, the local pastor could not help but be involved in the process of bringing a couple together. Particularly as concerned future marriages which were possibly within the prohibited degree of blood relationships, the ordinances urged couples to consult with their pastor, presumably the person in the community with the best understanding of the Old Testament and imperial

---

[62] 'Item, das sich niemands ahne vorwissen seiner eltern vorheiraten solle, welches wider gottliche, naturlich, keiserliche recht und der chur und furstlichen ordnung ist, und nicht zuzulassen, und wer das mit fördert, sol hertiglich gestrafet werden.' Ibid. I. 2, doc. 5; p. 27.

[63] The promises are *unkreftig und unbündig*. Ibid., doc. 9, p. 48.

[64] Ibid., doc. 40, p. 386.

[65] The articles prohibit 'heimliche winkelverlöbnis, sonderlich welche one vorwissen und bewilligung der eltern oder derer so an der eltern stat sind, geschehen'. Ibid., I. 2, doc. 1125, p. 572.

[66] Ibid., I. 1, doc. 34, p. 344.

[67] Ibid., I. 2, doc. 40, p. 386.

prohibitions, not to mention access to the relevant baptism and marriage records.[68] Saxon-Anhalt specified, in a 1572 ordinance, that the superintendent of each district should be aware of all proposed unions and consulted if there were any questions about a marriage.[69] Pastors, superintendents and, in some cases, even the consistory as a whole, were expected to regulate whether the couple could marry on account of blood relationships or other impediments to marriage.

The encouragement that Saxon marriage ordinances gave to pastors and other church officials to participate in the betrothals of their parishioners can be explained, I believe, by several factors. Almost always the input of a church official is requested to regulate whether the intended match is with a prohibited degree of blood relationship. Given the frequency with which the ordinances spelt out the permitted degrees of consanguinity, often providing tabular explanations and examples and rules of thumb, one can surmise that people in the sixteenth century found these rules difficult to follow. Particularly in rural areas with small populations and little immigration, it may have been difficult to compute the exact relationship in which people stood to each other.[70] Church records of baptisms and marriages provided one way to determine exact relationships. The presentation of the rules also made obvious the legislators' belief that the rules for computing consanguinity were difficult to follow and thus expert help in the form of a church official should be sought where possible. Perhaps the overriding consideration for encouraging people to consult with a pastor was the clear perception on the part of the framers of marriage ordinances that such matters were of utmost importance. The idea that marriages within forbidden degrees threaten the whole area with the wrath of God was indicated by a 1580 ordinance that prescribed exile for people who married within prohibited degrees, lest the crime of *blutschande* provoke God's wrath on the community as a whole.[71]

The reading of the banns, which, as has already been shown, was an integral part of the process of becoming engaged, was yet another way that the Saxon ordinances increased the number of participants required to make a betrothal valid. The parents and pastor of the pair had already indicated that they approved of the match, or at least that they could see

---

[68] For one example see the 1548 Merseburg 'Simple Instruction on Forbidden Persons and Degrees in Marriage', ibid., doc. 6, p. 34.

[69] Ibid., I. 1, doc. 125, p. 572.

[70] Luther also thought this was a problem and so suggested more stringent regulations on account of the simple people/rural dwellers: 'Man lest es auch wol zu grossen herrn in tertio [gradu] aber propter rusticos soll es in quarto bleiben . . . ' *TR*, 5, 156 (no. 5442 from summer or autumn 1542).

[71] Ibid., I. 1, doc. 40, p. 387.

no impediment to it. Other obvious impediments, such as a previous engagement or marriage by one party, could now be brought to public notice.

The Saxon marriage ordinances took betrothal seriously. An engagement could not be lightly entered into nor could it be easily broken off. The consistory threatened to invalidate betrothals made without parental permission or those which were within prohibited degrees of consanguinity. Equally, when children claimed to have been forced into an engagement against their wills, the consistory was empowered to invalidate the promise.[72] The disappearance of one party could also break an engagement but here the party who remained behind must consult with the consistory and wait until that body determined that the missing individual had no intention of returning or was dead. The 1586 Mansfield ordinance mandated a waiting period of a full year for such cases.[73] In all these cases, the dissolution or invalidation of a betrothal could only take place with the explicit permission of the consistory. The seriousness with which betrothal was regarded and the steps which the civil government took to safeguard this seriousness reflected a changed attitude toward the institutions of engagement and marriage.

Conclusions

Changes had certainly occurred in the general understanding of betrothal in all sections of sixteenth-century society. Two changes in particular are evident and in both cases the jurists expressed opinions that, although they were cognisant of Luther's teaching as well as the tradition that he rejected, differ from the laws as they were practised in Protestant communites. The church ordinances presented regulations regarding betrothal which drew on a variety of sources: the Bible and Luther, of course, but also the legal traditions of Protestant jurists and medieval canon lawyers. These regulations also demonstrated not only a society in transition – and there has never really been any doubt that sixteenth-century society was in transition – but one which was attempting to reorder the fundamental bedrock of its social organisations.

First, the church ordinances required engagement: betrothal was a necessary precursor to marriage. Engagement was an opportunity to work out the social ramifications of marriage once intention on both sides had been declared. As near as one can tell, engagement was only required by medieval canon law in those cases where the promise to

---

[72] Two examples are found in ibid., I. 2, doc. 6, p. 34 and doc. 9. p. 48.
[73] Ibid., I. 2, doc. 40, p. 206.

marry was made well in advance of the completion of the act. Luther appeared to demand engagement but he never made this claim explicitly and his elision of betrothal with marriage would seem to make the former superfluous. Kling and Beust discussed the issue of betrothal chiefly as it concerned the making of plans for the distant future. Kling, like Luther, slid present betrothal into marriage while Beust tried to keep even present betrothal and marriage separate. In the matter of the necessity of betrothal, the church ordinances and Luther's dwarf category of future contingent betrothals recapitulate Gratian's construct: betrothal was a period in which business can be conducted and when errors, it was hoped, could be prevented.

Second, the permission of parents, which Luther demanded in sharp contrast to the medieval tradition, emerged as a distinctive aspect of Protestant legislation on betrothal and marriage. The number of people who ideally consented to a promise to marry according to Luther and the Protestant legislators was six: the actual participants plus two sets of parents. Even in the medieval period engagement could hardly have come about because of a few hot words, yet in the sixteenth century the process had become far more clearly institutionalised. As we have seen, some communities established yet a further check on engagements; not only parental consent but also the permission of the pastor was required for a valid engagement. The circle of participants in a betrothal had widened greatly after the Reformation in comparison to what had gone before.

In the case of parental permission, the jurists examined in this chapter avoided taking a stand. Kling, who followed with some modifications the canonist's list of impediments to marriage, did not come to the issue; even when he discussed clandestine promises to marry the subject did not arise.[74] Beust also passed on a discussion of this topic. It could be, of course, that the issue of parental permission simply slipped the minds of these two writers. This, however, seems unlikely given the fact that the issue was at the top of most legislative agendas. It would seem that academic legal thinking remained tied to the basic structures as well as many of the guiding principles of canon law. A basic conservatism reigned (and reigns) in such circles.

This conservatism ignored the way both betrothal and marriage were utilised in the sixteenth century. The new legislation implemented in the wake of the Protestant Reformation changed the place of betrothal in the usual procedure of getting married. It made engagements necessary, public and invalid without the permission of the parents. In the course of these changes engagement became a way to keep order in the commu-

---

[74] See Kling, fo. 29ᵛ–31ᵛ.

nity. The requirement that engagement precede marriage gave the community as a whole – civil authorites via the pastor, extended family via
the parents – warning of an alliance about to be concluded. The necessity
of parental permission gave to parents as well as those willing or able to
put pressure on parents, a relatively easy way to end an engagement that
was for some reason not perceived to be optimal. Individuals lost the
ability to choose their future spouses without the approval of the wider
social context, which, in turn, came to be regulated by the state and its
representatives.

CHAPTER NINE

Ritual and Protestant Identity in Late Reformation Germany

Bodo Nischan

Steven Ozment, in his recent book *Protestants: Birth of a Revolution*, notes that 'the most challenging questions about the Reformation today have to do with its evolution through the sixteenth century as it passed from theology into sermon and pamphlet, from sermon and pamphlet into law and institutions, and then into the daily lives of ordinary people'.[1] Scholars have been far from unanimous in answering these questions. Many view the Reformation as a modest spiritual movement, easily manipulated by secular power and ineffective in creating a new and different kind of Protestant Christian.[2]

What impact, then, did the movement spawned by Martin Luther and John Calvin have on people's religious beliefs and practices? Or, put differently, how did those early, second and third-generation Protestants comprehend and express their historical identity? A closer look at piety in late Reformation Germany should provide some clues. It was during this period, bracketed by the Peace of Augsburg (1555) and the outbreak of the Thirty Years' War (1618), that more or less stable Protestant denominations started to emerge. Confessional consolidation entailed polarisation which often led to conflict. Nowhere was this more evident than in those principalities which had first experienced a relatively conservative Lutheran reform, in which many old religious practices were retained, and then, later in the century, a second reformation in which Calvinists claimed to discard the remaining 'popish relics' and 'leftover papal dung'. This had happened first in the Palatinate (1563), then in Nassau, Bremen, Anhalt (1590), Hesse-Kassel (1605), and also was attempted in Saxony (1587–91) and in Brandenburg (1613–15). The way people practised and experienced their religion was profoundly affected by these changes. Individuals generally had very little choice but to submit to the new court-imposed creed. But often they resisted, especially in

---

[1] S. Ozment, *Protestants: The Birth of a Revolution* (New York, 1992), p. 41.

[2] Best known and most widely debated is the conclusion reached by Gerald Strauss in his *Luther's House of Learning: Indoctrination of the Young in the German Reformation* (Baltimore, 1978), p. 299: 'A century of Protestantism had brought about little or no change in the common religious conscience and in the ways in which ordinary men and women conducted their lives.'

places where the process of confessionalisation had advanced to the point that a sense of denominational identity had started to emerge. Here it became increasingly difficult for rulers to apply the *cuius regio eius religio* formula, devised for the Peace of Augsburg, without provoking considerable opposition from the people.[3]

Popular religion, while the focus of much recent study, remains one of the most elusive and least understood topics in early modern history. Recent findings by anthropologists and folklorists suggest that ritual and ceremonial practices can yield important clues. Thus Robert Scribner has shown how 'by focusing specifically on liturgical forms and their varying components, we may be able to clarify our understanding of "popular religion" and to indicate the role it played in the considerable religious turmoil of the Reformation'.[4] Driving the pope and papal religion out of the hearts and minds of people, he has argued, turned the Reformation itself into a 'ritual process'.[5] Similarly, Peter Burke has suggested that 'ritual was even more important in the second stage of the Reformation [in] which the communities of the faithful had to be held together.'[6] As Germany's three major denominational churches – the Lutheran, Reformed, and Catholic – sought to consolidate their positions, 'rites usable as a distinctive confessional mark were either especially developed or suppressed', Wolfgang Reinhard has noted.[7] And Steven Ozment has found that 'although Protestantism had simpler religious rituals, each had suddenly become absolute, its importance enhanced by the reduction of religion to a claimed vital core'.[8]

---

[3] On the age of confessionalism, see E.W. Zeeden, 'Grundlagen und Wege der Konfessionsbildung in Deutschland im Zeitalter der Glaubenskämpfe', in his *Gegenreformation* (Darmstadt, 1973), pp. 85–134; H. Schilling (ed.), *Die reformierte Konfessionsbildung in Deutschland – Das Problem der 'Zweiten Reformation'*, SVRG, 195 (Gütersloh, 1986); Hans-Christoph Rublack (ed.), *Die lutherische Konfessionalisierung in Deutschland*, SVRG, 197 (Gütersloh, 1992); and H. Schmidt, *Konfessionalisierung im 16. Jahrhundert*, Enzyklopädie Deutscher Geschichte, 12 (Munich, 1992).

[4] R. Scribner, 'Ritual and and Popular Religion in Catholic Germany at the Time of the Reformation', *JEH*, 35 (1984), 48.

[5] Scribner, 'Ritual and Reformation', in R. Po-Chia Hsia (ed.), *The German People and the Reformation* (Ithaca, NY, 1988), pp. 122–44. Note also his 'Elements of Popular Belief' in T.A. Brady et al. (eds), *Handbook of European History, 1400–1600*, (2 vols, Leiden, 1994–95), I. 231–62, esp. 254.

[6] P. Burke, *The Historical Anthropology of Early Modern Italy* (New York, 1987), p. 230.

[7] W. Reinhard, 'Zwang zur Konfessionalisierung? Prolegomena zur einer Theorie des konfessionellen Zeitalters', *Zeitschrift für Historische Forschung*, 10 (1983), 266. Note also R. van Dülmen, 'Volksfrömmigkeit und konfessionelles Christentum im 16. und 17. Jahrhundert' in W. Schieder (ed.), *Volksreligiosität in der modernen Sozialgeschichte*, Geschichte und Gesellschaft, Sonderheft 11 (Göttingen, 1986), 14–30.

[8] Ozment, *Protestants*, p. 216.

To gain a clearer understanding of how sixteenth-century Protestants sought to comprehend and express their historical identity, this chapter will examine the relationship between ritual and confessional piety. The objective will be to show how Germany's early Lutherans and Calvinists used liturgy to define and distinguish themselves, first, from the old, the Roman Catholic, church and, second, from each other as separate Protestant denominational churches.

Ritual and Confessional Identity

Liturgy and ritual, both the followers of the Wittenberg and Helvetic reformers insisted, were essentially indifferent matters, adiaphora, that could be freely employed or omitted. The only problem was that they could not agree on just what constituted genuine adiaphora. The Lutheran position, refined in debate over the Leipzig Interim in the mid-sixteenth century, was formulated by Matthias Flacius Illyricus of Magdeburg. He rejected the liturgical compromises of the Interim that the victorious Catholics had sought to impose on the evangelicals after the Schmalkald War, noting:

> All ceremonies and ecclesiastical usages are free in themselves, as ever. But when they are imposed through coercion, or through the erroneous impression that they are required for worship, or through deceit, scandal, or public pressure from the godless, and when they do not benefit God's church in some way, but disrupt it and mock God, then they are no longer adiaphora.[9]

Flacius's 'general rule regarding ceremonies' was seconded by other Gnesio-Lutherans, notably Nikolaus Gallus,[10] also from Magdeburg, and Joachim Westphal of Hamburg.[11] It was also endorsed by the Formula of Concord (1577)[12] and frequently reiterated as churches were jousting for people's confessional allegiance. 'To distinguish ourselves

---

[9] Matthias Flacius, *Ein buch/von waren und flaschen Mitteldingen/Darin fast die gantze handel von Mitteldingen erkleret wird/widder die schedliche Rotte der Adiaphoristen* (Magdeburg, 1550), fo. Ai[b].

[10] Nikolaus Gallus, *Disputatio de adiaphoris et mutatione praesentis status pie constitutarum ecclesiarum* (Magdeburg, 1550?), fo. Cii[b]; and Gallus, *Das die gründe Nicolai Galli noch fest stehen/wider der Adiaphoristen Acta und Auszug . . .* (Regensburg, 1560), where he reiterates the formula: *In casu confessionis adiaphora fiunt necessaria, Hic fuit casus confessionis. Ergo adiaphora hic facta sunt necessaria*, fo. Bii[a].

[11] Joachim Westphal, *Des Ehrwirdigen vnd teuren Mans Doct. Martin Luthers seliger gedechtnis meinung/von den Mitteldingen . . .* (Magdeburg, 1550).

[12] See 'Konkordienformel, Solida Declaratio X: Von Kirchenbräuchen' in *Die Bekenntnisschriften der evangelisch lutherischen Kirche* (4th edn, Göttingen, 1959), pp. 1053–63; and *The Book of Concord*, ed. T. Tappert (Philadelphia, 1959), pp. 610–16.

from 'Anabaptists, Sacramentarians, Papists, Interimists, Adiaphorists, and others with novel and strange teachings . . . we are taking the right middle road by neither rejecting nor endorsing all ceremonies', explained Gallus.[13] Lutherans, observed Tilemann Hesshusen in 1585, were involved in a two-front war with 'Jesuits and Calvinists' in which ritual and ceremonial count.[14] Hesshusen cautioned people to beware of 'the wolf's howling of the Adiaphorists, who insist that our confession is not reflected in surplices or external garb and ceremonies'.[15] 'Ceremonies . . . serve to promote our true and pure teaching of the Holy Gospel', observed the Rostock superintendent Simon Pauli.[16] They enable us 'to distinguish true from false doctrine . . . and reveal our sectarian adversaries – Papists, Calvinists, and their ilk'.[17] Much the same, Balthasar Meisner, professor at Wittenberg, reminded his listeners that false prophets expose themselves not only by their erroneous teachings but also by their ceremonies: 'For heretics are in the habit of always using unique and strange church rites under the pretext . . . of Christian liberty.'[18] Liturgy and ritual thus had become much more than merely an indifferent matter for Lutherans in the late Reformation; they clearly were regarded as marks of confessional identity.[19]

Concurrently there had occurred another subtle but important shift in the way Lutherans were treating church usages, notably in regions where they were vying with Calvinists for people's confessional loyalty. Some of the very same liturgical practices which earlier critics of the Interim had condemned as 'Catholicising', many followers of the Augsburg Confession were now defending as a useful prophylactic against Reformed and other sacramentarian perversions. Old rituals are 'like a

---

[13] Gallus, *Disputatio*, fos Ciii[a]–Civ[b].

[14] Tilemann Hesshusen, *Postila. Das ist/Ausslegung der Evangelia/auff alle Feste und Apostel Tage/durchs gantze Jahr* (n.p., 1585), fos a5[b], b3[a].

[15] 'So ist auch der Adiaphoristen Wolffgeschrey nu fast wol bekant/wie sie jmerdar geruffen/das Bekenntnis stehe nicht im Chorrock/eusserlichen Kleidungen und Ceremonien/sondern nur in den hohen Artickeln des Glaubens', Tilemann Hesshusen, *Vom Bekenntnis des Namens Jhesu Christi für den Menschen* (Jena, 1571), fo. Ei[a].

[16] Simon Pauli, *Postilla. Das ist Ausslegung der Episteln und Evangelien/an Sontagen und fürnemsten Festen . . .* (Magdeburg, 1572), fo. 120[b].

[17] Michael Muling, *Isagoge Christiana. Christlicher und wolbegründeter Bericht: Welcher massen sich rechtgläubige Christenmenschen/gegen die Papisten/Calvinisten und andern Ketzerischen Schwermern/der Christlichen gebür nach verwahrlich bezeigen sollen* (Wittenberg, 1620), pp. 7–8.

[18] Balthasar Meisner, *Meditationes Sacrae, oder Geistliche Andachten/uber die Evangelien der Jährlichen Sonn- und Festtagen* (Frankfurt am Main, 1659), p. 403.

[19] On the development of Lutheran confessional identity in the post-Interim period, see R. Kolb, *Confessing the Faith: Reformers Define the Church 1530–1580* (St Louis, 1991), pp. 65–131.

good disciplinarian in that they provide helpful instruction on how to keep the true faith', thought Achatius, member of the Brandenburg consistory. He even published a lengthy compendium of excerpts from the writings of notable Lutherans to demonstrate that doctrinal orthodoxy and ceremonial traditionalism went hand in hand.[20] 'As long as the old ceremonies are kept in the Mark of Brandenburg, Calvinists also will be kept at bay', observed Elisabeth Magdalene,[21] sister of the archconservative elector Johann Georg (ruled 1571–98). In a book which he dedicated to the duchess, Zacharias Rivander of Saxony, where another reformation had just been aborted, he listed the marks whereby a 'simple layman' could easily spot a Calvinist minister. 'If he distributes Holy Communion without reverence . . . [and] runs to the altar like a hog to its trough . . . he surely is a secret sacramentarian.'[22] Similarly, Theodosius Fabricius of Göttingen in a history of the current communion disputes, which appeared in 1593, compared in separate columns the teachings and practices of Germany's three major denominations. His goal, the author explained, 'is not to contrast Protestants and Papists, but to compare the teachings of Lutherans with Zwinglians or Calvinists'.[23] Thus, for the year 1563 Fabricius's chronicle recorded: Heidelberg becomes reformed and Luther's catechism is eliminated. . . . Calvinists remove pictures from churches, abolish auricular confession, delete exorcism [from baptism] and numerous festivals, and discard altars and baptismal fonts.[24] Johann Olearius of Halle, who witnessed the introduction of Calvinism in neighbouring Anhalt in the early 1590s, thought that the new reformers were purposefully eliminating 'the public ceremonies of the mass that we [Lutherans] have kept to instruct people . . . florid descant, church organs, altars, wax candles, mass vestments, golden vessels, communion hosts, genuflecting as one approaches the Lord's Table, and similar practices'.[25]

---

[20] Achatius von Brandenburg, *Collecture und Ausszug auss den Christlichen/reinen/jetziger unserer zeit Lehrern/wie und warumb die Christlichen freyen/und ungefährlichen reinen Ceremonien . . . gehalten werden* (Frankfurt am Main, 1579), p. 207.

[21] Hieronymus Prunner, *Leichpredigt . . . Frawen Elisabeth Magdalena Gebornen Marggrefin zu Brandenburg/und Hertzogin zu Braunschweig und Lüneburg* (Frankfurt an der Oder, 1595).

[22] Zacharias Rivander, *Lupus excoriatus, Oder Der offentlichen vnd heimlichen Caluinsten/vnd aller Sacramentierer Wölffner Schaffspelz* (Wittenberg, 1591), fo. 60[b].

[23] Theodosius Fabricius, *Historia Certaminis Sacramentarii. Das ist/Historia des Streits Uber der gegenwart vnd Niessung des Leibes und Bluts Christi/vnter Brodt vnd Wein im Heiligen Abendmal des Herrn* (Magdeburg, 1593), fo. Aii[b].

[24] Ibid., fo. Eei[a].

[25] Johann Olearius, *Drey Predigten vom Unterschied der wahren Christlichen Lutherischen und falschen Papistischen und Caluinischen Religion . . . Sampt einer Vorrede vom Betrug und Lügen der Anhaltischen Scribenten* (n.p., 1591), p. 119.

Olearius's assessment was accurate for the Reformed, like the Lutherans, had come to view church rites and usages from a mostly confessional perspective.[26] Unlike the Lutherans, however, they had a much stricter notion of just what ceremonies were permitted. 'Those matters about which we have no commandment of God are in our liberty', John Calvin had observed; but he added, 'how much more true then, that which leads to stumbling, and serves as an instrument of idolatry and gives rise to misleading opinions, ought in no way be allowed'.[27] Carlos Eire has argued that, for the Genevan, 'the Reformation . . . was not so much one of doctrine, but one of piety, which involved profound social and cultural changes. To be properly "Reformed", a community would not only have to change its theology, but also its outward expression of faith.'[28] The results of this war against idolatry became most evident in late Reformation Germany. 'Because ceremonies indicate the confession one has either embraced or rejected, it is . . . most crucial that one shun and avoid all suspicious ones', insisted Anhalt's new reformers.[29] 'Exorcism [in baptism] . . . , altars, crucifixes, pictures, chasubles, mass vestments, capes, candles, etc. do [not] belong among Christian ceremonies' and therefore must go, observed Duke Johann Georg of Anhalt.[30] 'For the sake of the people the current emendation was neces-

---

[26] Not surprisingly, Catholics too treated ceremonies as a mark of confessional identity. Thus, Matthias Tympe, cathedral preacher at Münster, observed: 'Was sein die Tauffceremonien anders als eine bestättigung vnnd erklärung vnsers H. wahren Glaubens . . . Darumb wer diese und andere Ceremonien der Kirchen verachtet/der kompt allgemach dahin/dass er auch letzlich die Artickel des Glaubens/so durch solche Ceremonien angedeutet/illustriert/vnd herfür gestrichen werden/gering schätzet und haltet.' (Der Cermonien Warumb/Das ist/Lautere vnnd klare Vrsachen vnd ausslegungen der fürnemsten Ceremonien/welche auss einsprechung dess H. Geists bey dem H. Gottesdienst inn der gantzen H. Christenheit von alters her gleichformig vnd einhellig gebraucht werden' [Münster, 1609], pp. 1–2.)

[27] 'Premierement, ce qui ne nous est point commandé de Dieu, est en nostre liberté; d'avantage tout ce qui ne sert de rien à edification ne doit estre receu en l'Eglise; et s'il avoit esté introduict, il doit estre osté. Par plus forte raison, ce qui ne sert que à scandaliser, et est comme instrument d'idolatrie et de faulses opinions, ne doit estre nullement toleré. Or, il est certain, que le cresme, luminaire, et telles aultres pompes, ne sont point de l'ordonnance de Dieu: mais ont esté adioustées par les hommes.' 'La Forme d'Administrer le Baptesme' in Joannis Calvini Opera Selecta, ed. P. Barth and D. Scheuner (5 vols, Munich, 1926–62), II. 38.

[28] C.M.N. Eire, War Against the Idols: The Reformation of Worship from Erasmus to Calvin (New York, 1986), p. 233.

[29] Bericht und lehre Göttliches Wort/was von den Ceremonien unnd eusserlichen Kirchenbreuchen . . . zu halten sey (Zerbst, 1596), p. 50.

[30] Erinnerungsschrifft etlicher vom Adel und Städten/An den Durchleuchtigsten Hochgebornen Fürsten unnd Herrn/Herrn Johann Georgen/Fürsten zu Anhalt/Graven zu Ascanien/Herrn zu Zerbst un Bernburg. Sampt darauff erfolgten gnediger Verantwortung und erklärung (Amberg, 1597), fo. Div[a].

sary so that doctrine and ceremony alike will reflect the truth, and the many remaining superstitious rituals . . . will not mislead people any longer', declared Christoph Pezel of Bremen.[31] He told Count Johann VI of Nassau-Dillenburg that these reforms 'were urgently needed because Your Highness' lands are surrounded by Catholic territories and today's papists use these very ceremonies to attract people back to their religion'.[32] Similarly, the Reformed glossarist of the so-called Krell Bible, that appeared during Saxony's aborted second reformation, noted that ceremonies were 'instituted by God 1) as marks of the true confession whereby God's people are separated from all others, and 2) as a mutual bond for . . . God's churches'.[33] 'Our reformation', he went on to explain, 'affects both doctrine and ceremonies and . . . does away with pictures, altars, chapels, and similar practices that are either explicitly prohibited by the Word of God or else have become the cause of idolatry and scandal'.[34] Much like the Lutherans, the Reformed thus had come to see church rituals as a means, first, to delineate themselves from other denominations and, second, to build greater confessional loyalty and cohesion.[35]

The Theologians' Debate

Since the sacrament of the altar was the principal issue between Lutherans and Calvinists, liturgical variations in the celebration of the

[31] Christoph Pezel, *Auffrichtige Rechenschafft Von Lehr vn Ceremonien, So inn den Evangelischen Reformirten Kirchen/nach der Richtschnur Göttliches Worts angestellet* (Bremen, 1592), p. 162.

[32] Ibid.; fo. avᵃ.

[33] 'Commentary on Exodus 25,1', in *Die Fünff Bücher Mosis/Verdeutscht Durch D. Martin Luther. Darinnen/neben kurtzer Vorrede vber jedes Buch/Insonderheit ein jedes Capitel ordentlich in gewisse Versicul vnd Paragraphos, abgetheilet: Und mit darauff gerichteten Summarien: Auch fürnembsten Lehren/sampt einer jeden Lehre Nutz . . . Auff gnedigsten Befehl des Durchlauchtigsten vnd Hochgebornen Fürsten vnd Herrn/Herrn Christian/Hertzogen vnd Churfürsten zu Sachsen . . .* (Dresden, 1590), popularly known as the *Krell-Bibel*, fo. 72ᵃ.

[34] 'Commentary on II Kings 18,4', in ibid., fo. 39⁵ᵇ. On the second reformation in Saxony see also K. Blaschke, 'Religion und Politik in Kursachsen 1586–1591', in Schilling (ed.), *Reformierte Konfessionalisierung*, pp. 79–97; and E. Koch, 'Ausbau, Gefährdung und Festigung der lutherischen Landeskirche von 1553 bis 1601', in *Das Jahrhundert der Reformation in Sachsen. Festgabe zum 450 jährigen Bestehen der Evangelisch-Lutherischen Landeskirche Sachsens* (Berlin, 1989), pp. 195–223.

[35] On the Reformed view of rituals, see P. Münch, 'Volkskultur und Calvinismus. Zu Theorie und Praxis der "reformatio vitae" während der "Zweiten Reformation"', in Schilling, *Reformierte Konfessionalisierung*, pp. 291–307; and the above cited work by Carlos Eire (no.28).

Lord's Supper were bound to cause disagreement and controversy. To the Reformed the liturgical trappings of the traditional mass, which had been retained by the Lutherans, suggested an understanding of the Eucharist which was, to put it simply, papal and magical rather than evangelical. The main point over which they were arguing was the doctrine of Real Presence, specifically the teaching of the *communicatio idiomatum*, which many Lutherans cited to explain Christ's physical presence. Accordingly, the divine attributes of Christ's nature – his omnipotence, omniscience, and omnipresence – are communicated to his human nature so that, in the words of the Formula of Concord, he 'can be and is present wherever he wills', particularly in the communion elements.[36] The Reformed countered that a physical body could only be present in one place at any given time; since Christ has ascended into heaven, he certainly could not also be physically present in the bread and wine. They spoke derogatorily of the Lutheran dogma of 'ubiquity', 'which turns the sacrament into a miracle and opens the doors to old heresies'.[37] 'Ubiquity', the Reformed claimed, is like a poison that destroys the Gospel message; it is a first step towards Catholic transubstantiation and amounts to a return to the 'magical consecration' of the 'papal mass'.[38]

The Lutheran communion 'contains still many papal superstitions, yet does not observe the things Christ instituted and ordered us to do', the Reformed charged.[39] One rite specifically commanded, but omitted by the Lutherans, was the *fractio panis*, the ceremonial breaking of the eucharistic bread for distribution. Hardly any other rite – except exorcism in baptism – caused more arguments between Lutherans and Reformed than did the fraction. The issue, according to Lazarus Theodorus, 'was not whether Christ had broken the bread in the first communion service, but whether the bread had to be broken in the Calvinistic manner . . . and whether Christ had instituted and ordered it'.[40] The Reformed definitely thought so; the Lutherans clearly did not.

---

[36] 'Konkordienformel: Solida Declaratio, VIII: Von der Person Christi', *Bekenntnisschriften*, p. 1043; English translation from Tappert, *Book of Concord*, pp. 606–7.

[37] Technically, the Lutheran position after 1577 is more properly described by the terms *ubivolopresence* or *multivolopresence*; see H. Sasse, *This is my Body* (Minneapolis, 1959), p. 341; and T. Mahlmann, *Das neue Dogma der lutherischen Christologie* (Gütersloh, 1969), pp. 222–3.

[38] Johann Bergius, *Dass die Wort Christi noch veste stehen/Für die wahre seligmachende Gemeinschafft seines Leibes und Blutes im Heiligen Abendmahl . . .* (Berlin, 1624), pp. 204–38.

[39] 'Johann Georg to Simon Gedicke, Cölln/Sp., 8 September 1613', Universitätsbibliothek Göttingen, Germany, Cod. MS. hist. 189, I, fo. 80.

[40] Lazarus Theodorus, *Synopsis doctrinae Lutheranae et Calvinianae* (Frankfurt an der Oder, 1615), pp. 166–7.

Calvinists called it a 'holy eternal order' which assures the faithful communicant that the Lord indeed was crucified for each and all penitent Christians.[41] 'With their theatrical fraction the Calvinists do not merely wish to break the bread, but signify the absent body and deny the real presence of Christ', the Lutherans charged, correctly.[42] The renowned Heidelberg theologian David Pareus, for instance, favoured the fraction as a symbolic denial of the Real Presence.[43] Thus the *fractio panis* became an issue among second and third-generation Protestants, precisely because it mirrored underlying confessional differences. In a very real and graphic manner, that even the most illiterate churchgoer could readily comprehend, it symbolised the religious difference between the two Protestant confessions.[44]

While the Reformed wanted to see the fraction restored, there were other parts in the Lutheran communion which they wished to eliminate. 'Such things as candles, pictures, albs, chasubles, and mass vestments generally, are useless and vain papal relics that deform the Lord's Supper more than they adorn it', they insisted.[45] 'God wants all popish idols to be eliminated, not only from our hearts, but from our sight as well', proclaimed Martin Füssel.[46] Since these continue to be used by papists for idolatrous purposes, they must be cast aside immediately.

Just as they wanted to cleanse the Lutheran eucharist, Calvinists sought to eliminate Catholic vestiges from the baptismal service. Here too, underlying theological differences were involved: while the Lutherans emphasised the washing away of the guilt of sin in the sacrament, the Reformed viewed baptism as a sign of divine forgiveness. 'The quarrel between you and us', observed Theodor Beza to Jacob Andreae at Montbéliard in 1586, 'is whether holy baptism is a bath of rebirth and renewal in the Holy Spirit, or whether it is simply a sign that signifies and

---

[41] Martin Füssel, *Ceremoniae Christianae. Das ist/Kurtzer Bericht Von Lehr und Ceremonien Der Reformirten Kirchen der Chur Brandenburg Entgegen gesetzt/denen Ceremoniis Lutheranis* . . . (Frankfurt an der Oder, 1616), pp. 33–5.

[42] Simon Gedicke, *Antipistorius, oder Widerlegung des Calvinischen Politici Simonis Ulrich Pistoris in Seuselitz* . . . (Leipzig, 1620); and Gedicke, *Von den Ceremonien bey dem Heiligen Abendmahl/Christlicher Bericht* . . . (Berlin, 1613). See also Theodorus, *Synopsis*, p. 174.

[43] Werner Elert, *Morphologie des Luthertums* (2 vols, Munich, 1958), II. 272. On liturgy and the Reformed understanding of Christ's presence in the eucharist, see also L. Palmer Wandel, 'Envisioning God: Image and Liturgy in Reformation Zurich', *SCJ*, 24 (1993), 20–40.

[44] For additional information, see B. Nischan, 'The "Fractio Panis": A Reformed Communion Practice in Late Reformation Germany', *CH*, 53 (1984), 17–29.

[45] Job Friederich, *Ein gar kurtzer Bericht Von dem heutigen Religionsstreit und ärgerlichem Gezänck der Praedicanten* . . . (Frankfurt an der Oder, 1616).

[46] Füssel, *Ceremoniae Christianae*, p. 2.

seals our filial relationship to God'.[47] Lutherans accused Calvinists of having turned the sacrament into an empty symbol; the Reformed retorted that the Lutheran understanding amounted to a Catholic view of the sacrament. Liturgically these differences manifested themselves in exorcism and private baptism. Lutherans permitted both; the Reformed did not. Martin Luther had retained the rite of exorcism in his *Taufbüchlein* (1526) as a powerful prayer whereby the child's sinfulness and total dependence on God's grace is acknowledged.[48] Owing to the reformer's tremendous authority, the rite continued to be part of most Lutheran baptismal offices. The Reformed, emulating Bucer, Zwingli and Calvin, uniformly condemned exorcism as a 'papal relic'. The rite, they insisted, 'falsely testifies against God's eternal covenant of grace which includes also the unborn fruit of Christian parents'.[49] Exorcism, therefore, amounted to nothing more than 'monkish hocus pocus' which suggested a Catholic *ex opere operato* view of the sacrament in which man rather than God is the actor.[50]

The Popular Response

As the fraction had in the communion service, so exorcism had come to symbolise underlying confessional differences. Obviously the Lutheran and Calvinist theologians, who were debating the issues, understood these and other ceremonial differences. But what about the laity, the common people, those second- and third-generation Protestants? How deeply were they affected by the changes wrought by the Reformation? Did they too see the fraction in the Lord's Supper, or exorcism in baptism and other liturgical differences as major issues, and if so, why?

Our evidence is mostly anecdotal, but does provide important clues.

---

[47] *Acta Colloquii Montis Belligartensis* (Tübingen, 1587), p. 758. On the colloquy, see also J. Raitt, *The Colloquy of Montbéliard: Religion and Politics in the Sixteenth Century* (New York and Oxford, 1993).

[48] See Martin Luther, 'Das Taufbüchlein aufs Neue zugerichtet (1526)', in *D. Martin Luthers Werke. Kritische Gesamtausgabe* (vols 1–, Weimar, 1883–), XIX. 537–41. English translation in *Luther's Works*, ed. J. Pelikan and H.T. Lehmann (55 vols, St Louis and Philadelphia, 1955–73). LIII. 106–9. On Luther's understanding of baptism, see L. Gronvik, *Die Taufe in der Theologie Martin Luthers* (Göttingen/Zurich, 1968); and J. Trigg, *Baptism in the Theology of Martin Luther* (Leiden, 1994).

[49] *Gründlicher Beweiss/das der Exorcismus bey der heiligen Tauff wider die fürnembsten Heuptstück des Catechismi streite . . .* (Zerbst, 1591).

[50] Theodorus, *Synopsis*, pp. 101-11. For additional information, see B. Nischan, 'The Exorcism Controversy and Baptism in the Late Reformation', *SCJ*, 18 (1987), 31–51; and H.O. Old, *The Shaping of the Reformed Baptismal Rite in the Sixteenth Century* (Grand Rapids, MI, 1992), esp. pp. 120, 176, 285.

Let us look first at baptism: in the early 1590s, when the rulers of Saxony and Anhalt attempted to Calvinise the churches in their realms, they began by prohibiting the use of exorcism. People were 'aghast', for the deletion of the rite suggested that 'all who had been baptised with exorcism, had submitted to an idolatrous, magical, and devilish' ceremony, reported Georg Lysthenius, superintendent at Weissenfels.[51] Attempts to expunge the rite in Saxony 'caused much clamour and had many serious repercussions', noted one contemporary observer.[52] Many pastors simply refused to cooperate when asked to delete it. One country parson feared that 'the peasants in his village would stone him and chase him away if he dared to change the customary baptismal order'. In Zeitz a riot broke out when the people learnt that their pastor had been instructed to omit exorcism. At Naumberg, more than 200 people walked out of the cathedral when a minister, who had deleted the rite, tried to deliver a sermon. People refused to take communion from him; meanwhile neighbouring churches, where exorcism continued to be used, were overcrowded with communicants. St Othmar's in the suburbs often 'was so full that the pastor had to force his way in'.[53] Undoubtedly one of the most spectacular incidents occurred in Dresden, where a butcher, determined to have his daughter baptised in the proper Lutheran manner, appeared in the Hofkirche armed with a meat cleaver. He positioned himself next to the baptismal font and threatened to split the minister's head if he dared to omit exorcism from the baptismal formula.[54] The baby girl, it seems safe to assume, was baptised in the proper Lutheran manner.

The people of neighbouring Anhalt did not resort to cutlery, but showed equal zeal in the defence of the Lutheran formula. The duchy's rulers, Joachim Ernst and his son Johann Georg, had abolished the exorcism rite in 1589, first in the cities of Zerbst and Dessau and then throughout the realm. Townspeople, pastors and especially the knights objected bitterly, noting that 'it created divisions in our churches and anguish in the hearts of many pious Christians' and, what was worse, probably marked the beginning of a series of reforms that ultimately

---

[51] Georg Lysthenius, *An das Consistorium zu Leipzig. Drey unterschiedliche Schreiben/als nemlich eine Recusatio, Protestatio, Refutatio . . . wegen der jtzigen newen Wittenberger Theologen* (Magdeburg, 1592), fo. Biia.

[52] *Kurtzer aber wahrhaffter gründlicher bericht/Von dem Christlichen Leben/vnd seligen abschied des Durchleuchtigsten/Hochgebornen Fürsten vnd Herrn/Herrn CHRISTIANI, weyland Hertzogen zu Sachen . . .* (Dresden, 1595), fo. Div[a].

[53] Konrad Memmius, *Jacobi Franci Relatio Historica Quinquennalis . . . Anno 1590 biss 1595 . . .* (Frankfurt am Main, 1595), pp. 87–89.

[54] T. Klein, *Der Kampf um die Zweite Reformation in Kursachsen, 1586-1591*, Mitteldeutsche Forschungen, vol. 25 (Cologne/Graz, 1962), 166.

would lead to the principality's complete Calvinisation.[55] 'Now they are eliminating exorcism from baptism, then the altars will have to go, thereafter pictures and paintings, and finally all organs and singing.'[56] The outcome, according to this confessional dynamo theory, would be the end of Lutheranism in Anhalt. Shortly afterwards, in 1596, the Lutherans' worst fears materialised when 'in Anhalt's churches all pictures, Latin hymns, chasubles, surplices, . . . and altars were removed; in the Lord's Supper common bread replaced communion wafers and the fraction was reintroduced . . . while Luther's catechism gave way to the Heidelberg catechism'.[57]

Similar sentiments were expressed further east in confessionally divided Danzig where exorcism became an issue in the 1570s when the pastor and deacon of St Bartelmes, Gregor Schütz and Johann Krosling, publicly started feuding over the rite. Most of the parishioners – they proudly called themselves the *pusillos Christi* or the 'small flock of sheep' – sided with Schütz who defended the rite as a good evangelical practice. St Bartelmes on the outskirts of Danzig, where he preached regularly, soon became too small to hold all the people who flocked there to hear him. Women especially favoured the rite and 'preached in favour of exorcism in many private homes'. The controversy increasingly divided the city, but was temporarily squelched when Danzig's magistrates intervened ordering all pastors to retain the rite.[58] Since the city remained confessionally divided, the issue was far from resolved. It kept smouldering and, not surprisingly, erupted again a few days later when Thomas Fabricus, pastor of St Mary's, abolished first the exorcism rite, then auricular confession, and shortly afterwards started to simplify the communion liturgy.[59] When Johann Sigismund of Brandenburg converted to Calvinism in 1613 and sought to eliminate exorcism and other 'papal

---

[55] *Erinnerungsschrift etlicher vom Adel und Städten/An den Durchleutigsten Hochgebornen Fürsten unnd Herrn/Herrn Johann Georgen/Fürsten zu Anhalt* . . . (Amberg, 1597), fos ii[b]–vi[a]; and Johann Olearius, (ed.), *Stattliches/aussführliches und gar bewegliches Schreiben Der löblichen Ritterschrift im Fürstenthumb Anhalt/so mit der Calvinischen Reformation nicht zu frieden* (Halle, 1598), fos 2[a]–26[b]. See also Johann Olearius, *Wider den Calvinistischen Grewel der Verwüstung in des Fürstenthumb Anhalts Kirchen* (Halle, 1597), pp. 95–98.

[56] *Vom Exorcismo. Das dieser ohne verletzung des gewissens bey der Tauffe wol mag gebraucht und behalten werden. Etliche Tractetlein* (Frankfurt an der Oder, 1590), Vorrede.

[57] Johann C. Beckmann, *Historie des Fürstenthums Anhalt* (2 vols, Zerbst, 1680/1716), part 6, 134.

[58] Reinhold Curicke, *Der Stadt Dantzig Historische Beschreibung* (Danzig, 1686 [the unabridged edition; located at the Biblioteka Gdanska in Gdansk, Poland]), pp. 325–6.

[59] Christoph Hartknoch, *Preussische Kirchen-Historia* (Frankfurt am Main/Leipzig, 1686), p. 769.

relics', the populace there too reacted violently. The people of ducal Prussia, which the Hohenzollerns ruled as a Polish fief, criticised their ruler's new Reformed minister, Johann Bergius, for baptising children without the customary rite, noting that this 'was contrary to the Prussian church order and the duchy's constitution'.[60] The superintendent of Tilsit defended exorcism as a mark which separated true Lutherans from Calvinists and other 'ceremonial iconoclasts'.[61] 'In and by itself [*extra controversiam*] exorcism is really a minor matter', observed Nikolaus Blum of Saxony. 'But this ceremony becomes an issue when the people scream that it is papal, idolatrous, magical and devilish rite . . . ; then it cannot be omitted with a good conscience.'[62]

Most of the popular opposition to the court-sponsored Calvinism, however, was provoked by the Reformed communion service. Georg Mylius, professor at Jena, reported that people reacted to Christian I's liturgical reforms in Saxony by simply staying at home:

> The churches were emptier than they had ever been in this land. . . . There are quite a few who had not heard a single sermon in a year, some not even for several years. In many localities there were children who had not been baptised even though they were several months old. . . . People had such contempt for their new [Reformed] pastors that they compared them to Jews or Turks . . . and named their dogs after them.[63]

The communion liturgy generally, and the *fractio panis* specifically, also became a lively issue in Danzig. Over the objections of some parishioners the Reformed had introduced the fraction in 1593 at Holy Trinity Church, but could not do so elsewhere 'for fear that the common citizenry, who remained committed to the Augsburg Confession, would not tolerate it'.[64] Popular opposition also prevented the Calvinists from carrying out other reforms. Thus when they disposed of the Marian altar at St Peter's – on the grounds that it was rotten, worm-eaten, dilapidated and therefore unsafe – and replaced it with a Reformed communion table, 'several journeyman and some common rabble with axes and other

---

[60] 'Oberräte to Elector Johann Sigismund, Königsberg, 21 December 1614', Geheimes Staatsarchiv Preussischer Kulturbesitz, Berlin, Germany, Ostpr. Fo. no. 1230, fo. 22.

[61] Philipp Arnoldi, *Caeremoniae Lutheranae. Das ist/Ein Christlicher Gründlicher Unterricht von allen fürnembsten Caeremonien, so in den Lutherischen Preussischen Kirchen/in verrichtung des Gottesdienstes/adhibirt werde* . . . (Königsberg, 1616), fo. Bi[a] and pp. 210–28.

[62] Nicolaus Blum, *Leichpredigt/Uber den Custodierten D. Nicolaum Krell, Welcher den Neundten Octobris/wegen seiner verbrechung . . . öffentlich in Dressden enthauptet worden/Anno Christi MDCI* . . . (Leipzig, 1602), p. 23.

[63] Georg Mylius, *Kurtze/Doch augenscheinliche/Entwerffung der Calvinischen Comoedien in Meissen* . . . (Jena, 1593), fos. Ei[a]–Ei[b].

[64] Hartknoch, *Kirchen-Historia*, pp. 761–2.

tools stormed the church to rip down and hack into pieces the new Calvinist altar'. At Holy Trinity, where Calvinists had nailed the altar wings shut, 'a large number of craftsmen broke into the church with axes and guns, climbed up on the altar, pried it open with their axes . . . and then left it unlocked' for all to see. Everybody in Danzig, it seemed, was talking about pictures and altars, 'the common burgher often so impassionedly that words led to fistfights'.[65] Even when they enjoyed their greatest influence in the Hanse city a decade later, the Reformed did not dare to 'change the ceremonies because they feared the people'.[66] Calvinists claimed that their ceremonial reforms aimed at the 'unvarnished gospel truth', observed Johann Walther; 'yet what they really bring us is nothing more than a cobbled together, embellished, painted, varnished, sickeningly sweet, [yet] abominable, loathsome, corrupt and depraved untruth'.[67] Similar sentiments were voiced in other Prussian towns. At Thorn, the local parson was forced into early retirement by his congregation because he had urged his city's magistrates to introduce the fraction.[68] At Elbing the populace rebelled when their pastor 'abolished many ceremonies and replaced them with Reformed ones'.[69] In Marienburg people protested when their minister, Joachim Wendland, 'did away with the priestly surplice and chasuble, and would not allow any pictures in churches, but had people sing Lobwasser's psalms. He also objected to communion wafers, condemned altars, redivided the ten commandments in the Reformed manner, and did many other strange things. But the congregation most objected when he introduced the fraction of the bread.'[70]

Similarly, in Hesse people reacted with outrage to Landgrave Moritz's comprehensive restructuring of worship in the summer of 1605. At first he had recommended the fraction as 'merely an adiaphoron' but shortly afterwards 'required the rite as a necessary ceremony'.[71] Contemporaries were not surprised by the popular reaction. 'It is well known how Herr

---

[65] Curicke, *Dantzig*, pp. 353–5.

[66] Hartknoch, *Kirchen-Historia*, p. 779.

[67] Johann Walther, *Widerlegung Des newlich publiccirten und aussgesprengten Famosslibells Iacobi Adami, Calvinischen Predigers in S. Elisabeth Kirchen/darinn Er alle reine Evangelische/Lutherische Prediger zu Dantzig/mit ungrund und unwarheit ansticht und beschuldiget . . .* (Leipzig, 1613), p. 133.

[68] Hartknoch, *Kirchen-Historia*, p. 894.

[69] Ibid., p. 1005.

[70] Ibid., p. 1073. For additional information on the second reformation in Prussia, see M.G. Müller, 'Zur Frage der Zweiten Reformation in Danzig, Elbing und Thorn', in Schilling (ed.), *Reformierte Konfessionalisierung*, pp. 251–65.

[71] Balthasar Mentzer, *Trophaeum Calvinisticum: Oder Herrliche Siegzeychen dero Calvinischen Newlicher Zeit zu Marpurg aussgeschreieten unnd beschriebenen Victorien, uber der Sacramentirischen Analogia dess Calvinischen Brotbrechens . . .* (Giessen, 1608?), pp. 6 and 8.

Omnes will respond to such unnecessary innovations in church ceremonies . . . , especially when he suspects that they serve as a pretext for
false doctrine and error. The resulting tumult and rebellion [in August
1605] therefore should have come as no surprise', observed one
Lutheran.[72] People were convinced 'that a new creed, with a novel set of
commandments, a different baptism and communion . . . were about to
be introduced', admitted Moritz's Reformed advisors.[73] And, like the
Lutherans, they treated the *fractio panis* as a signal mark of the confession they were trying to establish in Hesse. After the suppressing of the
revolt, they therefore redoubled their efforts 'to instruct the common
man about the fraction ceremony, convince him, and liberate him from
evil and false preconceived suspicions'.[74]

While popular opposition could not stop Moritz from carrying out his
reforms in Hesse, it did block Elector Johann Sigismund's second reformation in Brandenburg. Here too the sacrament of the altar and its attendant ritual became the centre of much controversy and popular
opposition. Where the Reformed communion was introduced after 1613
in Brandenburg, disturbances often ensued. 'The common man',
observed one of the elector's Reformed councillors, 'was especially disturbed by the elimination of papal ceremonies in the Lord's Supper
which up to now had been retained and tolerated in our churches'.[75] In
some towns 'artisans mocked and ridiculed the Reformed by spreading
their coats on public streets and openly reenacting the fraction of the
bread'.[76] At Stendal 'they lampooned the Lord's Supper, as it was cus-
tomarily celebrated by His Electoral Highness and other Reformed, by
turning it into a carnival play'.[77] The centre of controversy here was one

---

[72] Helwig Garthe (ed.), *Gründlicher Ausführlicher Historischer Bericht Von dem Religionswesen im Fürstenthumb Hessen . . .* (Wittenberg, 1606), p. 296. On the 1605 uprising, see also Heinrich Leuchtner et al., *Nohtwendige Erzehlung/Der Motiven und Ursachen/warumb die zu Marpurg im Monat Iulio Anni 1605 beurlaubte Theologi und Prediger . . . die Ceremonien dess Brotbrechens im H. Abendmal . . . anzunemen sich bil-lich verweigert haben* (Giessen, 1606), pp. 54–73; and Wilhelm Dilich, *Hessische Chronica . . . aufs new übersehen/corrigiret und verbessert . . .* (2 vols, Kassel, 1608), II. 353–4.

[73] *Historischer Bericht/Der Newlichen Monats Augusti zugetragenen Kirchenhändel . . .* (Marburg, 1605), p. 19.

[74] Ibid., p. 37. On the second reformation in Hesse, see also G. Menk, 'Absolutistisches Wollen und verfremdete Wirklichkeit – der calvinistische Sonderweg Hessen-Kassels' in M. Schaab (ed.), *Territorialstaat und Calvinismus* (Stuttgart, 1993), pp. 164–238.

[75] Friederich, *Kurtzer Bericht.*

[76] Daniel H. Hering, *Verbesserungen und Zusätze zur Historischen Nachricht vom dem ersten Anfang der evangelisch-reformierten Kirche in Brandenburg und Preussen* (Halle, 1783), p. 62.

[77] 'Friederich Pruckmann to Johann Sigismund, Cölln/Sp. 22 October 1614', Zentrales Staatsarchiv, Merseburg, Germany (cited hereafter as ZStA), Rep. 47.16, fo. 163.

Peter Giessen, the town's newly appointed Reformed pastor. People jeered him in public, disturbed his sleep at night, and generally made life miserable for him through all sorts of mischievous tricks, at one point, for instance, 'even tying a horse by its tail to his door'. The agitation against Giessen crested when 'people ran through the streets at night with burning torches' mocking his faith and satirising the Reformed communion service.[78] Violence also erupted in the town of Küstrin where an aroused populace pelted the elector's new Reformed court pastors with rocks, snowballs and curses.[79] At Beelitz a riot broke out when the church organist dared to play a Reformed communion hymn (by Ambrosius Lobwasser); in the mêlée one of the Lutheran vigilantes threw a candelabra at the organist, 'missing him, but hitting and nearly killing his wife'.[80] And in Berlin, capital of Brandenburg, a major riot erupted in the spring of 1615 when the electoral court ordered the 'removal from the cathedral of all epitaphs, crucifixes, pictures, both altars . . . and the baptismal font.'[81] The enraged mob ransacked and looted the homes of the elector's new Reformed preachers. One of them, Martin Füssel, whom many blamed for the elector's apostasy to Calvinism, barely escaped alive. He was able to salvage only what he wore when he fled, so that for Good Friday services later that week, he appeared 'in the pulpit wearing only a green vest, his underwear, stockings, and a gown which he had borrowed'.[82]

These incidents – in Saxony, Anhalt, Brandenburg and Prussia – are significant because they illustrate how ceremony and liturgy in the late Reformation were treated as marks of confessional identity by both the religious leaders and the common people. Significantly, the Lord's Supper and the manner in which it was being celebrated remained, for Lutherans as much as for Calvinists and Catholics, the litmus test of confessional loyalty. People might not comprehend the subtle arguments of the theologians, but they certainly recognised the *fractio panis* as a Reformed ritual that suggested a Calvinist understanding of the sacrament just as they viewed exorcism as part of the Lutheran baptismal office.

---

[78] Johann C. Beckmann, *Historische Beschreibung der Chur und Mark Brandenburg* (2 vols, Berlin, 1751–53), II. 237–8.

[79] 'Johann Sigismund to Hauptmann of Küstrin, 3 February 1614', ZStA Rep. 47.16, fo. 43.

[80] 'Privy Councillors to Johann Sigismund, 23 March 1617', ZStA Rep. 47.16, ff. 271–2.

[81] *Collectio opusculorum historiam Marchicam illustrantium*, ed. Georg Küster (4 vols, Berlin, 1727–36), IV. 62.

[82] D.H. Hering, *Historische Nachricht von dem ersten Anfang der Evangelisch-Reformierten Kirche in Brandenburg* (Halle, 1778), p. 290. For a more detailed discussion of popular opposition to the second reformation in Brandenburg, see B. Nischan, *Prince, People, and Confession: The Second Reformation in Brandenburg* (Philadelphia, 1994), pp. 185–203.

The Reformation, these findings suggest, indeed did have a significant impact on people's religious awareness and perceptions. Not only the intellectual and governing elites, the common people too, it seems, had by the end of the century begun to develop a sense of denominational identity. In fact, people's confessional awareness at times could and did lead to excesses and misunderstandings, as was the case in 1593 at Peltzig in Saxony. There the newly appointed Lutheran pastor, Johann Heckelt, eager to stamp out all remaining vestiges of Calvinism and anything which earlier had contributed to its rise in Saxony, 'secretly removed' from the local church a painting of Philip Melanchthon whom many Lutherans now viewed as a crypto-Calvinist. But instead of applauding this as a demonstration of confessional orthodoxy, the townspeople and magistrates, who had not been consulted, interpreted it as a sign of sacramentarian iconoclasm. 'They were furious and demanded that the pastor return the painting to its accustomed place.'[83] No doubt, politics – the rivalry between the pastor and Peltzig city council – played a role in this dispute as it did in many other religious controversies of the period. But this in no way diminishes the importance of the confessional issue which clearly was the catalyst that had induced this confrontation.[84]

Such awareness of denominational identity in Germany continued to grow well into the seventeenth century, but then started to weaken during the Thirty Years' War. The war in which Emperor Ferdinand II's Catholic absolutism threatened Lutherans and Reformed alike with annihilation, encouraged both to focus less on their separate confessional identities and more on their common Protestant heritage. The flowering of pietism after the war, followed by rationalism at the end of the century, further helped break down the confessional barriers of the late Reformation, turning German Lutherans and Reformed into modern Protestants, *Evangelische,* as they call themselves to this day.

---

[83] Konrad Memmius, *Historiae Relationis Continuatio . . . Anno 1593* (Frankfurt am Main, 1593), fo. 9a; see also Memmius, *Relatio Historica Quinquennalis* (1595), p. 332.

[84] Note D. Döring, 'Ein bisher unbekannter Bericht über den "Calvinistensturm" vom 19/20.5. 1593 in Leipzig', *ARG,* 85 (1994), 205–19.

CHAPTER TEN

The Historiographical Origins of Calvinist Millenarianism

Howard Hotson

As befitted members of a movement which derives its name from protest, sixteenth-century Protestants often showed more unanimity in what they condemned than in what they professed. A good example of this tendency is their virtually unanimous rejection of the doctrine of millenarianism. By mid-century, all three main Protestant confessions had formally condemned it – Lutherans in the Augsburg Confession of 1530, the English in the Forty-Two Articles of Religion of 1552, and the Reformed in the Second Helvetic Confession of 1566 – and for the remainder of the century little dissent from this was raised by serious Protestant theologians.[1] So fully does it seem to have passed outside the ambit of theological debate, that in the concluding article of the Formula of Concord of 1577, where the numerous marginal heresies which had disturbed Lutheranism during the previous generation are gathered together and condemned, millenarianism is not even mentioned.[2]

If we turn to the seventeenth century, however, the situation becomes suddenly quite different. As early as 1613 we find it forcefully if briefly advocated by Johannes Piscator, the first man since Luther to translate the entire Bible into German and one of Reformed Germany's leading exegetes. In 1627 two classic expositions of it appeared simultaneously from two of the most universally learned Calvinists of their generation, Johann Heinrich Alsted in Herborn and Joseph Mede in Cambridge. And in the decades which followed, it attracted the attention of many of the greatest philosophers, pedagogues, poets and politicians of the Reformed world.[3]

---

[1] *Die Bekenntnisschriften der evangelischen-lutherischen Kirche* (2nd edn, Göttingen, 1952), 'Die Augsburghische Konfession', article 17, p. 72. *Die Bekenntnisschriften der reformierten Kirche*, ed. E. F. Karl Müller (Leipzig, 1903), 'Forty-Two Articles', article lxi, p. 521.30–35; *Confessio helvetica posterior*, article xi, p. 185.3–7.

[2] *Bekenntnisschriften der evangelischen-lutherischen Kirche*, 'Formula Concordiae', article xii, pp. 822–7. Cf. Johannes Wallmann, 'Zwischen Reformation und Pietismus: Reich Gottes und Chiliasmus in der lutherischen Orthodoxie', in Eberhard Jüngel, Johannes Wallmann and Wilfrid Werbeck (eds), *Verifikation. Festschrift für Gerhard Ebeling zum 70. Geburtstag* (Tübingen, 1982), pp. 187–205, here pp. 188–9.

[3] Piscator, *In Apocalypsin commentarius* (Herborn, 1613), esp. pp. 202–6, 246–59;

How did this transformation come about? Surprisingly, the question has been little studied. While scores of scholars have traced the influence of millenarianism on political and intellectual developments throughout the Calvinist world from the seventeenth century to the present day, its origins have yet to be systematically studied. The most extensive treatments of the subject are still to be found in general surveys of the English apocalyptic tradition,[4] and no sustained attention has been given to the complex nexus of exegetical, theological, philosophical, and historiographical problems raised by it. The problem is in fact far too complex and fraught with misconceptions even to be outlined here. Rather, this chapter offers a preliminary sketch of only one of these aspects as the first instalment of what is hoped will become a general investigation of the problem.

Millenarianism, strictly defined, is the expectation that the vision described in the twentieth chapter of the Book of Revelation of a thousand-year period in which Satan is bound and the saints reign is a prophecy which will be fulfilled literally, on earth, and in the future. It seems only self-evident, therefore, to seek the origins of the revival of millenarianism in burgeoning aspirations and brightening hopes for the terrestrial future. A number of influences, including the sociology of religion, the history of ideas, Marxist historiography, and cultural anthropology, have tended to encourage this approach; and most of the limited discussion of this problem to date has tended to adopt it.[5] It may

---

reprinted in *Commentarii in omnes libros Novi Testamenti* (Herborn, 1621), here pp. 1567–71, 1580–84. Alsted, *Diatribe de mille annis apocalyptics* (Herborn, 1627, 1630); German trans. by Sebastian Franck (Frankfurt, 1630); English trans. by William Burton, *The beloved city* (London, 1643). Mede, *Clavis apocalyptica* (Cambridge, 1627; revised 1632; frequently reprinted); English trans. by Richard More, *The Key of the Revelation* (London, 1643).

[4] Bryan W. Ball, *A great expectation: eschatological thought in English Protestantism to 1660* (Leiden, 1975), pp. 155–92; Richard Bauckham, *Tudor apocalypse: sixteenth century apocalypticism, millenarianism and the English Reformation* (Oxford, 1978), pp. 208–32; Katharine R. Firth, *The apocalyptic tradition in Reformation Britain, 1530-1645* (Oxford, 1979), pp. 204–54. Cf. Peter Toon (ed.), *Puritans, the millennium and the future of Israel* (Cambridge/London, 1970).

[5] The first influence derives from the tendency, stemming from Ernst Troeltsch, Max Weber, Richard Tawney and Robert K. Merton, to view Calvinism as a progressive ideology which helped to give rise to capitalism, democracy and modern science. See for instance I. Bernard Cohen (ed.), *Puritanism and the rise of modern science: the Merton thesis* (London/New York, 1990). Prominent illustrations of the other three are Ernest Lee Tuveson, *Millennium and Utopia: a study in the background of the idea of progress* (Berkeley/Los Angeles, 1949; New York, 1964); E.J. Hobsbawm, *Primitive Rebels* (New York, 1959); William M. Lamont, *Godly rule: politics and religion, 1603–60* (London, 1969). All the studies listed in the previous note, to one degree or another, fall prey to this easy assumption.

seem perverse, on the other hand, to search for the origins of Calvinist millenarianism in beliefs regarding the past. But the reasons for doing so are more compelling than they might at first seem. If the general surveys of English apocalypticism have told us anything, it is that millenarianism emerged from an exegetical and historiographical tradition which placed the millennium, not in the future, as the patristic millenarians had done, nor in the present, as the standard medieval interpretation maintained, but firmly in the past. One strand of the Calvinist revival of millenarianism can therefore be sought in the gradual exposure of the weaknesses of that tradition.

Before we can uncover its potential weaknesses, we must discover the basic logic which led most Protestants to place the millennium in the past. Like many of the most fundamental arguments underlying any cultural tradition, this logic was rarely if ever fully articulated by contemporaries. But its dominance of contemporary thinking is probably best explained by the fact that it derived directly from the central apocalyptic insight of the earliest reformers: the 'discovery' of Antichrist in the papacy. Although poorly studied outside English-language historiography, this idea played a role in contemporary Protestant thought which must not be underestimated.[6] Theologically, it comprehended the entire scope of Reformation protest in condemning the authority which ultimately guaranteed the non-scriptural doctrines and practices which Protestants rejected. Historically, it provided an urgently needed explanation of the defection of the established church from the Protestant understanding of the Gospel. Psychologically, it stiffened the Protestant revolt by placing it at the culmination of the cosmic struggle between God and Satan. Sociologically, it represented the apotheosis of late medieval anticlericalism, extending it to the apex of the clerical hierarchy and legitimising it in the strongest possible terms. Finally, nothing could have lent itself more readily to graphic representation, vivid dramatisation or popular comprehension than the simple dualism of Christ and Antichrist, which quickly established itself as 'one of the most lasting and

---

[6] The most comprehensive study remains Hans Preuss, *Die Vorstellungen vom Antichrist im späteren Mittelalter, bei Luther und in der konfessionalen Polemik* (Leipzig, 1906). An excellent more recent overview is Gottfried Seebass, 'Antichrist IV: Reformations- und Neuzeit', *TRE*, III (Berlin, 1978), 28–43. On the Continent, the most thoroughly studied aspect of this tradition is the crucial case of Luther, notably as integrated into Heiko A. Oberman's biography, *Luther: Mensch zwischen Gott und Teufel* (Berlin, 1982), English trans. by E. Walliser-Schwarzbart (London, 1989); most recently in William R. Russell, 'Martin Luther's understanding of the pope as Antichrist', *ARG*, 85 (1994), 32–44. For the English case, see Christopher Hill, *Antichrist in Seventeenth-century England* (London, 1971).

effective creations of evangelical propaganda'.[7] Wherever the Protestant rejection of the Roman church spread, therefore, the notion of the papal Antichrist spread with it, not least because it was one of the most potent bearers of that message. In a wide range of documents – including Melanchthon's apology for the Augsburg Confession, Luther's Schmalkald Articles, and confessions of the Bohemian Brethren and the English, Scottish and Irish churches – we find the identification of the papacy as the Antichrist treated as an article of faith.[8]

The 'discovery' of Antichrist in the papacy had direct implications for Protestants' understanding of their place in sacred history. A network of scattered biblical passages associated the figure of Antichrist with a final, terrible phase of apostasy and persecution which would be dramatically cut short by the coming of Christ in Judgement. One of the most vivid descriptions of this final period is in Revelation 20, where Satan, released from a thousand years of imprisonment, incites the nations to wage war against the saints, but is consumed by fire from heaven as Christ descends in Judgement. In Augustine's *City of God*, this brief period of Satan's release from bondage is explicitly identified with the final persecution of Antichrist; and in the dominant medieval tradition which derived from him, the reign of Antichrist was almost invariably situated in the brief interval between the end of the millennium and the Second Advent.[9] The further identification of the Antichrist with the papacy required, of course, the modification of the received interpretation in several important respects. The figure of Antichrist was expanded from a single son of

---

[7] R.W. Scribner, *For the sake of simple folk: popular propaganda for the German Reformation* (Cambridge, 1981), esp. pp. 148–89, here p. 149. The most famous example is of course the *Passional Christi und Antichristi*, reproduced in Luther, *Werke* (Weimar, 1888–; hereafter *WA*), IX. 677–715. For drama, see Ranier Pineas, *Tudor and early Stuart anti-Catholic drama* (Nieuwkoop, 1972) and Klaus Aichele, *Das Antichristdrama des Mittelalters, der Reformation und Gegenreformation* (The Hague, 1974). Even music proved an appropriate medium: *Der lxxix. Psalm, sein kurtz und rund in Reime gebracht, itzt in dieser letzten . . . zeit . . . zu singen, wider den Antichrist*, trans. J. Feder (n.p., 1546); Camillus Pulsictus, *Expositionis Psalmorum David omnium contra Antichristum . . . liber primus (-quintus)*(Venice, 1628).

[8] *Die Bekenntnisschriften der evangelischen-lutherischen Kirche*, pp. 234, 239–40, 246, 300, 364, 424, 430; cf. pp. 484–9, 488–9. *Die Bekenntnisschriften der reformierten Kirche*, ed. Müller, pp. 263.38–264.38, 536.31, 599.11; cf. pp. 32.16, 290.15, 666.7.

[9] The key passages are Matt. 24 (cf. Mark 13, Luke 21); 2 Thess. 2:3–11; 1 Tim. 4:13; 2 Tim. 3:1–5; 1 John 2:18, 22, 4:3; 2 John 7; and several passages from Revelation, esp. 20:7–10. On the received interpretation, see Augustine, *De civitate Dei*, XX. 12, 13 (*Corpus Christianorum Series Latina*, hereafter *CCSL*, XLVII. 721.9, 721.1); Bede, *De temporum ratione*, 71 (*Patrologia Latina*, ed. J. P. Migne, xc, 576–8); Kenneth Emmerson, *Antichrist in the middle ages* (Manchester, 1981), e.g. pp. 42, 56–7, 85, 86, 87, 129, 163, 167, 234; Bernard McGinn, 'Angel pope and papal antichrist', *CH*, 47 (1978), 155–73; and Gustav Adolf Benrath, 'Antichrist III. Alte Kirche und Mittelalter', *TRE*, III. 24–8.

Satan to an entire institution; his reign was extended from a mere three and a half years to a span of several centuries; and the millennium itself correspondingly contracted from the indefinite interval between the Advent of Christ and that of Antichrist to an identifiable historical period of a literal one thousand years. But the basic logical and chronological relationships between the millennium, the Antichrist, and the Second Advent remained essentially unchanged. Within the context of the received tradition within which Protestants worked, the appearance of the Antichrist could only mean that the millennium was over.

The Protestant reformers were not of course the first to associate the papacy with Antichrist: they themselves were fond of citing figures ranging from Dante, Petrarch and Bernard of Clairveaux to Joachim of Fiore, Savonarola, Wyclif and Hus.[10] Nor were they the first to unfold the implications of this identification for their understanding of the millennium. We find the idea that the millennium is over adumbrated in the late Middle Ages by Beguines, spiritual Franciscans and other heretics and papal critics, most notably John Wyclif.[11] It was from Wyclif's work that John Bale, the founder of the English Protestant apocalyptic tradition, derived the idea; and from Bale and a fifteenth-century Lollard treatise that the great English martyrologist, John Foxe, seems to have acquired it.[12] The Lollard *Commentarius in Apocalypsin*, which prompted Luther's reconsideration of the Book of Revelation and which he subsequently edited, argued that Satan had been loosed in 1033, one thousand years after the Resurrection and a similar interpretation can be found in Luther's writings.[13] Supported by authorities such as these and above all by the almost irresistible logic of the argument itself, this position became the basis of a remarkably broad consensus. Wherever the

---

[10] On Dante, see Piero Chiminelli, *La fortuna di Dante nella cristianità riformata* (Rome, 1921). On Joachim, see Marjorie Reeves, *The influence of prophecy in the latter middle ages: a study in Joachimism* (Oxford, 1969), pp. 107–8. On Savonarola, see Bruce Gordon's contribution in Volume 1 (Chapter 7). In general, see Emmerson, *Antichrist in the middle ages*, pp. 69–71, 206–7; Bauckham, *Tudor apocalypse*, pp. 103, 111–12; Ball, *A great expectation*, p. 132 n. 57; Firth, *Apocalyptic tradition*, p. 86.

[11] Bernard McGinn, *Visions of the end: apocalyptic traditions in the middle ages* (New York, 1979), index *s.n.* 'Antichrist'. Wyclif, *De solutione Satanae*, in *John Wyclif's Polemical Works in Latin*, ed. Rudolf Buddensieg (2 vols, London, 1883), II. 391–400.

[12] Bale, *The image of bothe churches*, in *The selected works of John Bale*, ed. Henry Christmas (Cambridge, 1849), p. 560. Foxe, *Actes and monuments* (London, 1563), p. 452. Cf. Bauckham, *Tudor apocalypse*, p. 74; Firth, *Apocalyptic tradition*, p. 47.

[13] *Commentarius in Apocalypsin ante centum annos aeditus*, ed. Martin Luther (Wittenberg, 1528), fo. 170ʳ. Luther's preface is WA, XXVI. 121–4. Cf. his *Vorrede auff die offenbarung S. Johannis* (1530), WA, *Die deutsche Bibel*, VII. 414.18–21, 416.29–38; *Supputatio annorum mundi* (1541), WA, LIII. 152–3; and Harvey Buchanan, 'Luther and the Turks, 1519–1529', *ARG*, 47 (1956), 145–50.

reformers' message spread, the notion of the papal Antichrist followed in its train; and wherever the latter idea established itself, the idea of a past millennium was almost bound to follow. Not all Protestants who condemned the papacy as Antichrist were equally outspoken regarding the millennium, but those who were almost invariably regarded it as a thousand-year period in the past history of the church.[14]

In what ways might the logic of this received opinion of a past millennium have been called into question? The most obvious question posed by this doctrine concerns the chronological location of the millennium. If the millennium represents a finite period of one thousand years in the past history of the church, then which period was it? The parameters within which exegetes could operate were relatively narrow: the *terminus a quo* was the Nativity of Christ and *terminus ad quem*, the discovery of Antichrist by the forerunners of the Reformation around AD 1300. It is not surprising, therefore, that within these relatively narrow parameters two basic hypotheses emerged: one beginning the millennium from about the time of the former *terminus*, the other ending it about the time of the latter one. Since the basic logic supporting these positions and the problems posed by them were somewhat different, it is best to consider them separately with reference to a few prominent examples, beginning with the more obvious of the two – the latter.

A classic instance of the latter interpretation of the millennium is the editions of Foxe's *Actes and Monuments* published in 1570 and thereafter, together with his *Eicasmi seu Meditationes in sacram Apocalypsin* of 1587. The most prominent of several periodisations expounded within those works is Foxe's division of the history of the Christian church into three main periods: two great periods of persecution bracketing a millennium of relative peace and security c. AD 300–1300. The first period of persecution under the pagan emperors lasts 294 years and comprises the ten great persecutions of the ancient church. The millennium of freedom from persecution, established by Constantine in the fourth century, ends with the loosing of Satan and the revival of persecution with Wyclif in the

---

[14] Ball, *A great expectation*, pp. 161–4, 276, mentions Arthur Dent, Hugh Broughton, Patrick Forbes and David Pareus. To this list could be added Sebastian Meyer, the mature John Bale, John Foxe, John Napier, Rudolph Hospinianus, John Prideaux, the young Alsted and a number of other writers. The few Protestant millenarians of the mid-sixteenth century (Franciscus Lambert, Coelio Secundo Curione, Giacopo Brocardo, Martin Cellarius-Borrhaus, Alfonsus Conradus of Mantua) are the exceptions which prove the rule: they were mostly ex-Franciscans or Italian converts and without exception operated within a Joachimist rather than an Augustinian frame of reference. See for instance Delio Cantimori, *Eretici italiani del cinquecento* (Florence, 1939); Reeves, *The influence of prophecy*, pp. 464–5, 481–3, 494–9; Bauckham, *Tudor apocalyptic*, pp. 24–5, 27–9, 213–21; Arno Seifert, 'Reformation und Chiliasmus: Die Rolle des Martin Cellarius-Borrhaus', *ARG*, 77 (1986), pp. 226–64, esp. pp. 251–5.

fourteenth. The ensuing second great period of oppression under the Antichrist is likewise destined to comprise ten persecutions and perhaps also to last 294 years, and will be followed immediately by the Second Coming and Last Judgement.[15]

The principal virtue of this dating of the millennium was its clarity, simplicity, and elegant symmetry. These characteristics derived from the simultaneous rejection of two of Augustine's major innovations in interpreting the millennium: not only did Foxe regard it as a literal thousand-year period; he also defined it in concrete, external, and therefore readily identifiable terms: the millennium for Foxe was a thousand-year period of relative freedom from persecution. In developing this view, Foxe's model was clearly Eusebius of Caesarea. Eusebius had not only written the classic history of the ten great persecutions of antiquity; he had also described the transformation wrought by Constantine in quasi-millenarian language.[16] The English martyrologist saw his task as complementing that of his great ancient predecessor and adapted the basic features of Eusebius's approach: he began the millennium, not from Christ, as Augustine had, but from Constantine; and he defined it in objective, demonstrable, external terms as a period of absence from persecution. It is therefore not inappropriate to term this first Protestant strategy in interpreting the millennium a modified Eusebian approach, modified that is by explicitly recognising the period after Constantine as the millennium and by restricting that period to a literal thousand years.

The admirable clarity and simplicity of Foxe's approach was not however without a serious disadvantage: it was vulnerable to disconfirmation of an equally straightforward empirical kind. Accumulating instances of ecclesiastical persecution, oppression, and suppression of the Gospel threatened to call it into question and it could thus be readily undermined by the advance of historical knowledge. Such accumulation was evident within Foxe's great work itself. The Latin editions of 1554 and 1559 opened with the persecution of Wyclif. The first English edition of 1563

---

[15] Foxe, *Actes and monuments* (2 vols, London, 1570), I. 1, 49, 120, 139, 144, 493–4, 909–10. Cf. the 1576 edn, pp. 101–2, and Bauckham, *Tudor apocalypse*, pp. 73–90, 221–4. The most recent discussion is Palle J. Olsen, 'Was John Foxe a millenarian?', *JEH*, 45 (1994), 600–624, here esp. pp. 606–10.

[16] Eusebius, *Tricennial orations*, esp. XVI. 3–8. Cf. *Ecclesiastical history*, X. 9; (*Patrologia Graeca*, ed. J.-P. Migne, XX. 1421–6, 901–6), and H.A. Drake, *In praise of Constantine: a historical study and new translation of Eusebius' Tricennial Orations* (Berkeley/Los Angeles/London, 1976), pp. 5–6, 51, 120–21. In dedicating the 1563 edition, Foxe presented himself as a Eusebius to Queen Elizabeth, who like Constantine had ended a great period of persecution. The first 135 pages of the 1570 edition are based closely on Eusebius. See William Haller, *Foxe's Book of Martyrs and the elect nation* (London, 1563), pp. 124, 130, 167–8.

added an 85 page preamble treating the earlier period, especially that after AD 1000. By 1570 this had expanded to over 1 000 folio columns, three-quarters of which were devoted to the period of the millennium itself. Foxe's increasingly convoluted attempts to work out a satisfactory chronology for this period are eloquent testimony to the problems this new material raised. Moreover, this first, historiographical problem was exacerbated by a second, exegetical one. The Apocalypse defined the millennium not in terms of an absence of persecution but as a period in which Satan was bound 'that he should deceive the nations no more' and in which the saints and martyrs 'lived and reigned with Christ' (Revelation 20:3–4). 'On any Protestant view', as Richard Bauckham has commented, 'the nations had been thoroughly deceived by both Islam and popery long before 1300: what began with Wyclif was their undeception rather than their deception'.[17]

The problems posed by this modified Eusebian conception of the millennium led directly to the intermediate attempts pursued around the turn of the century to salvage the notion of a past millennium without fully subscribing to a future one. A minor but revealing example is the exegetical efforts of Erasmus Williams. Williams shared with Foxe the view that the millennium was a literal period of one thousand years inaugurated by Constantine; but aware as he was of the defections, corruptions and persecutions of the ensuing period, he could not accept that the *following* period of one thousand years was the millennium. His solution to this problem was to assume that the millennium, although a literal period of one thousand years, was not a continuous period. Only the first quarter of this period had been played out after Constantine; the remaining 750 years of peace and prosperity for the church on earth were to be awaited in the future.[18]

A much more thoroughgoing attempt to avoid the historiographical and exegetical problems inherent in Foxe's interpretation was advanced by John Napier. Napier's basic innovation was to seek the defining characteristic of the millennium, not at the beginning of the period, but at its end. Foxe, rather inconsistently, had identified the foundation of the Ottoman Empire in 1300, rather than any episode in the history of papal persecution, as the event which marks the release of Satan from bondage.[19] From this identification Napier derived a new criterion to characterise the millennium: the absence, not of persecution, but of universal war.

---

[17] Bauckham, *Tudor apocalypse*, p. 222.

[18] Williams, 'Expositio revelationis sancti Joannis theologi', Bodleian Library, Oxford, MS Rawlinson A. 439; as discussed in Bauckham, *Tudor apocalypse*, p. 223.

[19] Foxe, *Actes and monuments* (1570), pp. 871-916; Olsen, 'Was John Foxe a millenarian?', pp. 608–9.

The exegetical basis of this interpretation was surprisingly firm. Revelation 20:7–8 prophesied that 'when the thousand years are expired, Satan shall be loosed out of prison, and shall go out to deceive the nations which are in the four quarters of the earth, Gog and Magog, to gather them together to battle'. In this passage, 'to deceive the nations' is the grammatical equivalent of 'to gather them together to battle'. By parity of logic, the binding of Satan that he might 'deceive the nations no more' could be interpreted as preventing him from stirring up universal warfare. 'Gog' and 'Magog', the nations which Satan deceives, had been identified by Luther, Bullinger, Bale and the Geneva Bible as the 'open' and 'secret' enemies of the church, and Napier followed this well-established Protestant tradition in identifying them as the Turk and the pope. Since the foundation of the Ottoman Empire and its assault on the eastern frontiers of Europe in 1300, therefore, Gog and Magog, the Turk and the pope, were engaged in a universal war in comparison with which, Napier maintained, 'all small civill warres, skirmishings and incursions, that occurred during these [previous] thousand yeares, were thought nothing but peace'. It was from stirring up such universal wars 'that *Sathan* was bound and restrained al the former 1 000 years, and not from stirring up of errors, heresies, martydom, and provincial warfare'. 'The Devils bondage a thousand yeares is no waies els', Napier concluded,'but from stirring up of univesall warres among the nations'.[20]

The historiographical advantages of this exegesis were no less attractive. Napier had defined the millennium in even more external terms than Foxe: his criterion was essentially secular and political rather than ecclesiastical, and its main protagonist was an alien interloper from outside the Christian world. This left Napier in perfect freedom to acknowledge the accumulating evidence of serious imperfections within the early as well as the late medieval church. The result, however, was the virtual inversion of the received notion of the millennium. It was not the saints who ruled the established church, in Napier's account, but the Antichrist. Satan may have been restrained, but during the entire millennium the Antichrist acted 'as his Lieftennant'. Persecution, therefore, far from being absent, became a characteristic feature of Napier's millennium: the martyrs who lived and reigned with Christ were those slain by Antichrist

[20] Napier, *A plaine discovery of the whole Revelation of Saint John* (Edinburgh, 1593), esp. pp. 59–64, 231–43; here pp. 64, 63. Accounts of Napier's interpretation include Ball, *A great expectation*, pp. 80–82; Firth, *Apocalyptic tradition*, pp. 132–49; R.G. Clouse, 'John Napier and apocalyptic thought', *SCJ* 5 (1974), 101–14; Paul Christianson, *Reformers and Babylon: English apocalyptic visions from the Reformation to the eve of the civil war* (Toronto, 1978), pp. 97–100; A. Williamson, *Scottish national consciousness in the age of James VI* (Edinburgh, 1979), esp. pp. 21–30. On Gog and Magog, see Bauckham, *Tudor apocalypse*, pp. 98, 110 47–8.

during the millennium for refusing to worship the beast or his image, who had already joined Christ in heaven. Meanwhile, the vast majority of contemporary souls were spiritually dead and 'lived not again until the thousand years were finished'. Stranger still, it was only upon Satan's release that these diabolical spiritual conditions began to improve:

> the whol outward visible church lay whollie as dead, and corrupted with Papisticall errours, and began not to bee raised up nor quickened by the word of life, till after the yeare of God, a thousande three hundred when that al these thousande yeares were outrun, and then began mo and moe to rise dayly from their former Antichristian errours.[21]

Advertently or not, Napier had turned the received conception of the millennium on its head. The thousand-year reign of the saints, as he described it, is not the best period of church history but the worst, and the loosing of Satan paradoxically marks a spiritual change for the better. Such an inversion of the very nature of the millennium arguably represents a more radical departure from established exegesis than millenarianism itself. It is doubtful whether the Laird of Merchiston fully grasped the consequences of his innovation, still more so whether he was enough of a theologian to defend them. Napier's secularisation of the defining characteristic of the millennium nimbly eluded exegetical and historiographical difficulties but crashed headlong into theological absurdities.

The resolution of this awkward consequence of the adaptation of the neo-Eusebian model seems to have been the chief objective of the next major English interpretation of the millennium, the eccentric exegesis of Thomas Brightman. Brightman's attempted solution capitalised on the fact that the period of one thousand years is mentioned six separate times in the twentieth chapter of Revelation. His principal innovation, drawing in turn on a suggestion made by Napier, was to distinguish two separate millennia from amongst these references: the millennium of Satan's binding, and the millennium of the saints' reign.[22] The first of these millennia conformed essentially to Napier's interpretation: between Constantine and the foundation of the Ottoman Empire, Satan was restrained from leading pagan rulers into war against the church, while the Antichrist, Satan's vicar, ruled the church in his stead. The fourteenth century thus saw the end of the first millennium, the loosing of Satan from bondage, the onset of the Turkish invasions from the east, and the beginning of the war of Gog and Magog. But it also witnessed the beginning of the second millennium with the first clear assaults of the resurrected Gospel on the

---

[21] Napier, *A plaine discovery*, pp. 234–5, cf. pp. 63–4.
[22] The passage cited above from Napier's *A plaine discovery*, p. 235.

empire of Antichrist which would culminate in the future overthrow of Babylon and the reign of the saints on earth.[23] Clearly, in Brightman's view, it was the best of times, it was the worst of times.

Brightman's interpretation is more satisfying as a solution to the problems inherited from Foxe and Napier than as an interpretation of the Apocalypse in its own right. Such an ingenious attempt to salvage a fatally wounded system reminds one of Tycho Brahe – the man who tried to adapt Copernican astronomy to Aristotelian physics by postulating that, while the other five planets orbited the sun, the sun itself, together with the moon and the fixed stars, revolved around the stationary earth. Brightman's double-jointed system enjoyed a *fortuna* similar to Tycho's: the author was highly regarded by subsequent exegetes, his book was frequently reprinted, and his system much commented upon; but he made few outright converts.[24] A generation of tinkering had produced a curious hybrid which succeeded in 'saving the phenomena' only at the cost of elegance, simplicity and intuitive plausibility. The chief importance of Brightman's strained solution, like Tycho's, lies in demonstrating the seriousness of the intellectual problem which provoked it. The *sententia recepta* of a past millennium was quite literally coming to pieces. Apocalyptic reckoning, like astronomical, was urgently in need of a bold new paradigm.

The historiographical shortcomings of the modified Eusebian approach were sufficiently obvious to relegate it to second place among the Protestant interpretations of the millennium. To avoid these problems, most Protestant exegetes dated the millennium from one event or another at the very outset of the Christian era: from the Resurrection, the preaching of the apostles, the destruction of the second temple by Titus, or the writing of the Apocalypse. This compelled them to follow Augustine also in defining the millennium in more internal and spiritual terms. But whereas Augustine had conceived the duration of the millennium as an indefinite period, this group of Protestant exegetes restricted

---

[23] Brightman, *Apocalypsis apocalypseos, ed est, Apocalypsis D. Joannis analysis et scholiis illustrata* (Frankfurt, 1609); translated as *A revelation of the Revelation* (Amsterdam, 1611, 1615), pp. 838–61, esp. 848–53. Accounts of Brightman's thought include Bauckham, *Tudor apocalypse*, pp. 139–43; Ball, *A great expectation*, pp. 82–4, 168–74; Christianson, *Reformers and Babylon*, pp. 100–106; Firth, *Apocalyptic tradition*, pp. 164–76; Robert G. Clouse, 'The apocalyptic interpretations of Thomas Brightman and Joseph Mede', *Journal of the Evangelical Theological Society*, 11 (1968), 181–93.

[24] The Latin version was published in Frankfurt (1609), Heidelberg (1612), Leiden (1616, 1644), and Cambridge (1644); the English translation in Amsterdam (1611, 1615). In addition to the evidence of Brightman's influence reported elsewhere, the commentaries in Alsted's *Trifolium propheticum* (Herborn, 1640) rely heavily on him. A rare disciple seems to have been Henry Finch: see Toon (ed.), *Puritans*, pp. 32–4.

it to a finite period of one thousand years ending some time in the eleventh century (the most popular dates being the pontificates of Sylvester II and Gregory VII). For the sake of convenience, we shall therefore refer to this second main approach as the modified Augustinian conception of the millennium.

Such a position coincided far better with the Erasmian humanists' and early reformers' sense that the teachings and practices of the Roman church most in need of reform were innovations of the past three or four hundred years. The codification of canon law, the development of scholastic theology, the inflation of papal pretensions to temporal supremacy, the multiplication of private masses, indulgences, Marian devotions, and many of the other most hotly contested 'human traditions' emerged for the most part during the period after 1050. As long as criticism of late medieval theology and worship remained relatively superficial, this interpretation remained acceptable. In the absence of readily accessible information on the earlier centuries of medieval church history, its limitations were dimly perceived. But the Reformation itself first radicalised the critique of medieval religion and then gave an enormous new impetus to the study of ecclesiastical and theological history. There were two sides to the Reformation debate and two sides to the historiographical aspect of it. Both were to raise serious problems for the Protestant conception of a past millennium.

The problems raised by Protestant historiography were essentially the consequence of the parasitic dependence of this conception on the doctrine of the papal Antichrist. As suggested above, the identification of the papacy as the Antichrist was strategically significant to sixteenth-century Protestants for several reasons. The notion of a past millennium was, by comparison, of secondary importance. Historical and exegetical defence and clarification of the latter idea thus tended to lag logically and chronologically behind the former, and this led to a serious problem: for zealous investigation into the origins of papal supremacy and the theological, liturgical and ecclesiastical usages associated with it soon revealed that they were rather older than the doctrine of a medieval millennium could comfortably accommodate.

The classic example of the zealous prosecution of historiographical warfare against the pope is doubtless the so-called *Magdeburg Centuries* and their presiding genius, Matthias Flacius Illyricus. Flacius set out to chart the progress of ecclesiastical decline from apostolic purity to antichristian depravity. But there was more to his project than this. He grasped clearly at the outset that evidence of ecclesiastical corruption would tend to discredit the papacy, which claimed to have led the church on earth since apostolic times through a visible and continuous succession of bishops, while leaving the Lutheran church, with its very different conception of the church as inward, invisible, and continuously assaulted by Satan, essentially unscathed. With all the passion of his fiery temperament, Flacius consequently set about unearthing, expounding and broadcasting every hint of scandal in the history of the ancient and medieval church to be found in the libraries of northern Germany and inspired a team of colleagues to do the same. For each of the first 13 centuries of church history, they collected and published material under some 15 broad headings, including such manifest scandals as persecutions, heresies, schisms and martyrs. Other chapters, such as doctrines, ceremonies, church government, and persons, assembled evidence of degeneration as well as perseverance. Parallel to the *Centuries*, Flacius assembled his famous *Catalogue of the witnesses of truth, who before our age have denounced the Roman Pontiff and his errors*, which likewise began at the beginning (with St Peter himself!) and devoted one-third of its 600 folio pages to denunciations of Roman errors before 1050.[25] Like most issues regarding continental apocalypticism in this period, the influence of these works on the apocalyptic tradition seems not to have been carefully studied, but it is unlikely that the single greatest Protestant historiographical undertaking of the sixteenth century could have strengthened the consensus that the millennium prophesied in the Apocalypse was fulfilled during the first millennium of the Christian church.

However unique in scale, in this crucial respect the celebrated history of Flacius and his colleagues was by no means unusual. A good example of an equally damaging large-scale history is the little-known project of Rudolph Hospinianus. In 1587 Hospinianus published in Zurich a folio volume *On the origin, progress, use and abuse of temples and of all things pertaining to them*. The very scope of the list of superstitions and corruptions discussed in the volume is unsettling: it includes the dedication of churches to saints, the building of shrines to house their physical relics, the veneration of the images introduced into these churches, the lies spread and miracles staged to enhance the numinous aura of these buildings and their contents, the consecration of images, altars, chalices, bells, holy water, and all the accumulating paraphernalia associated with the cult of saints, and the abuse of ecclesiastical benefactions, most notorious in the Donation of Constantine. Hospinianus, like the

---

[25] The title of the 'Magdeburg Centuries' is as follows: *Ecclesiastica historica, integram Ecclesiae Christi ideam, quantum ad locum, propagationem, persecutionem tranquilitatem, doctrinam, haereses, caeremonias, gubernationem, schismata, synodos, personas, miracula, martyria, religiones extra Ecclesiam et statum Imperii proliticum attinet, secundum singulas centurias, perspicuo ordine complectens* (13 vols, Basle, 1559–74). Flacius Illyricus, *Catalogus testium veritatis, qui ante nostram aetatem Pontifici Romano, euisque erroribus reclamarunt* (Basle, 1556). Heinz Scheible, *Die Entstehung der Magdeburger Zenturien* (1966).

Centuriators, charted the growth of abuses from apostolic times, and the origin of those noted here is perilously early: since the building of churches and the cult of martyrs received a tremendous impetus from the ending of persecution and the conversion of the Roman Empire, the age of Constantine quickly emerges from Hospinianus' study as the period in which most of these abuses began. Moreover, this volume was only the first instalment in a massive project treating the origin and spread of ecclesiastical malpractice generally. Similar patterns were revealed by the series which followed, which included folio volumes on the origins of monasticism, the use and abuse of the sacraments in the primitive church, and the rites and ceremonies surrounding Christian holidays (which were explicitly compared with those of Jews and pagans).[26] Clearly, Zwinglian critics of the Roman church were making their own distinctive contribution to the inadvertent critique of the idea of a past millennium.

The Catholic contribution, although late in coming, was naturally more direct. It was only around the turn of the century, precisely the years which saw the first falterings of confidence in the idea of a past millennium, that Catholics finally mounted a full-scale assault on the key premise of the Protestant tradition: the identification of the papacy as Antichrist. Cardinal Robert Bellarmine opened the assault with a systematic refutation of the now well-established Protestant position, embedded in his epoch-making *summa* of polemical theology, which forced it upon the notice of Protestants across Europe and provoked a torrent of indignant criticism.[27] An army of Jesuit polemicists followed, exposing the inconsistencies of the Protestant argument, rebutting the rejoinders to

---

[26] Rudolf Hospinianus, *De origine, progressu, usu et abusu templorum ac rerum omnium ad templa pertinentium, libri v* (Zurich, 1587); *De origine et progressu monachatus libri vi* (Zurich, 1588); *De origine, progressu, ceremoniis et ritibus festorum dierum Judaeorum, Graecorum, Romanorum et Turcarum libri tres* (Zurich, 1592); *Festa christianorum, hoc est de origine, progressu, ceremoniis et ritibus festorum dierum christianorum liber unus* (Zurich, 1593); *Historia sacrametaria, hoc est, libri quinque de coenae dominicae prima institutione, eiusque vero usu et abusu in primitiva ecclesia* (Zurich, 1598). Second editions were published between 1603 and 1612, typically *cum responsionibus ad Rob. Bellarmini, Caes. Baronii, . . . et sociorum eorum sophismata et argumenta, quibus idolatriam romanam defendere conantur*. Third editions appeared posthumously between 1669 and 1681 and were collected with his other works into his *Opera omnia* (7 vols, Geneva, 1681).

[27] Roberto Bellarmino, *Disputationes de controversiis Christianae fidei adversus hujus temporis haereticos* (3 vols, Ingolstadt, 1586–93), esp. I, iii, cap. 1: 'Disputatio de Antichristi' (Lyons, 1603 edn, I. 845–956). Edward A. Ryan, *The historical scholarship of Saint Bellarmine* (Louvain, 1936). A selection of literature on Antichrist stirred up by this work in England is catalogued in Peter Milward, *Religious controversies of the Jacobean age: a survey of printed sources* (London, 1978), pp. 131–6.

Bellarmine,[28] flinging the accusation of antichristianism back at their accusers,[29] refurbishing the medieval interpretation with an up-to-date scholarly apparatus, and developing the novel praeterist, futurist, and ahistorical readings of the Apocalypse which would eventually supersede the historical approach even among scholarly Protestants.[30]

Less direct in approach, but perhaps more damaging in effect, was the mounting Catholic historiographical effort of this period. The modern study of hagiography can be dated from the work of Laurentius Surius in the 1570s, and still more so from 1607, from which point we can trace the activities of that remarkable group of Jesuits, subsequently known as the Bollandists, who dedicated themselves single-mindedly to the collection and publication of all the authentic records of the lives of the saints.[31] In 1578 workmen digging a well in a vineyard outside Rome turned up even more concrete evidence of the early church's invocations of saints, prayers for the dead, and other practices concerned with death

---

[28] Literature in addition to Milward's list includes the following: Georg Scherer, *Bericht, ob der Bapst zü Rom der Antichrist zey* (Ingolstadt, 1585); John Gibbons, *Confutatio disputationis theologicae in qua Georgius Sohn . . . conatus est docere pontificem Romanum esse Antichristum* (Aug. Treu, 1589); Caspar Schoppe, *De Antichristo epistola* (Ingolstadt, 1605); Silvestre de l'Aval, *Les justes grandeurs de l'eglise Romaine, contre l'impieté de ceux qui nomment le Pape Antichrist* (Poitiers, 1611); William Walpole, *A treatise of Antichrist, conteyning a defence of cardinall Bellarmines arguments, which demonstrate that the pope is not Antichrist, against D. Downam who impugneth the same* (St Omer, 1613; reprint. English Recusant Literature, vol. 220, Ilkley, 1974); Jérémie du Ferrier, *De l'Antichrist et de ses marques contre les calomnies des ennemis de l'Eglise Catholique* (Paris, 1615); Richard Stanihurst, *Brevis praemunitio pro futurâ concertatione cum Iacobo Usserio . . . qui in suâ historicâ explicatione conatur probare Pontificem Romanum . . . verum & germanum esse Antichristum* (Douay, 1615).

[29] Leonard Lessius, *De Antichristo et eius praecursoribus disputatio* (Antwerp, 1611) and Edward Weston, *The triall of Christian truth . . . serving for the discoverie of heresie, and Antichrist in his forerunners and misteries of iniquitie* (Douay, 1614; reprint. English Recusant Literature, vol. 62, Menston, 1971) identify the Protestant heretics and schismatics as the forerunners of Antichrist.

[30] The most comprehensive restatement of the medieval tradition was Thomas Malvenda, *De Antichristo libri undecim* (Rome, 1604). The leading futurist commentary was Francesco de Ribera, *In sacram beati Ioannis Apocalypsin commentarij* (Antwerp, 1591?, 1592, 1593, 1603). The pioneering praeterist interpretation was Luis de Alcázar, *Vestigatio arcani sensus in Apocalypsin* (Antwerp, 1604). The most popular of many other Catholic commentaries seems to have been Basius Viegas, *Commentarii exegetici in Apocalypsin Ioannis apostoli* (Ebornae, 1599; reprint. 1601, 1602, 1603, 1606, 1613, 1615, 1617, 1630). Only passing notice of this entire Catholic response has been made in the literature: see Bauckham, *Tudor apocalypse*, pp. 140, 143, 236; Firth, *Apocalyptic tradition*, pp. 161–3, 171–7; Emmerson, *Antichrist*, pp. 210, 230.

[31] Laurentius Surius, *De probatis sanctorum historiis* (6 vols, Cologne, 1570–75). On the Bollandists, see René Aigrain, *L'hagiographie. Ses sources, ses méthodes, son histoire* (Paris, 1953); David Knowles, *Great historical enterprises* (London, 1963), pp. 1–32; H. Delehaye, *A travers trois siècles: L'uvre des Bollandistes 1615–1915* (Brussels, 1920).

and burial: the catacombs.[32] Caesar Baronius visited the catacombs and combined material from them with the findings of his own unprecedentedly thorough excavations in the Vatican library and archives. The result, his 12 volumes of *Ecclesiastical Annals*, was sufficiently explosive to vault the previously obscure Oratorian into the college of cardinals and almost into the Holy See itself.[33] Even the great Protestant scholar, Isaac Casaubon, upon assuming the task of refuting Baronius, was forced to concede that 'he is the first to bring to light from unknown hiding places a great many things which were quite completely unknown before'.[34] In the field of interconfessional polemic, such evidence began to aid the Catholic effort of reconversion in France and led successive Huguenot synods to tighten restrictions on the study of the church Fathers.[35] Its implications for the historical interpretation of the Apocalypse were surely no less direct. Having finally begun to marshall its vast resources, the Roman church was determined to reclaim its historical patrimony, to stamp its mark on the image of preceding centuries. As historical evidence mounted and a historiographical Counter-Reformation began, the conviction that the core Christian community had exemplified one or another narrowing norm of Protestant orthodoxy for an entire millennium after Christ became increasingly problematic.

A thorough investigation of the impact of such historical scholarship on the development of the apocalyptic tradition has yet to be undertaken, and there is certainly no room to pursue it here. But one need not look far for signs of disarray. In 606 Phocas murdered the Emperor Maurice, succeeded him as emperor, and subsequently granted the long-sought primacy of honour within the church to Pope Boniface III. Luther consistently recognised this event as the crucial date in the rise of the papal Antichrist and was followed in doing so by any number of Protestant historians and exegetes. The coherence of this view with that of a past millennium was obviously problematic. Luther sought to recon-

---

[32] Antonio Bosio compiled the classic account, published posthumously by Giovanni di Severano as *Roma sotterranea* (Rome, 1632). For an account of the discovery and the data uncovered, see G.B. de Rossi, *La Roma sotterranea cristiana* (3 vols, Rome 1864–77; reprint. Frankfurt am Main, 1966), esp. I. 12–46.

[33] Baronius, *Annales ecclesiastici* (12 vols; vols 1–9, Mainz, 1588–1601; vol. 10, Cologne, 1603; vols 11–12, Mainz, 1606–8), *ad annos* 57 ξ cxii, 130 ξ iii, 226 ξ viii, ix. Cyriac R. Pullapilly, *Caesar Baronius, Counter-Reformation historian* (Notre Dame, 1975); Hubert Jedin, *Kardinal C. Baronius. Der Anfang der katholischen Kirchengeschichtsschreibung im 16. Jahrhundert* (Münster, 1978).

[34] Casaubon, *De rebus sacris et ecclesiasticis exercitationes XVI. Ad Cardinalis Baronii Prolegomena in Annales et primum eorum partem* (Frankfurt am Main, 1615), fos e4^v–f1^r.

[35] Pontien Polman, *L'Element historique dans la controverse religieuse du XVIe siècle* (Gembloux, 1932), pp. 270–77. This magisterial work also provides the best general overview of the sixteenth-century phase of this development.

cile them by distinguishing between papal dominance of the church from 600 onwards and that of the empire, established around AD 1000.[36] More typical was the idea that Antichrist had only emerged gradually as the church declined; but as this solution was applied with increasing leniency, Antichrist gradually began to infiltrate the first Christian millennium. Hospinianus, for instance, continued to apply Revelation 20 to the thousand years after the Nativity; but by the time he reached Charlemagne he was already urging its imminent end, for Antichrist had been born in the time of Phocas and conceived in that of Constantine.[37] Other accounts of the *vita Antichristi* placed his birth earlier still: in the age of Constantine, in Pope Victor's excommunication of the Asian churches in the Pascal controversy of the second century, and still earlier.[38] As the history of ecclesiastical decline encroached upon the apostolic era, the web of apocalyptic allusion spread further until Antichrist, 'Mystery, Babylon the Great', became further identified with 'the mystery of iniquity' which, as Paul clearly testified, was already working at the time of the apostles.[39] By 1609, Thomas Brightman could write of the Antichrist:

> the Apostles could hardly make him keepe in his hornes, much lesse could their posterity doe it; who had lesse piety, knowledge, care, diligence, whose gifts also daily decaying more and more, made the man of sinne, to come & to growe up the more quickly .... Therefore thou also wast deceaved (ô Luther) Antichrist was come before thou supposeds, him to come.[40]

At the beginning of the century the ideas of the papal Antichrist and the

---

[36] Preuss, *Die Vorstellung vom Antichrist*, pp. 53, 194–5, 234–6; Polman, *L'Élement historique*, pp. 164–6; John M. Headley, *Luther's view of church history* (New Haven/London, 1963), pp. 192–4; Melanchthon, *Chronicon Carionis* (1532), *Corpus Reformatorum*, XII (Halle, 1844), col. 1072; Flacius et al., *Ecclesiastica historia*, VII (1564), cols 228, 244; Johannes Sleidan, *De quatuor summis imperiis libri tres* (1566), ed. M. Meibomius (Wittenberg, 1613), pp. 273–4.

[37] Hospinianus, *Historiae sacramentariae pars prior* (3rd edn, Geneva, 1681), fo. ¶4, pp. 162B, 251B, 283A.

[38] Joannes Himmelius, *Memoriale biblicum* (Jena, 1624); Alsted, *Thesaurus chronologiae* (Herborn, 1628), pp. 287–8, 382–8.

[39] Revelation 17:5; 2 Thessalonians 2:7; Alsted, *Definitiones theologicae* (Herborn, 1626), p. 76; 'Antichristus magnus est, qui operatur mysterium iniquitatis'. Cf. Philipp de Mornay, *Mysterium iniquitatis seu historia papatus . . . Asseruntur etiam jura imperatorum, regum, et principum christianorum adversus Bellarminum et Baronum* (Saumur, 1611). Cf. Andrew Willet, *Synopsis Papismi, that is, A Generall Viewe of Papistry: wherein the whole mysterie of iniquitie, and summe of Antichristian doctrine is set downe* (London, 1592).

[40] Brightman, 'The confuting of that counterfaite Antichrist, whom Bellarmine describeth'; a separate treatise within *A revelation of the Revelation* (1615), pp. 622–770, here pp. 648–9, 654–5.

past millennium had seemed mutually supporting; by the end of the century they had begun to undermine one another.

Such problems as these require far closer analysis than can be given here. What is clear, however, is that for all the doubts that could be raised about the location and nature of the past millennium, the fully fledged millenarian had a robust answer. Alsted and Mede, the two figures most responsible for the instauration of millenarianism within the Calvinist world, were both extremely well versed in material of this kind and employed it in the elaboration and defence of their position. Alsted's *Thesaurus chronologiae* of 1624 contains a veritable anthology of such material, including a chronology of the *testium veritatis* based directly on Flacius, another of the *mysterium iniquitatis* derived from de Mornay, and further chronologies of heresies, persecutions, sects, schisms, popes, monks, and scholastic theologians, each of these chronologies tended to demonstrate the omnipresence of difficulties which the church had suffered throughout history.[41] In his most important millenarian treatise, the *Diatribe de mille annis apocalypticis*, published three years later in 1627, Alsted redeployed this material into an assault on the modified Augustinian conception of the millennium:

> Some say that these thousand years here mentioned began with the overthrow of the *Temple*, and *Jewish* Worship; . . . Now let us see what a fine exposition this is. *Jerusalem* was overthrown by *Titus* in the 69. year of *Christ:* Here then let us begin the *Epocha* of these thousand years, so that they may end in the year of *Christ* 1069. Now let there be conferred with this whole course of time the *Conversion* of the *Nations*, the stinck of *Heresies*, the defection and seduction of *Mahomet*, the *Mystery of Iniquity*, and lastly the *persecution* of the *Godly*; and then let it be shewn how *Satan* reigning all this while so powerfully, was bound for a thousand years, and seduced not the *Nations*.[42]

The revised view of Napier and Brightman was no less vulnerable to this kind of historical criticism. In his *Trifolium propheticum*, written in 1633, Alsted directly challenged Brightman's contention that Constantine had so repressed the heathen rulers that they were unable to persecute the church for a thousand years. The repeated invasions of Western Europe by Goths, Vandals, Vikings, Saracens and Tartars are only the more familiar of the heathen invasions which the church suffered between 300 and 1300: Alsted also outlined the much greater mis-

---

[41] Alsted, *Thesaurus chronologicae* (Herborn, 1624; revised and expanded 1628, the year after the *Diatribe* was published), esp. pp. 278–398.

[42] Alsted, *The beloved city*, p. 36; *Diatribe*, pp. 77–8. His immediate opponent here is David Pareus's *In divinam Apocalypsin . . . Johannis commentarius* (Heidelberg, 1618), as can be seen by comparing the Latin text with Pareus, *Operum theolgicorum exegeticorum tomi I, pars quarta* (Frankfurt am Main, 1647), p. 811.b.D.

eries imposed by heathen empires on the ancient Christian communities of North Africa, the Near East, Asia Minor, and Eastern Europe. 'I truly wonder', he concluded, 'that men of judgement can so delude themselves that they earnestly assert that the thousand years begin from the death of Christ or from Constantine, or from I know not what other point, since history contradicts these assertions.'[43] Most academic millenarians advanced this kind of objection at greater or lesser length: the pietist chiliast, Georg Lorenz Seidenbecher, drawing on Alsted and others, elaborated it exhaustively in 1660 for over 200 pages.[44]

Joseph Mede was scarcely less well-versed in historical material of this kind, and developed it to equally devastating effect in perhaps his second most important work. Fourteen years after the publication of his *Clavis apocalyptica*, Mede published an extraordinary synthesis of this diverse material under the title, *The Apostasy of the Latter Times . . . or the Gentiles' Theology of Daemons revived in the Latter Times amongst Christians* (1641). The apostasy referred to here is of course that most fully described in 2 Thessalonians 2:2–12, which had long since been closely associated with the final persecution of Antichrist. Developing this idea on the basis of 1 Timothy 4:1–3, Mede argued that this apostasy consisted, in effect, of precisely those unacceptable aspects of Catholic devotion which had been traced back into late antiquity. His subtitle mentioned the *Worshipping of Angels, Deifying and Invocating Saints, Adoring of Reliques, Bowing down to Images and Crosses, etc.* His text itself adds further antichristian practices to this list, including the legends (or 'lies') of medieval hagiography, counterfeit miracles, forgeries such as the Donation of Constantine, the idolatry of the mass, the prohibition of marriage for priests, enforced abstinence from meat, and other aspects of the monastic profession. More audaciously still, he argued that each of these forms of piety represented a satanically inspired perversion of the substance and forms of truly Christian religion into those of pagan idolatry. Satan had not been restrained from 'deceiving the nations' or preventing the gentiles from converting to Christianity. On the contrary, he had deceived the established church itself, converting it into a 'gentile theology' with a pious veneer. Moreover, the period which Mede identified as these 'Latter Times' corresponded closely with the neo-Eusebian conception of the millennium: it began somewhere between 365 and 455

---

[43] Alsted, *Trifolium prophecticum* (Herborn, 1640), p. 2148.

[44] Waremundus Freyburger (= G. L. Seidenbecher), *Chiliasmus sanctus: qui est sabbatismus populo Dei relictus* (Amsterdam, 1660), pp. 39–280. Many other millenarians make similar points: Alfonsus Conradus Mantuanus, *In Apocalypsin D. Ioannis Apostoli commentarius* (Basle, 1574), p. 483; Piscator, *Commentarius*, pp. 250–51; *Commentarii*, p. 1581.b; Nathaniel Homes, *The resurrection revealed* (London, 1661), p. 456 (as quoted in Ball, *A great expectation*, p. 163).

and would continue for 1260 years.[45] Where Foxe had expected to find a thousand-year reign of the saints, Mede could see only a 1 260-year reign of Satan. The inversion begun by Napier was complete.[46]

It may well be, therefore, that the modified Augustinian strategy only postponed the historiographical failure of the doctrine of the past millennium. But in addition to the type of problems shared with the neo-Eusebian model, it created further historiographical difficulties of its own. The third verse of Revelation 20 foretold that Satan, after his millennium of bondage, 'must be loosed a little season.' Augustine and the dominant medieval tradition interpreted a number of related scriptural passages to mean that the reign of Antichrist would be a mere 1 260 days or three and a half years.[47] Foxe's suggestion that the second great period of persecution might last as long as the first was straining this passage somewhat; but the modified Augustinian position virtually doubled the length of this interval once again. The millenarians of subsequent decades would see this as one of the most obvious inadequacies of the received interpretation. As Alsted, drawing on Piscator, complained,

> if these thousand years were expired in the year of Christ 1069, it follows that these 557 years, which have passed from that time to this present year 1626 is a *little season*, . . . but these 557 years cannot be said to be a *little season* in regard of 1 000 years, seeing they contain rather more then half thereof.[48]

No less intractable than these historiographical problems were this interpretation's inherent theological difficulties; for what precisely, in such circumstances, was the defining characteristic of the millennium? Obviously, it could not be the clear, external mark which the Foxe had used – persecution – for the first and most exemplary third of the millennium corresponded with the first great period of persecution. If Augustine was to be followed in beginning the millennium with Christ,

---

[45] The fifth, revised edition of *The Apostacy* is in *The works of Joseph Mede*, ed. J. Worthington (2 vols, 3rd edn, London, 1672), I. 621–93. On the chronology, see especially 655–62.

[46] Napier had already argued that Antichrist's reign extended roughly from 300 to 1560 AD (*A plaine discovery*, p. 64). Brightman elaborated a characteristically baroque variation on this theme (*A revelation of the Revelation*, pp. 356–64, 404–12, 451–2). Mede's position differs from theirs in only two basic respects: this period is not the reign of Satan's lieutenant but of Satan himself, and therefore the millennium does not begin at the same time.

[47] Dan. 12:7, Rev. 11:2–3; 12:6, 12; 13:5. Augustine, *De civitate Dei*, XX. 8, 13 (CCSL, XLVIII. 713.37–9, 722.3–4). Emmerson, *Antichrist in the middle ages*, pp. 43, 45, 95, 100, etc.

[48] Alsted, *Diatribe*, p. 78 (translation adapted from *The beloved city*, p. 36). Piscator, *Commentarius*, p. 250; *Commentarii*, p. 1581.b. Cf. Bellarime, *De controversiis*, I. 875C–D.

he would also have to be followed in defining the nature of it in internal, spiritual terms. If such modification could be achieved, it would be very attractive: like Augustine himself, the Protestant exegete could calmly contemplate all persecutions, corruptions, heresies and invasions which the church had suffered, safe in the knowledge that the kingdom of Christ in which the saints reigned lay within. But the reformers' limitation of the millennium to a literal thousand-year period in the distant past posed a serious obstacle to adopting such a view. Suppose that one held with Augustine that the freedom and blessedness of the church during the millennium pertained not to external conditions but to the internal states of the consciences of the faithful alone. What then was the condition of the church after the *end* of this period? Were the consciences of the righteous no longer free or at peace? Suppose, following John Bale, that the angel who descended from heaven to bind the Devil in Revelation 20:1–3 is to be understood as Christ himself, who descended from the Father with all power in heaven and on earth to bind 'that old serpent' who had deceived Adam and Eve and thereby to redeem mankind.[49] Is this redeeming work to be restricted to a mere thousand years? The earliest Calvinist millenarian, Alfonsus Conradus of Mantua, identified this problem precisely: the 'nations' which Satan is prevented for a thousand years from deceiving cannot possibly be the elect, for even after the millennium he will be powerless to deceive them.[50] Augustine asks essentially the same question in the *City of God*: 'Now if the binding and shutting up of the Devil means that he cannot lead the Church astray, will his unloosing mean that he can do so again? God forbid! For he will never seduce that Church which was predestined and chosen before the foundation of the world.'[51]

We thus encounter an awkward asymmetry in the Augustinian interpretation: the binding of Satan prevents him from leading the true church astray, but the loosing of Satan does not allow him to deceive God's people once again. What then can the loosing of Satan mean? Augustine provides no fully adequate solution to this problem. His best argument is that, although those already converted to Christ when Satan is released will not be harmed by him, his persecution will be so devastating that no new souls will be converted.[52] Augustine can afford to take this position because, in his view, as we have seen, the 'little season' for which Satan is

---

[49] Bale, *The image of bothe churches*, pp. 560–61, 564–9.

[50] Conradus, *Commentarius*, p. 483.

[51] Augustine, *De civitate Dei*, XX. 8 (*CCSL*, XLVIII. 712.1–5), trans. Henry Betteson (Harmondsworth, 1972), p. 910.

[52] Augustine, *De civitate Dei*, XX. 8 and 13 (*CCSL*, XLVIII. 711.96–715.125, 721.1–723.69).

released will be only three and a half years long. For neo-Augustinian Protestants, whose 'little season' was now half as long as the millennium itself, this was scarcely an option: the last generation of believers would have died in the twelfth century. Other solutions were scarcely more appealing. Napier, following another hint from Augustine, argued that while the period of Satan's bondage is to be taken as a literal thousand years, the millennium of the saints' reign is to be understood as the 'perfect' time representing the entire interval between the First and Second Advents.[53] Brightman's still more awkward distinction of two separate millennia offered another solution to the problem. Once again, the millenarians had a far simpler alternative to such tortured exegesis. Their millennium could be clearly defined as a period of both external peace and internal felicity which need not be squared with the awkward facts of history for the simple reason that it was yet to come. When the external reign of the saints is overthrown by the final period of Satanic tyranny, their internal peace and felicity will also be briefly disturbed. But Christ will shorten the days of this final persecution for the sake of his elect and will consume Satan with the brightness of his coming.

Careful study of other strategies for defending the notion of a past millennium is called for, but even without pursuing them further the basic dilemma is clear. If the millennium is regarded as a thousand-year period now past, then the question of its chronological location naturally arises; this question can only be resolved by reference to some definite criterion and both of the two general standards available proved inherently problematic. The external criteria of Eusebius, Foxe, Napier and Brightman – whether freedom from persecution, invasion, war, or corruption – were vulnerable to empirical disconfirmation. The more historical knowledge accumulated, the less exemplary previous church history was revealed to be. The internal criteria of Augustine or Bale, on the other hand, were equally vulnerable to rational refutation. The more theological attention was applied to the problem, the less tenable the very notion of a spiritually defined past millennium became. External criteria could not, it seems, be extended to an entire thousand-year period. Internal criteria could not be restricted to a mere thousand-year period. The spiritualised, Augustinian conception of the nature of the millennium could only be fully harmonised with the spiritualised, Augustinian conception of the duration of the millennium.

Recognition of this dilemma provides an altered perspective on the problem of the origins of Calvinist millenarianism. The logic which first drove senior seventeenth-century Reformed theologians to place the mil-

---

[53] Napier, *A plaine discovery*, pp. 234–5, 239–40. Augustine, *De civitate Dei*, XX. 7, 8 and 13 (*CCSL*, XLVIII. 710.55–80, 721.1–722.17, 723.54–68).

lennium in the future is not to be found merely in soaring expectations for the future, much less in radical programmes of political transformation. It must also be sought in the theological and historiographical difficulties encountered by their sixteenth-century predecessors in attempting to find somewhere else to put it, the difficulty, that is, of assessing their place in sacred history, of establishing a historical identity.

Index

The index is for both volumes (indicated by Roman numbers I and II) and contains names, places and themes which appear in the main text, not in the footnotes. Although chapter one appears in both volumes, it has not been indexed twice. All references in the index to I: 1–22 are also valid for volume II.